The Grammar of Chinese Characters

Anybody who reads or writes Chinese characters knows that they obey a grammar of sorts: though numerous, they are built out of a much smaller set of constituents, often interpretable in meaning or pronunciation, that are themselves built out of an even smaller set of strokes. This book goes far beyond these basic facts to show that Chinese characters truly have a productive and psychologically real lexical grammar of the same sort seen in spoken and signed languages, with non-trivial analogs of morphology (the combination of potentially interpretable constituents), phonology (formal regularities without implications for interpretation), and phonetics (articulatory and perceptual constraints). Evidence comes from a wide variety of sources, from quantitative corpus analyses to experiments on character reading, writing, and learning. The grammatical approach helps capture how character constituents combine as they do, how strokes systematically vary in different environments, how character form evolved from ancient times to the modern simplified system, and how readers and writers are able to process or learn even entirely novel characters. This book not only provides tools for exploring the full richness of Chinese orthography, but also offers new ways of thinking about the most fundamental question in linguistic theory: what is grammar?

James Myers is Professor of Linguistics at National Chung Cheng University, Taiwan. He has published numerous articles applying quantitative and experimental methods to grammatical issues in Chinese and other languages, and has also (co-)edited volumes on sign language, empirical grammatical research, and Chinese linguistics.

Routledge Studies in East Asian Linguistics

The Grammar of Japanese Mimetics
Perspectives from Structure, Acquisition and Translation
Edited by Noriko Iwasaki, Peter Sells, and Kimi Akita

Southern Min
Comparative Phonology and Subgrouping
Bit-Chee Kwok

The Grammar of Chinese Characters
Productive Knowledge of Formal Patterns in an Orthographic System
James Myers

For more information about this series, please visit www.routledge.com/Routledge-Studies-in-East-Asian-Linguistics/book-series/RSEAL

The Grammar of Chinese Characters
Productive Knowledge of Formal Patterns in an Orthographic System

James Myers

LONDON AND NEW YORK

First published 2019
by Routledge
2 Park Square, Milton Park, Abingdon, Oxon OX14 4RN

and by Routledge
52 Vanderbilt Avenue, New York, NY 10017

Routledge is an imprint of the Taylor & Francis Group, an informa business

© 2019 James Myers

The right of James Myers to be identified as author of this work has been asserted by him in accordance with sections 77 and 78 of the Copyright, Designs and Patents Act 1988.

All rights reserved. No part of this book may be reprinted or reproduced or utilised in any form or by any electronic, mechanical, or other means, now known or hereafter invented, including photocopying and recording, or in any information storage or retrieval system, without permission in writing from the publishers.

Trademark notice: Product or corporate names may be trademarks or registered trademarks, and are used only for identification and explanation without intent to infringe.

British Library Cataloguing-in-Publication Data
A catalogue record for this book is available from the British Library

Library of Congress Cataloging-in-Publication Data
Names: Myers, James (Linguist), author.
Title: The grammar of Chinese characters : productive knowledge of formal patterns in an orthograhic system / by James Myers.
Description: Abingdon, Oxon ; New York, NY : Routledge, 2019. | Series: Routledge studies in East Asian linguistics | Includes bibliographical references and index.
Identifiers: LCCN 2018060182 | ISBN 9781138290815 (hardback) | ISBN 9781315265971 (ebook)
Subjects: LCSH: Chinese characters. | Chinese language—Writing. | Chinese language—Grammar. | Chinese—Orthography and spelling.
Classification: LCC PL1171 .M94 2019 | DDC 495.11/1—dc23
LC record available at https://lccn.loc.gov/2018060182

ISBN: 978-1-138-29081-5 (hbk)
ISBN: 978-1-315-26597-1 (ebk)

Typeset in Times
by Apex CoVantage, LLC

Printed and bound in Great Britain by
TJ International Ltd, Padstow, Cornwall

Contents

	List of figures	vi
	List of tables	viii
	Preface	x
1	Chinese character grammar: the very idea	1
2	Character morphology	43
3	Character phonology and phonetics	73
4	Corpus-based evidence for character grammar	120
5	Experimental evidence for character grammar	160
6	Implications and applications	203
	Index	229

Figures

1.1	The exponential growth of character inventories	5
1.2	Proportion of character types in oracle bone script (ca. 1200 BCE), bronze inscriptions (1046 BCE), Warring States script (403 BCE), small seal script (221 BCE), and early regular script (220 CE)	9
1.3	Hierarchy of character-internal parts	12
1.4	OFTEN (TSL), rotating motion repeats	20
1.5	HABIT (TSL, northern dialect), rotating motion repeats	20
1.6	MIDDLE (TSL)	21
2.1	Variation in radical position in semantic-phonetic characters	52
2.2	The interaction of character token frequency with semantic radical position on idiosyncratic allomorphy rates	59
3.1	The role of semantic radical dimensions in alternative positions	78
3.2	The interaction of left-edge stroke shape and main character axis	98
3.3	Writing path for standard stroke order in 正	110
3.4	Writing paths for standard stroke orders in 十 and 十	111
3.5	The learning of the Western stroke order convention for +	112
4.1	Growth curves for three character formation operations, empirical and projected	124
4.2	Growth curves for single-edge semantic radicals in semantic-phonetic characters	125
4.3	The percentage of characters formed via reduplication in oracle bone script (ca. 1200 BCE), bronze inscriptions (1046 BCE), small seal script (221 BCE), and regular script (220 CE)	132
4.4	Popeye studying 'Chinese'	152
5.1	The rough location of the Visual Word Form Area (in the fusiform gyrus)	164
5.2	Sample prime/target pairs in the second semantic radical judgment experiment	180
5.3	Acceptance rates (top) and log reaction times (bottom) as a function of grammaticality, constituent type, and character axis	182
5.4	Acceptance rates (top) and log reaction times (bottom) for items with a horizontal axis and non-radical constituents as a function of grammaticality and constituent reduction	183

Figures vii

5.5 Acceptance rates (top) and log reaction times (bottom) for non-lexical characters with reduplication as a function of grammaticality, lexical status of reduplicative structure, and reduplication shape 187
5.6 Competing risks regression for the reduplication experiment 189
5.7 Examples of bizarre experimental stroke groups 190
5.8 Acceptability of curving at the left edge vs. elsewhere 191
5.9 Acceptability of stroke prominence in prosodic head (right or bottom) vs. elsewhere 192
5.10 Acceptability of leftward hooking on a vertical stroke as the function of prosodic position (head = right vs. nonhead = left) and the presence of strokes at its top 193
5.11 All materials in the second stroke-based acceptability judgment experiment 194
5.12 Acceptability of curving and leftward hooking as a function of stroke position 194
5.13 Acceptability of leftward hooking on vertical strokes as a function of its position and the presence of strokes on top of it 195
6.1 Coarse-grained and fine-grained views of Chinese character reduplication 207
6.2 The learning of traditional Chinese characters by Taiwanese school children 212

Tables

1.1	The character for 'fish' *yú*	5
1.2	Xu Shen's six character categories in *Shuowen*	7
1.3	The sizes of proposed inventories of basic character constituents	12
1.4	Simple character strokes and their traditional names	14
2.1	Iconic character formation	47
2.2	Where characters have their radicals	51
2.3	Where radicals prefer to appear in semantic-phonetic characters	52
2.4	Radical position and idiosyncratic allomorphy rate (per number of characters)	57
2.5	Radical position and variation in idiosyncratic allomorphy in semantic-phonetic characters	57
2.6	Bottom-edge 火/灬 in semantic-phonetic and compound characters	57
3.1	Effect of semantic radical dimensions on position	77
3.2	Effect of idiosyncratic allomorphy on radical dimensions	80
3.3	Frequencies of character reduplicative templates	82
3.4	Parameters for the simplest character strokes	85
3.5	Some other simple character strokes	85
3.6	Some complex strokes	86
3.7	Stroke interactions in two- and three-stroke characters	88
3.8	The relationship between curving and constituent dimensions	97
3.9	The effect of asymmetry and top contact on leftward hooking	101
4.1	Estimated productivity for character types	123
4.2	Estimated productivity for radical positions in semantic-phonetic characters	124
4.3	Reduplication in oracle bone script	133
4.4	Reduplication in small seal script	133
4.5	The treatment of reduplication in character simplification	140
5.1	The results of Xiao and Treiman (2012)	162
5.2	Sample materials from Hsiao and Cottrell (2009)	165
5.3	Sample materials from Chen *et al.* (1996)	166
5.4	Sample materials from Taft and Zhu (1997), Experiment 3	167
5.5	Sample materials from Tsang and Chen (2009)	168
5.6	Sample target characters used in Chen and Cherng (2013)	169

Tables ix

5.7	Sample materials from Feldman and Siok (1997)	170
5.8	Sample materials from Feldman and Siok (1999)	171
5.9	Sample materials and schematic results from Yeh and Li (2002)	175
5.10	Sample materials from Sun and Yan (2006)	175
5.11	Two sets of test items in the semantic radical judgment experiment	179
5.12	Sample filler items in the judgment experiment	179
5.13	Sample materials used in the reduplication judgment experiment	185
5.14	Sample materials from the first stroke-based acceptability judgment experiment	190

Preface

The idea for this book was born around 30 years ago, when my training as a graduate student of linguistics collided with the long lists of characters I was asked to memorize in my first-semester Chinese class. It seemed obvious to me that characters were amenable to the same sorts of structural analyses that my linguistics teachers were asking me to do in the phonology and morphology exercises. The fact that characters are visual seemed irrelevant, since our department also had people studying the structure of sign languages, which even by then had long been recognized as having genuine grammars. So, in a fit of sophomore rebelliousness, I decided to take on the linguist's traditional taboo against orthography (writing system conventions) and wrote up some manuscripts arguing that Chinese characters have a grammar too. I soon learned that this was hardly an original insight and started building up a small library of linguistic research on orthography, the most treasured of which was (and still is) Jason Chia-Sheng Wang's 1983 University of Wisconsin–Madison Ph.D. thesis, *Toward a generative grammar of Chinese character structure and stroke order*.

Then I wrote my own dissertation on something completely different, got a job, and focused on what I thought would be more 'respectable' research.

Among the reasons for my returning to Chinese character grammar after so many decades, the most important is technology. While Wang had to handwrite all of his examples, I now have Unicode at my disposal, not to mention a cornucopia of free Web databases and a burgeoning experimental and computational literature. My own age may be a factor as well; I feel less pressure now to avoid peculiar research topics.

Character grammar is indeed a peculiar idea. When I presented some of my results at a recent conference, an attendee simply wanted to know if I was serious (well, yes). Another conference rejected my abstract outright, with one reviewer writing that "[t]here is no parallel between orthographies, created by man and to be learnt/taught explicitly, on the one hand, and human language, which is precisely acquired by any child without explicit learning/teaching," and another commenting more succinctly that "[t]his paper does not deal with linguistic matters, it only discusses graphic and orthographic points." (I respond to both misconceptions in the first chapter, by the way.) Of course, other readers and listeners have been much kinder, but I do not take a positive reception for granted. It takes a lot

Preface xi

of evidence and argumentation to make the case for Chinese character grammar, which is why this book is a book and not a pamphlet.

Given this, my book's title may seem to beg the question, but I see nothing wrong with starting from the assumption that characters really do have grammar and then seeing how far we get. If my approach does a disservice to linguistics or to Chinese, its inadequacies should quickly become unbearable. In this and in all else, I will let my readers be the judge. Some may even read the book as a *reductio ad absurdum* against the very notion of grammar itself, taking it to show how clever sophists can apply it to a domain that 'obviously' has no 'real grammar' (though for the record, I do not endorse this interpretation myself).

The title also fails to clarify that this book focuses primarily on traditional Chinese characters as used in Hong Kong, Macao, and Taiwan (as well as Kinmen and the rest of the Republic of China). I do discuss the simplified characters used in the People's Republic of China, Singapore, and most Chinese-teaching programs across the world, not only because more readers are likely to be familiar with them, but also because they are often studied in contemporary corpus-based and psycholinguistic research, two of my data sources. Traditional characters still belong at the center of my argument, however, because the characters created, revived, or adapted for the simplified standard comprise only a tiny subset of the whole, and because traditional characters have had a lot more time to evolve as a system (albeit under the influence of prescriptive dictionaries and the like). Fortunately, when I do get to simplified characters, we will see that their grammar is virtually identical to that of traditional characters anyway.

Earlier, I noted the role that technology played in the creation of this book, but of course human assistance has been even more important, and many people did their best to help me avoid the inevitable pitfalls of an unconventional and interdisciplinary synthesis of well-trodden research areas. Naturally, none of those who I thank below should be held responsible for any errors that remain, let alone my conclusions.

The first people to give me advice were the readers of my graduate school manuscripts: Jean Ann, Diana Archangeli, David Basilico, Paul Bloom, Tom Bourgeois, Lee Fulmer, Mike Hammond, Masahite Ishihara, James McCawley, Shaun O'Connor, Paul Saka, Marcus Taft, and Wendy Wiswall, with my then-and-still-colleague Jane Tsay (蔡素娟) being particularly helpful (she even handwrote some of my examples). After I revived the project in Taiwan, an army of lab assistants helped me create experimental stimuli, run experiments, find and check references, and try to catch my mistakes (along with assisting on unrelated projects), among them Yu-Chu Chang (張佑竹), Kuei-Yeh Chen (陳奎燁), Pei-Shan Chen (陳佩姍), Tsung-Ying Chen (陳宗穎), Yan-Jhe Ciou (邱彥哲), Guo-Ming Hong (洪國銘), Chiung-Wen Hsu (許瓊文), Zi-Ping Hsu (徐子平), Yu-Guang Ko (柯昱光), Wen-Chi Lin (林玟綺), Mei-Jun Liu (劉美君), Chia-Wen Lo (羅佳雯), Hsiao-Yin Pan (潘曉音), Si-Qi Su (蘇思綺), Pei-Fen Tu (杜佩芬), Han-Te Wang (王涵德), Chen-Tsung Yang (楊振宗), and Yu-Shan Yen (顏郁珊). Our few hundred experimental participants were of course also essential. All of this assistance, and much else besides, was supported by grants from the xii *Preface*

Republic of China's National Science Council/Ministry of Science and Technology (NSC 97–2410-H-194–067-MY3, NSC 97–2410-H-194–067-MY3, MOST 103–2410-H-194–119-MY3, MOST 106-2410-H-194–055-MY3). Tsung-Ying Chen (陳宗穎) collaborated on some of the experiments reported here, Shihkai Liu (劉世凱) redrew the Taiwan Sign Language examples, various tips were supplied by Thomas Bishop, Jung-hsing Chang (張榮興), Daniel Hole, Norbert Kordek, Robert Ladd, Victor H. Mair, and Lian Hee Wee (黃良喜), and feedback on my more recent work was given by Chia-Ying Lee (李佳穎), Yu-Hsuan Lin (林雨萱), Jim Tai (戴浩一), and Jane Tsay (蔡素娟), as well as by journal reviewers, conference abstract reviewers, and conference attendees, not to mention the reviewers for Routledge. I am particularly grateful to Ariel Cohen-Goldberg for inviting me to present at his workshop on Grammatical Approaches to Written and Graphical Communication at the 2012 meeting of the Cognitive Science Society, which made me think that I should finally do something a bit more serious with my old character stuff. Finally, Wolfgang Behr, Hsin-Chin Chen (陳欣進), Zev Handel, and Niina Zhang (張寧) gave me invaluable and detailed comments on large portions of the manuscript itself.

James Myers
Chiayi
February 17, 2019

1 Chinese character grammar
The very idea

1.1. Introduction

Chinese characters have a rich grammar; this grammar is productive and psychologically real and is formally similar to the morphology, phonology, and phonetics of natural spoken and signed languages. The purpose of this book is to convince readers that these strange ideas are not only worthy of serious consideration but shed new light on the nature of Chinese characters and grammar themselves.

Before describing character grammar and the evidence for it, I use this first chapter to review some key background questions. What are Chinese characters, and how have they traditionally been studied (Section 1.2)? What is 'grammar,' and what sorts of evidence can help test hypotheses about it (Section 1.3)? How would a Chinese character grammar relate to the grammars that have previously been proposed for other areas beyond speech (Section 1.4)? Indeed, the idea of Chinese character grammar itself is not new, so how does my proposal differ from earlier ones (Section 1.5)?

1.2. Chinese characters: an overview

To see why the idea of Chinese character grammar is so plausible, one only needs to consider a few simple facts: literate readers and writers know thousands of them (taxing rote memory), their forms are not derivable from their meanings or pronunciations (implying purely orthographic knowledge), their numbers have increased exponentially over the centuries (implying productive coinage), and they can be systematically decomposed into smaller units important for character production and recognition. None of these banalities are news to those who habitually read and write characters, even if 'grammar' is not necessarily the label that would spring to mind.

For the benefit of readers less familiar with characters, I briefly unpack these facts, looking first at the more basic ones (Section 1.2.1), then turning to character-internal structure (Section 1.2.2). More conventional reviews can be found in many places (e.g., in English: Bottéro 2017; Feng 2016; Handel 2017; Qiu 2000; Yin 2016; in Chinese: Hsu 1991; Su 2001; Wang 2001).

2 *Chinese character grammar*

1.2.1. Character basics

The most basic questions about characters concern their use, development, and current status, so I start with these here, in Sections 1.2.1.1, 1.2.1.2, and 1.2.1.3, respectively.

1.2.1.1. Character use

Chinese characters (漢字 *hànzì*) are written symbols (technically, graphs or glyphs) that almost always represent a single spoken morpheme (hence a single syllable) in Sinitic languages, including Mandarin. They have also been adapted and modified for other Sinitic languages like Cantonese and non-Sinitic languages like Japanese (where they are known as kanji), Korean, Vietnamese (prior to the introduction of romanization), and other neighboring languages (see Handel 2019).

As a simple example of how Chinese orthography works, consider the sentence in (1). It would normally be written without any spaces, added here to make room for the glosses (note that, throughout the book, I generally give only one gloss and pronunciation per character, though both may vary historically and in contemporary use; note also that CL = classifier, SUF = suffix). The pronunciations are given in Pinyin (漢語拼音 *Hànyǔ pīnyīn*) romanization, including tone diacritics. The text runs left to right here, according to modern convention, but traditionally Chinese text was (and often still is) written vertically downward or horizontally right to left. Aside from the morpheme-by-morpheme and syllable-by-syllable correspondences with the characters, a number of other orthographic features are visible: word boundaries (e.g., around 句子 *jùzi* 'sentence') are not marked; each character fills roughly the same-sized square area; the similar-sounding characters 子 and 字 share a formal element (子), as do the apparently unrelated characters 這, 個, and 句 (口).

(1) 這　　個　　句　　　　子　　　有　　　八　　　個　　　字
　　　zhè　*ge*　*jù*　　　*zi*　　*yǒu*　　*bā*　　*gè*　　*zì*
　　　this　CL　sentence　SUF　have　eight　CL　character
　　　'This sentence has eight characters.'

This simple picture can be complicated in any number of ways. For example, disyllabic morphemes do exist, and they are often written with a pair of characters sharing a constituent, as in (2a) (see also Section 2.3.1.4) or, more commonly, simply by reusing existing characters for their pronunciations, as in loanwords like (2b). Much more rarely, a single character may be used to represent a polymorphemic (and thus polysyllabic) spoken word (Mair 2011), as in (12c) (see Section 4.4.3).

(2) a 葡萄 *pútáo* 'grape'
　　　b 沙拉 *shālā* 'salad' (*沙 shā* 'sand,' 拉 *lā* 'pull')
　　　c 卅 *sà/sānshí* 'thirty' ('three-ten,' more commonly written 三十)

Chinese character grammar 3

For historical reasons, some Chinese characters are ambiguous in meaning and/ or pronunciation, as illustrated in (3) (for other effects of historical change on characters, see Sections 2.2 and 4.3.1.1).

(3) a 银行 *yínháng* 'bank' (literally 'silver-<u>store</u>')
     b 行人 *xíngrén* 'pedestrian' (literally '<u>walk</u>-person')

Since Chinese characters generally represent spoken morphemes, never ideas directly, they are not 'ideograms' (Boltz 2017a; DeFrancis 2002; Erbaugh 2017). However, the default character-morpheme-syllable correspondence makes it appropriate to call them 'logograms' (graphical representations of words, or more precisely, morphemes), or more generally, 'glyphs' (as used for ancient Egyptian or Mayan words). Still, classifying the system strictly as exclusively 'logographic' is somewhat controversial (DeFrancis 1989; Handel 2013, 2015; Unger 2014, 2016) because characters can also be used as a syllabary, as in loanwords (see also Section 4.3.1.1).

The precise number of characters is difficult to estimate (Anderson 2017) because many are variants or were originally invented outside of China, and characters have continued to be coined into the modern era. The Unicode standard (see Section 1.2.1.3) contains over 75,000 characters, and the database of the Chinese Document Processing Lab (2011) contains over 165,000, but most educated readers are only familiar with a small portion of these. Hue (2003) estimates that the typical college student in Taiwan knows a bit over 5,000 characters, along with strategies for guessing the meanings and pronunciations of others (see Section 1.2.2.2).

1.2.1.2. Character history

The history of Chinese characters seems to have begun before 1200 BCE in the Shang kingdom, around modern Henan province (Boltz 1986, 2017b). This makes them much younger than Egyptian hieroglyphs (attested before 3000 BCE) but slightly older than the earliest forms of Roman letters, which developed from the Egyptian-inspired Phoenician alphabet (invented by 1000 BCE) (Simons 2011).

The earliest surviving corpus of indisputable Chinese characters consists of questions and answers carved on flat animal bones (e.g., oxen shoulder blades or turtle shell bellies), as part of a divination ritual in which hot rods were applied to create portentous cracks. This system is thus called the oracle bone script (甲骨文 *jiǎgǔwén* 'shell and bone script'; Venture 2001, 2017). Like Egyptian hieroglyphs, the symbols were relatively picture-like, but also like Egyptian, they were not literally pictographic (Boltz 2006a) because they were already abstract and associated, as least as memory aids during rituals, with a spoken language (known from somewhat later writings to have a sophisticated syntax; see, e.g., Herforth 2003). Most relevantly for the notion of character grammar, from the earliest stages many characters were already productively created by combining other characters (see Section 4.3.1).

An important milestone came in 100 CE with the compilation of around 10,000 characters and variants by Xu Shen (許慎 *Xǔ Shèn*) in a work often referred to

4 Chinese character grammar

simply as *Shuowen* (說文解字 *Shuōwén jiězì*, roughly 'Explaining graphs and analyzing characters'; see Bottéro and Harbsmeier 2008 for context and caveats). As suggested by the title, it was not just a character list but also a treatise on character structure, one that remains influential today (see Section 1.2.2). It described the character system prevalent during China's first imperial dynasty, the Qin (221 to 206 BCE), which has come to be known as the small seal script (小篆書 *xiǎozhuànshū*) because of its usage in identification seals.

By the time Xu wrote his magnum opus, the small seal script had actually been supplanted by so-called clerical script (隸書 *lìshū* 'slave script'). Starting around a century after Xu, this evolved into the regular script (楷書 *kǎishū*) of today, the longest-lived script standard in Chinese history. Regular script looks strikingly different from its predecessors: its mostly straight lines are easier to produce with an ink brush than the flowing curves of small seal script.

Today small seal and clerical script are mainly used for artistic purposes, along with later-derived calligraphic styles like semi-cursive script (行書 *xíngshū* 'running script') and the even less legible shorthand-like cursive script (草書 *cǎoshū* 'grass script'). The invention of moveable woodblock printing brought the Song typefaces (宋體 *Sòngtǐ*, where 體 *tǐ* is literally 'body' but here connotes 'style'), named after the dynasty (960–1279), though following Japanese typographic conventions they are also called Ming (明體 *Míngtǐ*), after a later dynasty (1368–1644). Song typefaces (or 'fonts,' in the terminology of word processing programs) are the ones encountered most often by readers, at least until modern times, when sans serif typefaces (黑體 *hēitǐ* 'black style') became popular for street signs, newspaper headlines, and now the internet. For more on Chinese character styles (in calligraphy and typesetting), see Gu (2017), Tseng (1993), Palmer (2015), and Wilkinson (2000); I regret not being able to incorporate much on the calligraphic tradition in this book, particularly its insights into low-level character structure.

The most recent major change is the system of simplified characters (簡體字 *jiǎntǐzì* 'simple style characters,' or 簡化字 *jiǎnhuàzì* 'simplified characters,' respectively, 简体字 and 简化字 in the system itself), which was developed in the People's Republic of China, primarily in the 1950s and 1960s, and is now used worldwide, aside from Hong Kong, Macao, and Taiwan (Li 1996; Li 2017; Handel 2013; Wiedenhof 2017). This system is traditionally contrasted with what in English are traditionally called traditional characters (the Chinese terms, 正體字 *zhèngtǐzì* 'proper style characters' or 繁體字 *fántǐzì* 'complex style characters,' do not mention tradition but are just as politically tinged). However, as compared with earlier script changes, this latest change was relatively minor: simplified characters (or constituents) were mostly adopted from existing character variants and calligraphic styles, with somewhere between 45 percent (Wiedenhof 2017) and 65 percent (Tsai and Tai 2018) remaining identical to their traditional counterparts (see also Ministry of Education of the Republic of China 2011). While most of this book focuses on traditional characters, the implications of simplification for character grammar is discussed in Section 4.3.2 and in various places in Chapter 5.

Table 1.1 The character for 'fish' *yú*

Oracle bone	Small seal	Clerical	Regular	Song	Sans serif	Simplified regular
𩵋	魚	魚	魚	魚	魚	鱼

Note: The oracle bone example comes from Academia Sinica (2018).

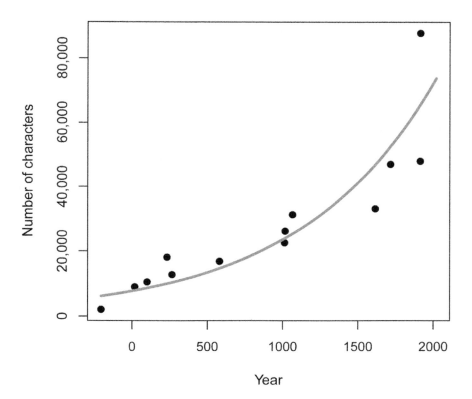

Figure 1.1 The exponential growth of character inventories

Examples of the script styles I have mentioned are shown in Table 1.1. Throughout this book I use brush-pen-like regular typefaces when citing character examples and Song typefaces when using, as opposed to exemplifying, Chinese in the text.

Over all these historical periods, new characters continued to be coined, indeed at an exponential rate. I mean this quite literally: as shown in Figure 1.1, if we plot character dictionary sizes by the year in which they were compiled (based on data in Yip 2000, p. 19), the best-fitting curve is mathematically exponential ($B = 0.001$, $SE = 0.0002$, $t = 6.9$, $p < .0001$, where B estimates the slope of the line predicting the logarithm of the number of characters, SE represents the standard

6 Chinese character grammar

error or noisiness of the estimate, $t = B/SE$ measures how far the estimate is from the null result of zero, and p is the probability that these results could arise by chance, where by convention $p < .05$, or 5 percent, indicates statistical significance). Of course, the size increase may also be due to the incorporation of ever more obsolete and variant characters by obsessive scholars; Handel (forthcoming) found only 585 characters in the modern traditional character computer standard that were not already attested in a major eighteenth-century dictionary, and most of these ended up having even earlier attestations or were otherwise suspect. After all, why invent new characters when the inventory of the spoken monosyllabic morphemes that they represent is itself relatively fixed? Nevertheless, the accelerating rate at which characters came out of the woodwork is reminiscent of biological growth and is thus consistent with the independently demonstrable fact that characters are generally coined via constrained constituent recombination (see Sections 4.2.1, 4.4.2, and 4.4.3).

While character history has long been a central focus of character research, it is not the focus of this book (for further reiterations of this crucial point, see Sections 1.3.1.2, 1.3.2, 1.5.2, and 2.2). Of course, modern character patterns arose in the past, but history is not destiny; regular script is dramatically different from earlier character systems (see Section 4.3.1), and it is not helpful to dismiss its quite systematic reanalyses as mere 'corruptions' (訛變 *ébiàn*), as character historians sometimes do. Moreover, modern readers and writers take modern and not ancient characters as the starting point for their productive generalizations (as demonstrated in Chapters 4 and 5).

1.2.1.3. Characters in the modern world

My sudden jump from ancient history to statistical modeling at the end of the previous section exemplifies much of contemporary character research. Computers have not only made it possible to compile and analyze enormous databases of Chinese text (Huang and Qi 2017; McEnery and Xiao 2016; Zhang 2016), but also to encode, decompose, and recognize characters in print or handwriting (Chan 2003; Dai, Liu, and Xiao 2007; Hsieh 2006; Kordek 2013; Su 2013). Chinese characters, along with the related systems used in Japan and Korea, are now included (as part of the so-called CJK Unified Ideograph component) in the Unicode system, which attempts to provide distinct digital codes for every unit in every living writing system and continues to expand (e.g., Burkimsher 2018).

Computers have also had a huge impact on how Chinese is written. Chinese typewriters were already highly sophisticated a century ago (Mullaney 2017), but computer software now allows even a minimally skilled Chinese writer to call up any desired character, or even multicharacter word, in just a few keystrokes (Wittern 2017). Most typists use a code representing pronunciation (e.g., with Pinyin romanization or the older onset-and-rime-based 注音符號 *Zhùyīn fúhào* system still used in Taiwan), but others prefer one indicating orthographic form rather than pronunciation, in particular the Cangjie (倉頡 *Cāngjié*) and Wubi (五筆 *Wǔbǐ*) input systems.

Chinese character grammar 7

Technology has also played an essential role in the rapid development of psycholinguistic and neurolinguistic research on characters, by making it easier to design, run, and analyze experiments on reading, writing, and learning to read and write. Chinese psycholinguistics began with studies on individual characters (Myers 2017a), and this remains a major research line today (see reviews in Liu and Wu 2017; Perfetti, Liu, and Tan 2005; Su and Law 2017; Tao and Healy 2016). In Chapter 5, I review the subset of this literature most relevant to character grammar.

1.2.2. Character structure

Now that I have put characters into context, it is time to look inside them. I first review the traditional classification of character types (Section 1.2.2.1) and describe their semantic and phonetic components (Section 1.2.2.2), then other character components (Section 1.2.2.3), and finally strokes (Section 1.2.2.4).

1.2.2.1. Character types

A key claim of the *Shuowen* analysis of Xu Shen (though it precedes him) was that all characters can be classified into six basic types, an idea called 六書 *liù shū* ('six writings'). Later scholars have proposed their own systems, with a larger or smaller number of classes and subclasses (e.g., Behr 2010; Boltz 2017c; Novotná 1962; Qiu 2000), but Xu's immensely influential system will suffice for our purposes. Table 1.2 illustrates Xu's principles with his own examples; the characters, pronunciations, and translations reflect modern Chinese (the English glosses for Xu's terms are from Qiu 2000, p. 152, though scholars disagree on exactly what some meant at the time).

Table 1.2 Xu Shen's six character categories in *Shuowen*

Chinese term	Rough English gloss	Examples	
指事 *zhǐshì*	'indicate things'	上	*shàng* 'above'
		下	*xià* 'below'
象形 *xiàngxíng*	'resemble form'	日	*rì* 'sun'
		月	*yuè* 'moon'
形聲 *xíngshēng*	'form and sound'	江	*jiāng* 'river'
		河	*hé* 'river'
會意 *huìyì*	'conjoining meanings'	武	*wǔ* 'martial'
		信	*xìn* 'trust'
轉注 *zhuǎnzhù*	'evolving and deriving'	考	*kǎo* 'examine' (obsolete: 'elderly')
		老	*lǎo* 'aged'
假借 *jiǎjiè*	'loan-borrowing'	令	*lìng* 'to lead'
		長	*zhǎng* 'leader'

8 *Chinese character grammar*

The first two categories are essentially iconic, in that they represent ideas or entities through metaphor or physical similarity. The last two actually relate not to character structure but to character etymology, via formal modification or reuse of existing characters to represent new spoken morphemes. It is thus only the two middle categories that are grammatically relevant, since they involve the recombination of synchronic character components. The difference between these two types lies in what I will call their EXTERNAL INTERPRETATIONS. 'Form and sound' characters combine a component indicating pronunciation with one hinting at meaning; such characters are thus often called SEMANTIC-PHONETIC characters (also called 'phono-semantic,' 'radical-phonetic,' 'picto-phonetic,' or 'phonograms').

The logic in Xu's two examples for this type is illustrated in (4). Unfortunately, these examples are complicated by a couple of issues. First, sound change has obscured the earlier similarity in pronunciations between character and phonetic component; Zhengzhang (2013) reconstructs the Old Chinese pronunciations of 江 and 工 respectively as /kroːŋ/ and /koːŋ/, and those of 河 and 可 respectively as /gaːl/ and /kʰaːlʔ/ (the reconstructions of Baxter and Sagart 2014 are also near-homophone pairs). Second, in the modern characters the semantic component changes dramatically in shape (as discussed further in Chapters 2, 3, and 4).

(4)   a 江 *jiāng* 'Yangtze River' = 氵(水) *shuǐ* 'water' + 工 *gōng* 'work' (phonetic)
       b 河 *hé* 'river' = 氵(水) *shuǐ* 'water' + 可 *kě* 'can' (phonetic)

In the other type of decomposable character in Xu's typology, 'conjoined meanings,' all of the components are interpreted for their meaning, as illustrated with his examples in (5), which are again less than ideal. Not only are the semantic analyses unclear (traditionally understood as stopping a weapon and standing by one's speech, respectively), but both have been argued by modern scholars to have been originally coined as semantic-phonetic characters (albeit with pronunciations now obscured through sound change), uncontroversially in the case of 信 (e.g., Qiu 2000, p. 155) and contentiously in the case of 武 (see Boltz 2006b; Boltz 1994 argues against Xu's entire 'conjoining meanings' category, while Bottéro 1996 and Sampson and Chen 2013 defend the mainstream view). In any case, I will use the term SEMANTIC COMPOUND for the kind of character that Xu thought that these exemplified, since modern readers do often see characters this way (see, e.g., Section 4.4.3).

(5)   a 武 *wǔ* 'martial' = 止 *zhǐ* 'stop' + 戈 *gē* 'dagger-ax'
       b 信 *xìn* 'trust' = 亻(人) *rén* 'person' + 言 *yán* 'speech'

A subtype of Xu's 'conjoining meanings' category that will prove grammatically quite interesting is what I will call REDUPLICATION (more traditionally known as 叠體字 *diétǐzì* 'stacked-body characters'; see Behr 2006, p. 86; Liu 2008, pp. 5–7, for many other terms). Not only do the meanings of the reduplicated forms in (6) relate to the meanings of the repeated constituent, but as noted by

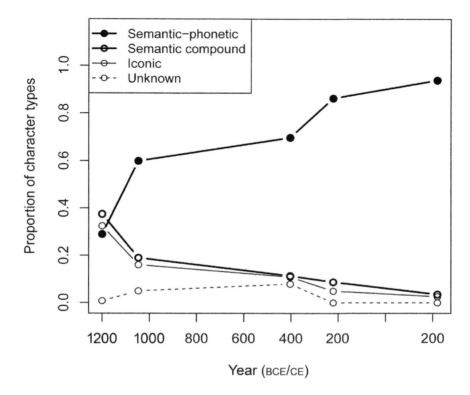

Figure 1.2 Proportion of character types in oracle bone script (ca. 1200 BCE), bronze inscriptions (1046 BCE), Warring States script (403 BCE), small seal script (221 BCE), and early regular script (220 CE)

Source: Based on Huang (2003, p. 3, Table 1).

Behr (2006), the reduplication itself is meaningful, typically being associated with ideas like plurality, repetition, and attenuation.

(6) a 木 *mù* 'wood, tree'   林 *lín* 'forest'
    b 火 *huǒ* 'fire'   炎 *yán* 'blazing'
    c 日 *rì* 'sun'   晶 *jīng* 'glittering'

Of all character types, semantic-phonetic characters are by far the most productive and have been for millennia. Figure 1.2, based on Huang (2003, p. 3, Table 1), plots the proportions of character inventories for Xu's first four categories (combining the two iconic types into one and adding an 'unknown' category for the older systems) as they evolved over time. The years represent the onset of the political era associated with each script: oracle bones of the Shang king Wu Ding; bronze inscriptions, traditionally associated with the Western Zhou, though they actually emerged earlier (Chu 2004); Warring States writing; the small seal script

10 *Chinese character grammar*

of the Qin; and the regular script of the Cao Wei. Similar values are given by Hsu (1991, p. 118). The dominance of the semantic-phonetic type is clear: only in the very oldest period do the others form a substantial portion of the character inventory. By the end of Huang's historical survey, over 90 percent of all characters were semantic-phonetic, around the same as for modern characters (an oft-cited reference is Zhou 1978, who estimates that around 80 percent of simplified characters remain transparently semantic-phonetic).

1.2.2.2. Semantic radicals and phonetic components

Another influential feature of *Shuowen* was to group characters by a shared component that came to be called the 'radical' in English. The term 'radical' is not ideal; not only does the Chinese 部首 *bùshǒu* literally just mean 'group heading' (see Behr and Söderblom-Saarela 2018 for further history and critiques), but I argue in Chapter 2 that radicals behave more like affixes than the 'roots' implied by the term's etymology. Handel (forthcoming) suggests that it would be more appropriate to call them 'classifiers,' for reasons I also review (and endorse) in Chapter 2. Nevertheless, I have decided to retain the familiar English term RADICAL to avoid imposing an analysis before I have argued for it and to reduce the burden on the reader's memory (after all, polysemous terminology is hardly radical).

The *Shuowen* character set was organized around 540 radicals, but it was the much later *Compendium of Standard Characters from the Kangxi Period* (康熙字典 *Kāngxī zìdiǎn*), completed in 1716 CE and named after the Qing dynasty emperor who ordered it (Winter 2017), that popularized the now-standard set of 214 radicals still used for traditional characters (simplified characters have a somewhat different set; see Section 4.3.2). These radicals include many that Handel (2019) calls merely LEXICOGRAPHIC, being simple but arbitrary graphical elements chosen solely for indexing purposes, as illustrated in (7) (the dictionary of Lin 1972 took this approach to an extreme, classifying all characters via a mere 50 form-based 'radicals').

(7) a 丘 *qiū* 'mound' (lexicographic radical: 一 *yī* 'one')
     b 也 *yě* 'also' (lexicographic radical: 乙 *yǐ* 'second')

However, the traditional radical list also contains many genuine SEMANTIC RADICALS, which relate to the whole character's meaning. In this book, I restrict this term to semantic-phonetic characters; of course, semantic compounds are also comprised of semantic components in a more general sense, but they behave differently from semantic radicals in some ways (see Sections 2.3.1 and 2.3.2). Some researchers, especially psycholinguists, extend the term 'radical' to all character constituents, even those uninterpreted in meaning or pronunciation, but in this book, 'radical' only refers to the lexicographic or semantic radical, and virtually always the latter.

The other part of a semantic-phonetic character is called the PHONETIC COMPONENT, since it relates to the character's pronunciation ('phonetic element' is also

Chinese character grammar 11

seen, but this misleadingly implies that they must be indivisible). As I use the terms, then, the semantic radical and phonetic component both have external interpretations in the modern spoken language, unlike individual strokes and other types of stroke groups. Some more or less transparently interpretable semantic-phonetic characters are shown decomposed into their semantic and phonetic components in (8); I return to the issue of transparency in Section 2.2.

(8) a 時 *shí* 'time' = 日 *rì* 'day' + 寺 *sì* 'temple'
     b 花 *huā* 'flower' = ⁺⁺ (艸) *cǎo* 'grass' + 化 *huà* 'change'
     c 鵬 *péng* 'roc (mythical bird)' = 鳥 *niǎo* 'bird' + 朋 *péng* 'friend'
     d 梨 *lí* 'pear' = 木 *mù* 'wood, tree' + 利 *lì* 'benefit'

Since semantic radicals are typically combined with constituents that are characters in their own right, including those that were previously created in the same way, it is common to find recursively decomposable structures like that in (9). The recursive nature of character structure has often been noted (e.g., Chuang and Teng 2009; Harbaugh 1998; Ladd 2014; Sproat 2000), but it is still remarkable to find an orthographic system with this hallmark of grammatical architecture (see Section 1.3.1.3).

(9) 燙 *tàng* 'scalding hot' = 火 *huǒ* 'fire' + 湯 *tāng* 'soup'
     湯 *tāng* 'soup' = 氵 (水) *shuǐ* 'water' + 易 *yáng* 'yang (male principle)'

1.2.2.3. Other character constituents

Missing from traditional character analysis is what to do with the many character components that appear across characters but provide no information about the (modern) meaning or pronunciation. That diachronic change has created this situation so frequently is itself interesting from the perspective of character grammar, since it suggests that character compositionality is irresistible even when it obscures etymology and is irrelevant to the recording of spoken language.

I will use CONSTITUENT as a neutral term that includes not only interpreted constituents, like semantic radicals and phonetic components, but also synchronically uninterpreted ones, while not precluding further decomposition into still smaller constituents. Non-decomposable constituents are BASIC CONSTITUENTS, though as we will see shortly, they have yet to be defined to everyone's satisfaction; other terms in the literature include 'formatives' (Wang 1983), 'logographemes' (Lui *et al.* 2010), and 'stroke patterns' (Chen, Allport, and Marshall 1996). If it is not clear whether a group of strokes should even be considered a constituent, I will use the even more neutral term STROKE GROUP. Figure 1.3 summarizes my hierarchy of terms (not pictured are lexicographic radicals, which include semantic radicals but not phonetic components, yet need not even be stroke groups; see Section 1.2.2.2).

The obvious fact of character decompositionality does not imply that basic character constituents must form a well-defined set. Table 1.3 demonstrates how much the proposed constituent inventories for traditional characters, simplified

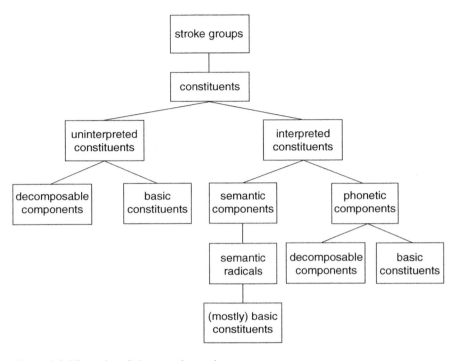

Figure 1.3 Hierarchy of character-internal parts

Table 1.3 The sizes of proposed inventories of basic character constituents

System	Source	Inventory size
Traditional	Lui *et al.* (2010)	249
	Chinese Document Processing Lab (2011)	441
	CNS 11643–2 (see Chuang and Teng 2009)	517
	Lu *et al.* (2002)	644
	Morioka (2008)	667
Simplified	Lu (1991) (cited in Guder-Manitius 2009)	347
	Fei (1996) (cited in Guder-Manitius 2009)	384
	Xiao (1994) (cited in Guder-Manitius 2009)	423
	Ministry of Education of the People's Republic of China (2009a)	514
	Ministry of Education of the People's Republic of China (1997)	560
Japanese	Stalph (1989)	485
	Kawabata (2010)	593

characters, and Japanese kanji vary in size (see Kordek 2013, pp. 74–77, for discussion of some of these).

Proposed constituent inventories generally start from the reasonable assumption, adapted from morphological theory, that one cannot segment off a group of strokes unless the remainder is itself a constituent or a combination of constituents. This is about as far as the consensus goes, however. As Kordek (2013, p. 75) notes, one source of disagreement is 'graphical variant forms' (which I will analyze in Chapters 2 and 3). For example, the constituents in (10) all differ in one way or another as free characters vs. character-internal components. Researchers seem to consider the difference in (10a) too drastic to treat the constituents as the same (though readers and writers still know that they are related), while they generally treat variants that differ only in size, as in (10b), as identical. It is the intermediate degrees of shape change, as in (10c–d), where constituent inventory proposals tend to disagree.

(10) a 水 vs. 河 (氵)
     b 口 vs. 如
     c 木 vs. 相
     d 且 vs. 助

Proposed constituent inventories also differ in whether they allow constituents to overlap. For example, most proposals would reject a synchronic decomposition like that in (11).

(11) 東 *dōng* 'east' = 木 *mù* 'wood, tree' + 日 *rì* 'sun'

However, the ultimate reason for disagreement among inventory proponents may simply be that they are attempting the impossible. Diachronic reanalysis has resulted in many modern characters that are not fully decomposable, just as in the lexicons of spoken and signed languages. Moreover, grammatical systems and lexical inventories complement each other. Since the latter cannot be determined without analyzing the former, and since grammar and the lexicon are both empirical psychological issues, they cannot be stipulated by committee. I return to all of these points in later chapters.

1.2.2.4. Strokes

When we finally reach the lowest level of modern character structure, the stroke, we return to an area where traditional analyses have had much to say. The basic strokes in regular script have long been recognized and named, as illustrated in Table 1.4.

Moreover, characters are not supposed to be sketched freely like pictures, but rather written out, stroke by stroke, in a particular sequence, each stroke having its own direction. For example, the character in (12a) is often used as a tally

14 *Chinese character grammar*

Table 1.4 Simple character strokes and their traditional names

Stroke	Traditional name	Examples	
﹨	點 *diǎn* 'dot'	太	寸
一	橫 *héng* 'horizontal'	三	十
丨	豎 *shù* 'vertical'	十	中
㇀	提 *tí* 'rise'	子	氺
﹨	捺 *nà* 'press down'	八	木
㇒	撇 *piě* 'throw away'	千	才
㇅	彎 *wān* 'bend'	川	月
㇄	鉤 *gōu* 'hook'	丁	事
㇂	斜 *xié* 'slant'	戈	心

Note: Stroke images from https://commons.wikimedia.org/wiki/Category:CJK_strokes (by user 'Cangjie6'), licensed under the Creative Commons CC0 1.0 Universal Public Domain Dedication. Variation in stroke form will be discussed in Chapter 3.

marker (counting in units of five), with the strokes being added one by one in the order shown in (12b), the horizontal lines drawn left to right and the vertical ones downward. I discuss stroke direction and order in Sections 3.4.1 and 3.6.2, respectively.

(12) a 正 *zhèng* 'proper'
      b 一 丁 千 疒 正

1.3. Grammar

To be clearer on what the notion of character grammar might entail, we should step back and reconsider the notion of grammar more generally. In this section, I first sketch out what seem to me to be its essential properties (Section 1.3.1) and then review how grammatical claims are tested (Section 1.3.2).

1.3.1. The nature of grammar

As scholars in several cultures have discovered semi-independently (Section 1.3.1.1), grammar is a psychologically real phenomenon (Section 1.3.1.2) allowing language to be productive (Section 1.3.1.3) in accordance with abstract principles (Section 1.3.1.4).

1.3.1.1. The discovery of grammar

All cultures have notions about how language works (e.g., Hunter 1982), and the profession of grammarian predates Aristotle in ancient Greece (Hovdhaugen 1982) and Pāṇini in ancient India (Cardona 1994). The ancient Chinese studied grammar as well, with a particularly sophisticated theory of phonology, influenced by contact with Sanskrit tradition (Downer 1963; Malmqvist 1994). Chinese linguists were not entirely uninterested in morphosyntax, the most enduring analytic framework being the dichotomy between so-called empty words (虚字 *xūzì*, i.e., grammatical morphemes) and full words (實字 *shízì*, i.e., content words), but if classical Chinese linguists had little to say about grammar beyond phonology, it is only because morphology and syntax are harder to become aware of in Sinitic languages. Unlike Greek and Sanskrit, Chinese has never had (much) inflection and is written with morpheme-sized units; both of these features obscure morphological relations and syntactic distinctions.

The idea that orthography makes linguistic patterns visible also explains why the one grammatical domain (besides phonology) where Chinese linguists excelled was in character analysis, as emphasized by Wang (1989). By any measure, Xu Shen's *Shuowen* is a linguistic masterpiece, and the ever more sophisticated character compendia and analyses that followed reveal how natural it is for the inquisitive human mind to recognize that language is systematic, even written language.

1.3.1.2. Psychological reality

Psychological reality is a fraught term for reasons explained in Section 1.3.2 (see also Myers 2017b), but it does capture an important idea: whatever else grammars may be, they are (neuro)psychological things. This idea predates linguistics; even in folk tales, thinking animals are talking animals. Language is also linked to thought in the otherwise quite different scholarly traditions of ancient India, China, and Greece and remains so in the works of Humboldt, Wundt, Sapir, Whorf, Chomsky, Halliday, and Langacker. Even when synchronic patterns are explainable by language history (see, e.g., Blevins 2004 for phonology as history), linguistically constrained mental processes are still necessary to explain how they arose in the first place (see, e.g., Kiparsky 2006 for a critique of Blevins). Without psychology, language history cannot even explain itself, let alone the productive abilities of present-day speakers and signers.

Psychological reality does not depend on conscious awareness; most fluent speakers and signers would be hard pressed to explain why they speak/sign one way and not another. It also does not preclude the universally acknowledged fact that language is social, since sociolinguistic skills still reside in individual minds (Labov *et al.* 2011). Grammar need not even be fully distinct from language use. In the case of syntax, where novel sentences must be parsed or constructed on the fly, Neeleman and van de Koot (2010) argue that it is impractical to the point of impossibility for mental grammar to be consulted like a textbook; it is much more efficient to build grammatical knowledge directly into the language processor

16 *Chinese character grammar*

itself. That is, as in the famous multi-level model of cognition advocated by Marr (1982), grammar is merely an efficient way of describing what the language processor is 'designed' to do. Experiments confirm that real-time processes really do 'know' grammar: the mental sentence parser skips syntactic islands when probing for *wh*-movement gaps (Phillips and Wagers 2007), regular and irregular verbs are treated differently in lexical access (Pinker and Ullman 2002), and consonant clusters are 'corrected' in the mind's ear when they violate phonotactic constraints (Berent *et al.* 2007).

1.3.1.3. Productivity

Speakers and signers are capable of understanding and producing linguistic forms that they have never encountered before, something impossible by rote memory alone. Productivity is sometimes linked to the more technical notion of recursion, which relates, roughly speaking, to building a new member of a class out of an existing member of this class, or at least building a new class member in a predictable way (see, e.g., Fitch 2010).

Character grammar would have to be a lexical grammar, however, and productivity is more constrained in the lexicon; syntax can generate an unlimited number of sentences, but people are much more cautious about accepting new words. Nevertheless, Di Sciullo and Williams (1987, p. 3) were clearly joking when they parodied the conventional linguistic view that "the lexicon is like a prison – it contains only the lawless, and the only thing that its inmates have in common is lawlessness." There are endless debates about how precisely one should balance the regular and the rote, but it is doable: some take the position that lexical grammar is fully productive like syntax, but can only fill in information not already fixed by memory (e.g., Di Sciullo and Williams 1987; Harley and Noyer 1999; Pinker and Ullman 2002), and others the opposite position that grammatical regularity actually arises from the coalescence of many similar lexical memories (e.g., Blevins 2006; Bybee and Hopper 2001; Jackendoff and Audring 2016).

In either case, the result is that in a lexical grammar, productivity is intrinsically gradient, with processes ranging from very productive to very unproductive (Bauer 2001). When quantifying gradient productivity, lexical frequency becomes important. Token frequency counts the number of times a particular lexical item is encountered (e.g., *it* has a higher token frequency in English than *id*). By contrast, type frequency counts the number of items in the mental lexicon that conform to some pattern, and this makes it more relevant to grammatical analysis (Perfors, Ransom, and Navarro 2014). For example, most English verbs form the past tense with -*ed*, and this high type frequency makes it highly productive in novel forms (Pinker and Ullman 2002). The fact that most of the exceptions to this regularity are of high token frequency (e.g., *see*, *eat*, *run*) results from the protective effect of rote memory. Chapters 4 and 5 provide copious evidence for the productivity of character grammar, with gradient productivity highlighted particularly in Section 4.2.3.

1.3.1.4. Abstractness

Grammars, even lexical grammars, are abstract in at least three ways: they are non-iconic, amodal, and modular.

An iconic representation is one with elements and relations that map relatively straightforwardly onto the real-world situation that it represents (Simone 1995). While iconicity plays some role in language, it cannot subsume abstract grammar. One specific instance of this is the hallmark of grammar known as the duality of patterning (Hockett 1960): human language does not merely combine meaningful elements to express ideas derivable from their combination, as in syntax and morphology (i.e., iconically mapping complex forms to complex meanings), but it also combines meaningless elements merely to make arbitrary lexical distinctions, as in phonology. Presumably the meaningless regularities of phonology are useful in some indirect way; for example, shrinking the space of phonologically well-formed morphemes reduces the burdens of morpheme learning and processing.

Second, grammar is not tied to a particular physical modality (i.e., input and output). When a speaker or signer transmits a word to another, both producer and recipient feel that it is the 'same': the two directions of language processing need to meet somewhere in the middle, in some sort of amodal form (if only virtually, at the top of Marr's levels). Bever (1975) suggested that children develop grammar precisely in order to mediate between language production and comprehension; Pickering and Garrod (2013) discuss similar ideas. Momma and Phillips (2018), after noting that in the case of syntax "the claim that the parser and the generator share the same grammar . . . is not especially controversial" (p. 237), argue that these input and output systems themselves may share mechanisms.

Finally, grammar is not only amodal but also modular, that is, relatively independent of other components of cognition, and is itself divisible into relatively independent subcomponents like syntax, morphology, and phonology, with phonetics lying at the margins of grammar proper. While the idea that these terms refer to distinct things is as old as the terms themselves, grammatical modularity is not absolute; I have already admitted that there is no sharp line between grammar and the lexicon. These are well-known challenges, however, and so there are established approaches for dealing with them (see Section 1.3.1.4, as well as Section 3.5). Experimental evidence relating to all three aspects of character grammar abstractness is reviewed in Section 5.2.1.

1.3.2. Evidence for grammar

As Rey (2014, p. 243) points out, "Anything is, of course, evidence of whatever best explains it." Hence, there is no *a priori* privileged source of evidence about grammar; any relevant empirical observation should be considered, from simple linguistic descriptions to high-tech brain scans.

To put it tautologically, there are exactly two types of empirical observations: experimental and everything else. In linguistics, the latter type typically comes in corpora of natural language productions. Corpus analysis has the advantage of

18 *Chinese character grammar*

providing relatively direct information about natural (non-manipulated) language production, even for dead languages. For example, the fact that there are more words in the English dictionary (a corpus-derived database) ending in *-ness* than *-ity* suggests that *-ness* affixation is (or at least was) more productive than *-ity* affixation. This conclusion is strengthened when one compares the proportion of low-token-frequency words formed in these two ways in large text corpora (e.g., Baayen and Renouf 1996), since rare words are potentially novel coinages (see Section 4.2.2 for details and caveats). Similarly, no English words start with /bn/, few start with /sf/ (e.g., *sphere, sphincter, Sphynx*), and many start with /bl/ (e.g., *black, blue, blind, blood, blow*), suggesting that English phonology favors certain consonant clusters over others. I apply arguments of this sort to characters in Chapters 2 and 3, and particularly in Section 4.2.

However, a corpus is generally given to the researcher as is, which may prove frustrating if initial hypotheses are suggested by preliminary analyses with no way to follow them up. Corpus gaps also pose an inferential challenge. If the corpus size is large enough and the construction simple enough, it is possible to interpret a gap by calculating the probability of the construction being absent by chance alone (e.g., Stefanowitsch 2006), but corpora are not always large enough nor constructions simple enough. The most important limitation of corpus analysis, for lexical grammar in particular, is that it is impossible to be sure if a corpus pattern is part of synchronic grammar and not merely a historical relic. This is the primary reason why Ohala (1986) argues that experiments are superior to corpus evidence when testing phonological hypotheses, and the same point applies to morphology.

Fortunately, if grammar is what language is trying to do, then any psycholinguistic or neurolinguistic experiment should reflect grammatical knowledge. For example, psycholinguists who study lexical access often use the lexical decision task, where participants are shown real and fake words and must decide which is which, and the naming task, where participants name pictures or read aloud written words. While such experimental paradigms have taught us a lot about how real words are looked up in memory, they can also tell us what participants expect words to be like. In the lexical decision task, for instance, the more word-like the nonwords, the slower and more inaccurately they will be rejected. The wordlikeness of real words also matters (e.g., *blink* vs. *sphere*), even when rote memory factors like token frequency are taken into account. In Section 5.2, I apply this logic in reinterpreting the existing character reading literature from a grammatical perspective.

The most direct experimental test of grammar, however, is simply to ask participants for acceptability judgments for nonexistent forms. While it is true that acceptability is affected by factors other than grammatical status, numerous experiments have demonstrated their robustness, even in linguistic judgments by non-linguists (Myers 2017c). This method is highlighted in Section 5.3.

1.4. Grammar beyond speech

My examination of character grammar builds on previous extensions of grammar beyond spoken language, above all the natural sign languages of the world's many

Chinese character grammar 19

Deaf communities (Section 1.4.1; the capitalization indicates that these are cultural groups). Some researchers have also applied grammatical notions to nonlinguistic cultural artifacts (Section 1.4.2) and to orthography itself (Section 1.4.3).

1.4.1. Sign language grammar

Sign languages are, in fact, my major inspiration for exploring Chinese characters from a grammatical perspective, and not only because they are also visual (an oft-noted similarity: see, e.g., Flaherty 2003; Fok and Bellugi 1986; Fok *et al.* 1991; Steinberg 1986). Since the revolutionary work on American Sign Language (ASL) by Stokoe, Casterline, and Croneberg (1965), a vast and ever-growing literature on sign language, from grammatical descriptions (e.g., Jepsen *et al.* 2015; Myers 2017d) to corpus analyses (e.g., Schembri *et al.* 2013) to diachronic change (e.g., Senghas, Kita, and Özyürek 2004) to cross-linguistic typology (e.g., Sandler and Lillo-Martin 2006) to psycholinguistic experimentation (e.g., Emmorey 2001), has demonstrated that sign languages are natural human languages in their social and communicative functions, in their neuropsychological underpinnings, and above all in their grammars. Sign utterances are arranged into sentences with hierarchical structure and syntactic classes (Neidle *et al.* 2001), words (signs) may be composed of smaller meaningful parts and are inflected to indicate things like plurality, person, and aspect (Aronoff, Meir, and Sandler 2005), and even monomorphemic words are decomposable into smaller basic parameters (locations, movements, and handshapes, themselves built out of features like joint bending) that are modified in context (Brentari 1998) and realized in syllable-like structures (Sandler 2008).

Contemporary linguists thus have no doubt that sign languages have syntax, morphology, and even phonology. It may seem odd to apply the term 'phonology' to silent languages; Stokoe himself felt that way, offering instead the neologism 'cherology' (from the Greek word for 'hand'). The term did not catch on, however, because phonology is not physics but psychology. Exactly as in spoken languages, sign phonology deals with lexically contrasting features, prosodic grouping, and predictable changes in form that are semantically neutral and cannot be ascribed to physiology alone (e.g., Brentari 2011), while sign phonetics deals with articulation and perception (e.g., Napoli, Sanders, and Wright 2014; Wilcox 1992).

As an example of sign phonology, Battison (1978) observed that in most two-handed signs in ASL, either both hands have the same handshape, or else the non-dominant hand (e.g., the left hand for right-handed signers) takes one of a small number of simple handshapes, like a fist or an open palm. Eccarius and Brentari (2007) extended these observations to two-handed signs in Hong Kong Sign Language and Swiss German Sign Language, and Lee (2016) did likewise for Taiwan Sign Language (TSL), as illustrated with the examples in Figures 1.4 and 1.5 (from Tsay, Tai, and Chen 2017).

While in a physical sense nothing in spoken languages remotely resembles these constraints, at an abstract level they exemplify a familiar phonological phenomenon: the complementary filling in of features via assimilation or via defaults.

20 *Chinese character grammar*

Figure 1.4 OFTEN (TSL), rotating motion repeats

Source: Redrawn by Shihkai Liu from video images in Tsay *et al.* (2017), with permission.

Figure 1.5 HABIT (TSL, northern dialect), rotating motion repeats

Source: Redrawn by Shihkai Liu from video images in Tsay *et al.* (2017), with permission.

In many languages, vowels are oral by default, but become nasalized when adjacent to nasal consonants (e.g., English *cat* [kʰæt] vs. *can* [kʰæ̃n]), and in languages with tone spreading, a tone is filled in by default when spreading does not occur (e.g., Yip 2002; Wee 2019). The handshapes on the non-dominant hand fit this universal pattern as well, since the defaults tend to be unmarked, being the easiest to articulate and the most frequent within and across sign languages (Ann 2006). In Section 3.4.2, I discuss a similar trade-off between defaults and assimilation in Chinese character strokes.

Despite their separate histories and lack of mutual intelligibility, sign languages are much more similar to each other than spoken languages (Sandler and Lillo-Martin 2006). This is partly due to the way they are learned, more often from their Deaf contemporaries than from their parents, who are usually hearing. This splintering of cross-generational transmission makes it hard for idiosyncrasies to accumulate, while marked properties tend to be smoothed over as young minds re-impose default settings (Singleton and Newport 2004). This smoothing need not be instantaneous; Sandler *et al.* (2011) show that the very young Al-Sayyid Bedouin Sign Language, despite being richly expressive, has only just begun to develop duality of patterning. As reviewed in Section 4.3, Chinese character grammar has also increased in sophistication over the centuries, though due to the permanent record that it leaves, it is much more constrained by history than sign language grammar.

Chinese character grammar 21

Another obvious feature of signed languages is modality: they are manual and visual rather than oral and auditory. This is why sign languages compensate for the relative slowness of their large articulators (compared to speech) by marking affixation with simultaneous morphemes, attested though less common in spoken languages (McCarthy and Prince 1994). This trick allows the rate of information flow to be virtually identical in spoken and signed languages (Bellugi and Fischer 1972; Myers, Tsay, and Su 2011). We will see that Chinese character grammar is quite different in this regard (Section 2.3.1.2).

The visual modality has led to the greater use of iconicity in signed as compared with spoken languages (Armstrong 1983; Eccarius and Brentari 2010; Stokoe 1991; Taub 2001; Thompson, Vinson, and Vigliocco 2010; Vinson *et al.* 2015). Sign languages embedded in Chinese cultures even make use of the rich iconic resources afforded by the manual-visual modality to borrow Chinese characters into the sign lexicon (Ann 1998), as illustrated in Figure 1.6 with the TSL sign based on 中 (*zhōng* 'middle').

While its ubiquity in sign languages confirms that iconicity is a natural part of human language, the point I made earlier, about grammar being fundamentally abstract, still holds (see Section 1.3.1.4 and Davidson 2018 for other arguments). One indication of this is the mutual unintelligibility of unrelated sign languages; visual metaphors vary cross-linguistically (Emmorey 2014) and signs also tend to become less iconic over time (Aronoff, Meir, and Sandler 2005; Frishberg 1975). The limited role of sign iconicity is also suggested by the observation that children

Figure 1.6 MIDDLE (TSL)

Source: Redrawn by Shihkai Liu from video images in Tsay *et al.* (2017), with permission.

22 *Chinese character grammar*

begin to process signs as symbols long before they recognize iconic gestures (Namy 2008); iconicity only becomes productive after further cognitive development (Baus, Carreiras, and Emmorey 2013; Namy, Campbell, and Tomasello 2004). For example, young Deaf children can be as confused about the referents of deictic pronouns like 'I' and 'you' as are hearing children, even though this contrast involves quite transparent pointing gestures (Meier 1991). Moreover, when iconicity comes into conflict with purely phonological constraints, phonology generally wins (Emmorey 2014; Frishberg 1975; Sandler *et al.* 2011). We will see that the role of iconicity is similarly limited in Chinese characters (Section 5.2.1.1).

The existence of natural human languages in the visual-spatial modality has led some to conclude that signing must have been selected for in the course of biological evolution, and since manual gestures are articulatorily and neurologically simpler than speech vocalizations (and are also observed in other primate species), signing must have emerged prior to speech (e.g., Corballis 2002). The major sticking point for this speculation is well-known (e.g., Deacon 1997): why and how was sign language replaced by spoken language in the vast majority of the species? At the very least we must posit some sort of neural leap across the modality divide, but once we grant that, a much simpler solution becomes apparent: the human language faculty has always been at least partly amodal. Speech may be more practical than signing (it can be used in the dark, around obstacles, and when working with both hands), so specialized systems may have evolved for it in particular, but the core of human language remains untied to any one modality. Once this flexible neural system evolved, it may have become as trigger-happy as our face-processing system (which detects 'faces' anywhere, even in clouds), automatically switching on whenever it encounters any sufficiently complex communication challenge (see Section 6.2.3). Since communication runs both ways, feedback loops then lead to the grammatical system itself becoming ever more intricate (the main focus of Deacon 1997).

Crucially, an amodal capacity for grammar would not only explain sign languages but would also predict that grammar should appear beyond both speech and sign, a point I turn to next.

1.4.2. Grammar beyond language

Only fitful attempts have been made to apply grammatical notions to other human activities. Perhaps the most robust application beyond language is the grammar of music, though this may simply be the grammar of language in disguise; Pinker (1997) and Patel (2012), among others, have claimed that music is a mere side-effect of neurocognitive systems that evolved for language (Levitin 2006 disagrees). In any case, musical structure involves decomposition into notes, hierarchical constituent structure, and transformations (e.g., embellishment), making it possible to analyze it using formalisms adapted from syntax and prosody (e.g., Lerdahl and Jackendoff 1985; Temperley 2001; Van der Werf and Hendriks 2004; Yan 2005).

The production of music links it to another area where grammars have been proposed: motor control. Novembre and Keller (2011) and Charnavel (2016) describe grammars of action for musical performers and dancers, respectively. In earlier studies on the grammar of action, Goodnow and Levine (1973) and Ninio and Lieblich (1976) formalized what they called syntactic principles describing the regularities and hierarchically structured plans in the way children copy simple line drawings, though in Section 3.6.1, I argue that their results are actually more reminiscent of phonetics than syntax.

Grammars have also been proposed for the visual arts, with more or less formal grammars of narrative drawings (Munn 1973), architecture (Glassie 1975), and abstract designs (Hatcher 1974; Korn 1978; Kress and Van Leeuwen 1996; Washburn and Crowe 1988). Cohn *et al.* (2012) have even analyzed comic strips in a discourse grammar and tested their analyses in neuroimaging experiments. While all of the research lines mentioned here are worth further exploration, in Section 6.2 I give reasons for thinking that the sophistication of Chinese character grammar depends on a confluence of unusual properties; grammar need not be a universally applicable concept.

1.4.3. Orthographic grammar

Besides speech and signing, writing seems like the best candidate for a grammatical approach (Section 1.4.3.1), and this insight has led to a multifaceted literature on orthographic grammar (Section 1.4.3.2).

1.4.3.1. The nature of orthography

Bloomfield (1933, p. 21) expresses a view that preceded him and remains widespread today: "Writing is not language, but merely a way of recording language by means of visible marks." Of course, Bloomfield was wrong about many things (on p. 39 he expresses the mistaken belief that sign languages are either "merely developments of ordinary gestures" or "based on the conventions of ordinary speech"), but his linguistic misgivings about orthography are well justified. This may be a surprising admission in a book arguing for Chinese character grammar, but writing truly does differ from spoken and signed languages in significant ways.

Writing is superfluous: all physically capable humans speak or sign, but not all read and write, and even literate people do not communicate solely via writing. Writing is also subservient: by definition, all true orthographic systems are designed to record the components of spoken language (features, phonemes, moras, syllables, morphemes), not ideas directly (Aronoff, Berg, and Heyer 2016; Sampson 1985; Sproat 2000). Reading and writing are generally assumed to require explicit training, quite unlike the way spoken and signed languages are effortlessly absorbed by children from their environment. If orthography has grammar, then, it is one that is almost always learned as a second language; phrases like "native Chinese reader" are misleading. Writing can also survive outside of the mind in a way that speech and signing cannot (at least prior to the invention of mechanical sound and image recording), making it feel more like a physical artifact than a purely mental thing. The previous two points mean that

24 *Chinese character grammar*

orthography is subject to a greater degree of prescriptivism and historical inertia than speech and signing. Finally, the invention of writing is far too recent and literacy too rare to matter to the evolution of brain structure; language may be innate (Pinker 1994), but writing certainly is not. Put together, such observations strongly suggest that orthographic systems cannot share exactly the same sort of natural grammar as spoken and signed languages.

Despite Bloomfield, many linguists study orthography, but most are not particularly interested in the idea of orthographic grammar (e.g., Coulmas 1989, 2003), and some even seem to base their interest in orthography precisely on the fact that Bloomfield would not approve (see, for example, Harris 1995, 2000; Sampson 1985, for arguments that orthography is theoretically important; and the same authors, Harris 1981; Sampson 2007, for arguments that grammar in general is a myth).

For all that, orthography still has undeniably grammar-like properties. The many mismatches between written and spoken forms, even in alphabetic systems, suggest that some orthographic knowledge must be independent of speech. Householder (1971) goes so far as to argue that since it is easier for literate English speakers to derive pronunciations from spellings than the other way around, writing has actually become the primary form of language for them (see Aronoff 1994a for related ideas). Literate language can also take on a life of its own, as demonstrated dramatically by the survival of written classical Chinese centuries after anything like it was spoken in everyday life. Indeed, while difficult, it is not impossible to read and write a language that one does not speak at all (see Section 6.3.1.2). Some Chinese linguists have gone so far as to suggest that even spoken Chinese grammar is intrinsically character-based, with no level corresponding to morphologically complex words (e.g., Huang, Wang, and Chen 2018; Wang 2008; though see Behr 2018; Myers 2017e; Xu 2018 for defenses of the mainstream view that Chinese does indeed have words, like every other language on the planet).

Orthographic knowledge must also be psychologically real and productive. This is most obvious in the case of alphabetic orthographies, where functional regularities allow readers to pronounce nonsense forms like *blick*, but Chinese readers can also make reasonable guesses about the pronunciation and meaning of unknown characters, based on their phonetic components and semantic radicals. The idea that such skills derive solely from explicit instruction is an insult to the learners' own pattern-finding minds. School-taught rules (like "*i* before *e* except after *c*" for English spelling) are notoriously unreliable anyway, so it is fortunate that children are quite capable of picking up and generalizing orthographic regularities on their own (Pacton *et al.* 2001; see more on orthographic learning in Section 6.3.1.1). Educators and dictionary-makers may have greater influence on orthography than on spoken language, but even they feel the pressure of the 'invisible (writing) hand' of the masses (Crystal 2012; Wiedenhof 2017).

Productive orthographic knowledge is also abstract, in the same three ways addressed earlier (Section 1.3.1.4): it is non-iconic, amodal, and modular. As we have already noted, orthographic systems never involve actual pictures (Boltz 2006a; Jespersen and Reintges 2008); true icons and ideographs are restricted to usages like mathematical notation and signage (Chang 1987; Chang *et al.* 1987;

Chao 1961, 1968). Orthography also depends on amodal mental representations in order to link writing with reading and back again. For example, Naka (1998) found that children are better able to remember novel symbols if they have had practice writing them themselves (see also Sections 5.2.1.2 and 6.3.1.1).

As for modularity, orthography seems to depend on specialized knowledge. Even though neural modules for reading and writing cannot be innate, experience with any orthographic system trains certain brain areas more than others (Jobard, Crivello, and Tzourio-Mazoyer 2003; Perfetti, Cao, and Booth 2013; Rastle 2007), and consistent with amodality, similar brain networks are used for both reading and writing (Perfetti and Tan 2013). The brain even distinguishes symbols used for language, like letters, from those used for other purposes, like numbers (Anderson, Damasio, and Damasio 1990). A key component in the reading network has become known as the Visual Word Form Area (VWFA) because it becomes particularly active when discriminating between orthographic forms, regardless of the precise nature of the writing system (Cohen *et al.* 2000; Dehaene and Cohen 2007; Dehaene and Cohen 2011; McCandliss, Cohen, and Dehaene 2003). Dehaene and Cohen (2007, 2011) argue that the VWFA originally evolved for recognizing fine detail in objects and faces, analytical skills that proved essential when orthography was invented. I return to the VWFA in Section 5.2.1.3.

1.4.3.2. Approaches to orthographic grammar

The grammar-like aspects of orthographic have led some linguists to attempt to formalize the structure of orthographic systems. Sometimes the formalism has been taken to a mathematical extreme. For example, Sproat (2000) argues that all orthographic systems have 'regular grammars,' as the term is used in the branch of mathematics called formal language theory: new constituents are created only by concatenating or repeating old constituents, not by movement, counting, or more complex processes (Fitch and Friederici 2012; Moll, Arbib, and Kfoury 2012). If correct, this puts orthographic grammars into the same class as spoken and signed language morphology and phonology, in contrast to the more powerful grammatical algorithms needed for syntax (Heinz and Idsardi 2011). I return to Sproat's model in Section 1.5.

In a more quantitative approach to mathematical grammar, Eden (1961) plotted what he saw as the elementary curves of English cursive handwriting, allowing entire words to be expressed as formulas; Teulings, Thomassen, and van Galen (1986) adopted a similar approach. Köhler (2008) analyzed orthography using mathematical tools developed for the study of fractals, in which complex structure is repeated at a finer level of detail, while Altmann (2008) attempted to unite formal and quantitative approaches to writing into a single framework.

Other research lines have simply transferred the techniques of traditional grammarians to orthography. We have already seen in Sections 1.2.2 and 1.3.1.1 that even ancient Chinese linguists (and calligraphers) analyzed characters like descriptive grammarians. In modern scholarship, the 'grapheme' has become the standard term for the basic written unit in an orthographic system (e.g., <t> in English <top>),

26 *Chinese character grammar*

analogous to the phoneme as basic sound unit in a spoken language (e.g., /t/ in English [tʰɑp]) (Bazell 1956; Bhatt 1988; Catach 1986). Graphemes also include the mora-based hiragana and katakana symbols in Japanese orthography, as well as the character constituents in Chinese orthography (though see Section 3.2 for challenges).

Graphemes do not necessarily act like phonemes in every respect (Daniels 1991; Kohrt 1986); in particular, graphemes in the world's orthographic systems are too diverse to form anything like an International Graphetic Alphabet. But there are no direct parallels to phonemes in signed languages either (the hand-shapes? the fingers?), and more generally, it is unreasonable to expect identity across systems with very different functions and physical modalities. This would be a problem for the notion of orthographic (or even sign language) grammar only if grammars are defined not by systems but by inventories, a misguided idea that I already challenged in Section 1.2.2.3.

In any case, grapheme-to-phoneme correspondences are psychologically real even in semi-transparent alphabetic systems like that of English (Kessler and Treiman 2003), and form-sound patterns affect Chinese reading as well (as reviewed in Section 5.2.2.2). There are even orthographic parallels to allophonic variation, with context-dependent 'allographs' seen not only in handwriting, but sometimes in mechanical printing as well (e.g., the Greek letter for /s/ is written <ç> word-finally but <σ> elsewhere; similar allographic patterns are found in modern Arabic, and even early English typesetting: Nash 2001). Predictable variation in Chinese character constituent form will be highlighted in Chapters 2 and 3.

To illustrate just how phonology-like even purely orthographic regularities can be, consider an extensive argument from McCawley (1994) (see also Albrow 1972; Venezky 1967). He starts by observing that English orthography requires changing a word-final <y> into <i> when a suffix is added, as in (13a); my additional examples in (13b) show that it also applies with consonant-initial suffixes, and those in (13c) demonstrate its productive extension to nonwords (from Lewis Carroll's nonsense poem 'Jabberwocky' in *Alice Through the Looking-Glass*). Despite having no effect on pronunciation, this pattern looks very much like phonology, where word-final position often has a special status.

(13) a carry ~ carrier   spy ~ spies   dry ~ dried
      b happy ~ happiness worry ~ worrisome merry ~ merriment
      c slithy ~ slithier   mimsy ~ mimsier

McCawley goes on to show that this alternation is blocked before the suffix -*ing*, as in (14a); my additional examples in (14b) show that the blocking is triggered by any <i>-initial suffix, confirming his analysis of this as a form of dissimilation.

(14) a carry ~ carrying   spy ~ spying   dry ~ drying
      b baby ~ babies ~ babyish

McCawley then links this pattern with another one noted by Albrow (1972), whereby English content words virtually always have at least three letters, in

Chinese character grammar   27

contrast to function words, as shown by the minimal pairs in (15a). A few content words do have only two letters, but most of these have very high frequencies and abstract semantics, making them similar to function words, as illustrated in (15b), or else are abbreviations (15c), foreign borrowings (15d), or end in <x> (perhaps treated as the two-letter <ks>) (15e).

(15) a bee vs. be   inn vs. in   buy vs. by   two vs. to
      b sew vs. so   dew vs. do   toe vs. go
      c Ed Al ad
      d id
      e ox ax (cf. axe)

One intriguing aspect of this pattern not mentioned by McCawley is its similarity to the prosodically motivated minimal word constraints of spoken language phonology (Demuth 1996). But he does point out that the three-letter restriction interacts with the <y> ~ <i> alternation. In the words in (16a), <y> actually alternates with <ie>, as if <y> must be lengthened to <ie> when unsuffixed in order to reach the three-letter minimum. This analysis is illustrated by contrasting a 'derived' two-letter stem in (16b) with a lexically specified three-letter stem in (16c).

(16) a die ~ dying   lie ~ lying
      b <dy> + Ø   →   <die>   [expanded]
         <dy> + <ing>   →   <dying>
      c <dry> + Ø   →   <dry>   [expansion unnecessary]
         <dry> + <ing>   →   <drying>

Linguists have also applied grammatical ideas to letter-internal structure. Primus (2010) observes that three of the five lower-case Roman vowel letters contain closed loops (<a>, <e>, <o>) and the two that do not (<i>, <u>) both happen to represent high vowels. A series of studies, beginning with Watt (1975) and extending most recently to Watt (2015), has argued for purely formal letter regularities as well. For example, when capital Roman letters are not symmetrical along the vertical axis as in (17a), they almost always face rightward (i.e., have flatter and simpler left edges) as in (17b), aside from the ambiguously facing letters in (17c) and the sole leftward-facing letter in (17d). Remarkably, when Jameson (1994) experimentally presented English readers with invented capital letters, some almost as zany as those in Dr. Seuss's classic children's book *On Beyond Zebra* (Geisel 1955), those that conformed to Watt's generalizations were judged as significantly more plausible as 'new letter' candidates.

(17) a A   H   I   M   O   T   U   V   W   X   Y
      b B   C   D   E   F   G   K   L   P   Q   R
      c N   S   Z
      d J

28 *Chinese character grammar*

1.5. Character grammar

I am hardly the first person to think of Chinese characters in grammatical terms (Section 1.5.1), though I strike off in a somewhat different direction (Section 1.5.2).

1.5.1. Previous approaches to character grammar

As we saw in Section 1.2, even traditional Chinese lexicography implicitly assumes that characters have grammar. In recent decades, this idea has been made explicit in a number of studies.

The least abstract, and thus least grammar-like, looks at the meaning of constituent combinations. Chou, Hsieh, and Huang (2007) and Hsieh (2006) describe computer frameworks that exploit semantic radicals to map out semantic classes and relations among characters; List, Terhalle, and Schulzek (2016) give a more informal version of the same idea. Taking a different but related tack, Yau (1978, 1983) argues that the treatment of constituents in the oracle bone script reflected universal constraints on the conceptualization of argument relations. For example, in the oracle bone character in (18) (taken from Academia Sinica 2018), showing a hand grasping an ear, Yau claims that the ear icon was drawn before the hand icon, reflecting the same operand-before-operator order he observed when he asked people to draw a hand reaching for a ball (ball first). Unfortunately, Yau's analysis could at best only apply to a small number of characters (oracle bone script already contained a large proportion of semantic-phonetic characters, as well as semantic compounds far more abstract than this one), and more seriously, research on the physical oracle bones themselves (Venture 2001; Wan 2017) shows that characters were actually carved quite differently from Yau's speculations.

(18)   𠂤取 *qŭ* 'take'

The next stop on the way to abstract character grammar are studies of the frequencies of character constituents and their combinations. These include Stalph (1989), whose analysis of Japanese kanji also quantified how many constituents can appear together and in which positions, Bohn (1998), who also modeled constituent and stroke frequencies as a function of general mathematical laws, and Kordek (2013), who extended both of the above studies in mathematical models of constituent combinations (see Section 4.2 for more on quantitative corpus-based character analyses).

More grammar-like yet are notational schemes for indicating how character constituents are put together. The simplest is the set of so-called Ideographic Description Characters in Unicode, listed in (19a) (see Kordek 2013, pp. 91–117, for other schemes of this general sort). The analysis is quite superficial, however. For example, I demonstrate in Chapter 2 that the characters in each of the sets in (19b–d) actually have entirely different structures, and as mentioned earlier in Section 1.2.2.3, the overlapping structure in (19e) is generally not even considered decomposable in most of the literature.

Chinese character grammar 29

(19) a ▢ ▢ ▢ ▢ ▢ ▢ ▢ ▢ ▢ ▢ ▢ ▢
      b ▢ 忙 刻 林
      c ▢ 花 煮 多
      d ▢ 州 街 琳 鴻
      e ▢ 東 (cf. 木 日)

Other character description projects also take the hierarchical structure of character construction into account. The Chinese Character Decomposition project (Wikimedia Commons 2017) decomposes all of its characters into two parts (the second being empty if it is a simple constituent or involves reduplication), which through recursive searching allows for full decomposition, albeit only to constituents that may also be free characters. The Character Description Language (Bishop and Cook 2007) makes it possible to encode novel characters and even novel constituents.

While such projects remain more focused on database development than on grammar per se, Sproat (2000) is specifically interested in the latter. As discussed earlier (Section 1.4.3.2), he posits that all orthographic systems have regular grammars (in the mathematical sense of formal language theory). To demonstrate this in Chinese characters, he must first convert two-dimensional character structure into linear strings. The recursive structure of Chinese characters makes this easy, as illustrated by the linearization of the character in (20a) as (20b) (from Sproat 2000, p. 36); A → B means "A is concatenated to the left of B" and A ↓ B means "A is concatenated above B."

(20) a 鱗 *lín* 'fish scale'
      b 魚 → [米 ↓ [夕 → 牛]]

Sproat's full set of concatenation symbols makes it possible to linearize characters that at first sight would seem to require center-embedding, an impossibility in a regular grammar. For example, the character in (21a) has a semantic radical on the left edge (亻, reduced from 人), while the phonetic component on the right is decomposable into a vertically arranged pair of constituents (including the radical ⁺⁺, reduced from 艸) and then another constituent on the right (the radical 攵, reduced from 攴). This can still be linearized without center-embedding as in (21b), where A ← B means "A is concatenated to the right of B."

(21) a 儆
      b 亻 → [攵 ← [⁺⁺ ↓ 句]]

Sproat's system also includes a symbol for surrounding concatenation, whereby A ⊙ B means 'A surrounds B,' as illustrated in (22). I briefly return to Sproat's system in Section 3.3.2.

(22) a 囚
      b 囗 ⊙ 人

30 *Chinese character grammar*

The earliest studies to explicitly invoke the modern linguistic notion of grammar for Chinese character structure seem to be Rankin (1965) and Rankin and Tan (1970) (see also Fujimura and Kagaya 1969). Unfortunately, when Rankin's model is remembered today, it is primarily as an object lesson in how *not* to analyze characters. For example, Rankin (1965, p. 16) considered the character pairs in (23) to be related via affixation of a stroke, but as Wang (1983, p. 59) points out in a scathing critique, this is as misconceived as deriving English <white> from <while> through a similar 'affixation.'

(23) a 天 *tiān* 'day'   矢 *shǐ* 'arrow'
      b 夫 *fū* 'husband'   失 *shī* 'lost'
      c 干 *gān* 'dry'   午 *wǔ* 'noon'

However, simply as an empirical observation there does seem to be a genuine pattern here. It is just that the more appropriate parallel seems to be with phonology, not morphology, since it relates to constituent form rather than interpretable decompositionality (see Section 1.5.2 and Chapters 2 and 3 for the distinction). Citing other types of patterns, Ladd (2014) makes the parallels between character structure and phonology more explicit by asking whether Chinese characters show duality of patterning, though his own answer is equivocal (see Section 3.2). Also inspired by phonology, Goldberg and Cohen-Goldberg (in preparation) argue that stylistic variation in characters (see Section 1.2.1.2) is amenable to a formal grammatical analysis in terms of the degree of faithfulness of surface to underlying forms; I discuss the issue myself in Section 4.4.1, but come to rather different conclusions.

By far the most thorough grammatical analysis of Chinese characters, however, at least prior to the present book, is Wang (1983). I cannot praise this work highly enough, and it is a shame that, if cited at all, it is usually only in passing (e.g., see critiques in Stalph 1989, pp. 42–48; Kordek 2013, pp. 118–119). As we will see in Chapters 2 and 3, Wang made numerous empirical observations that fit neatly into my own analytical framework, including those relating to semantic radical position, stroke alternations, and stroke order. Moreover, even though Wang states that he based it solely on his own intuitions as a writer and reader of traditional Chinese characters, I show in Chapters 4 and 5 that his empirical observations usually hold up when we test them with statistical analyses of large corpus-derived samples and psycholinguistic experiments.

Admittedly, Wang (1983) is overly dependent on the generative grammar of his era (in particular Chomsky and Halle 1968), with hard-to-read formal notation, absolutist rhetoric about the proper goals of linguistics, and the tacit assumption that the lexicon only interacts with grammar via underlying representations and lists of exceptions (ignoring gradient productivity, for example; see Section 1.3.1.3). Otherwise my primary objection to Wang's approach is that he does not go far enough, missing some generalizations and the broader generalizations that subsume them, including parallels with spoken and signed languages. He also puts undo focus on stroke order, which, as I will argue in Section 3.6.2, is not a core part of character grammar.

Chinese character grammar 31

1.5.2. The morphology, phonology, and phonetics of Chinese characters

While I do not assume that a character grammar must follow the conventions of generative linguistics, I agree with Wang (1983) that this grammar is a cognitive system, reflecting the actual mental knowledge involved in the coinage, modification, learning, reading, and writing of characters. My primary focus is on the knowledge of present-day readers and writers, but even ancient characters once lived in the minds of actual people, as they created, reinterpreted, and restructured them as systems. Character history is an overlapping series of character grammars, and a character grammar is what learners have generalized from the character inventory that history has bequeathed them at any particular point in time.

Going beyond Wang (1983), I also claim that Chinese character grammar is structured much like spoken and signed grammars, making it a lexical grammar divided into three major domains: morphology, phonology, and phonetics. The difference between morphology and phonology is that the former is (potentially) interpreted by the higher levels of language, whereas the latter is interpreted only physically. In the case of CHARACTER MORPHOLOGY, the higher-level linguistic systems are the meanings and pronunciations that the characters represent (not just meanings, as in the case of spoken and signed morphology). A character-internal stroke group is therefore morphemic if it is a basic constituent that is reliably associated with a meaning (the semantic radical in a semantic-phonetic character or a semantic component in a semantic compound) or a pronunciation (a simple phonetic component in a semantic-phonetic character), though some uninterpreted constituents may potentially earn morphemehood by being salient in other ways (see Section 2.2). Other concepts relating to character morphology that we have already seen include decomposition, recursion, and reduplication; many more will be discussed in Chapter 2.

CHARACTER PHONOLOGY may be sensitive to character morphology but not the other way around, since it constrains constituent-internal elements like stroke types and regulates constituent position and modification without affecting character interpretation. Aspects of character phonology that have already been alluded to include duality of patterning and alternations in constituent shape; many more will be discussed in Chapter 3. To avoid potential confusion, keep in mind that in this book 'phonology' always refers to a mental system (in speech, signing, or orthography, as I will indicate explicitly), never merely 'pronunciation,' which is the term I will use for the spoken interpretation of characters.

Finally, CHARACTER PHONETICS relates to characters as psychophysical entities, in both visual and manual modalities. Concepts relating to character phonetics that we have seen so far include physical and perceptual constraints on character form and stroke order, which will be discussed more fully at the end of Chapter 3. Again, to head off possible misunderstandings, I should emphasize that 'character phonetics' refers exclusively to the mechanics of character production and perception, even though I also retain the unrelated traditional term 'phonetic component,' which does indeed relate to pronunciation.

32   *Chinese character grammar*

Given the ineliminable irregularity of any lexical system, we cannot expect these three domains to be any more distinct in Chinese characters than they are in the lexicons of spoken and signed languages; the humble goal of this book is simply to apply familiar grammatical notions to characters, not to refight old battles over grammatical theory itself. For example, if we accept that morphological alternations may be so idiosyncratic that the alternative forms must simply be memorized (e.g., English *see ~ saw*), then we leave open the possibility that even what seems like quasi-regular phonology (e.g., English [i:] ~ [ɛ] in *thief ~ theft, leave ~ left, deep ~ depth*) may (sometimes) actually be morphologically conditioned allomorphy (Bermúdez-Otero and McMahon 2006; Kiparsky 1982). We will encounter tricky cases of this sort in character grammar as well (e.g., Section 3.5).

It is also notoriously difficult to distinguish strictly between phonology and phonetics (Cohn 2007), with researchers pointing to subphonemic or gradient articulatory features that are language-specific or even word-specific (Gahl 2008; Pierrehumbert 2002), raising the possibility that phonological knowledge may itself be encoded primarily in phonetic terms (Hayes, Kirchner, and Steriade 2004). Again, the fact that these issues also arise in character grammar, as we will see in Section 3.6, is no strike against it, merely an acknowledgment that grammatical theory itself is not complete.

Finally, I must emphasize that the grammar I sketch is indeed merely a sketch; I do not intend it to be comprehensive, nor do I formalize it to the degree required by a computer program, let alone a generative linguist. One reason is practical: a comprehensive grammar of Chinese character form would likely fill up a book much longer than this one, leaving no room for the corpus-based and experimental evidence that I believe is crucial to my argument. I also do not want to put off readers unfamiliar with, or even distrustful of, formal linguistics. Most importantly, however, I hope that the very sketchiness of my grammar will inspire some readers to extend the project even further.

1.6. Summary

I am not merely claiming that the tradition started by Xu Shen's *Shuowen* was actually grammatical analysis all along, as interesting as that claim may already be. I also argue that an overtly grammatical approach to characters allows us both to make better sense of familiar facts and to reveal hitherto neglected patterns. If characters have a lexical grammar like that of spoken and signed languages, then it should be psychologically real, productive, and abstract, and there should be components similar to morphology, phonology, and phonetics. We have already seen evidence supporting all of these predictions: modern readers know too many characters to rely solely on rote memory (and can guess the likely meanings and pronunciations of unknown ones), writers have productively coined thousands of characters over the centuries, character knowledge bridges input and output systems, is not reducible to iconicity, and depends on specialized skills, characters are recursively decomposable into externally interpreted constituents, and, at another level of patterning, also show purely formal regularities that interface with the characters' physical forms.

To flesh all this out, I start in the following two chapters by applying the traditional grammarian approach of analyzing patterns in the lexicon: Chapter 2 describes character morphology (character morphemes and operations like affixation, compounding, and reduplication), and Chapter 3 describes character phonology and character phonetics (holistic structure, stroke features, stroke combinations, stroke alternations, and articulatory and perceptual constraints). Since merely being attested in the lexicon does not entail that a pattern is psychologically real, the next two chapters turn to more rigorous types of evidence: Chapter 4 looks at corpus data (quantitative measures of productivity, historical change, variant characters, and contemporary character creation), and Chapter 5 looks at experimental data (psycholinguistic and neurolinguistic experiments on reading, as well as new experiments designed specifically with grammatical hypotheses in mind). Finally, Chapter 6 considers possible explanations for character grammar and its possible real-world applications.

References

Academia Sinica, 2018, 小學堂文字學資料庫 [Primary school text database]. http://xiaoxue.iis.sinica.edu.tw/, accessed 11/17/2018.

Albrow, K.H., 1972, *The English writing system: Notes toward a description*, Longman, London.

Altmann, G., 2008, "Towards a theory of script", in G. Altmann and F. Fan, eds., *Analyses of script: Properties of characters and writing systems*, pp. 149–164, Mouton de Gruyter, Berlin.

Anderson, M.M., 2017, "Number of characters", in R. Sybesma, W. Behr, Y. Gu, Z. Handel, C.T.J. Huang and J. Myers, eds., *Encyclopedia of Chinese language and linguistics*, vol. 3, pp. 255–259, Brill, Leiden.

Anderson, S.W., Damasio, A.R. and Damasio, H., 1990, "Troubled letters but not numbers: Domain specific cognitive impairments following focal damage in frontal cortex", *Brain*, 113(3), pp. 749–766.

Ann, J., 1998, "Contact between a sign language and a written language: Character signs in Taiwan Sign Language", in C. Lucas, ed., *Pinky extension and eye gaze: Language use in Deaf communities*, pp. 59–99, Gallaudet University Press, Washington, DC.

Ann, J., 2006, *Frequency of occurrence and ease of articulation of sign language handshapes: The Taiwanese example*, Gallaudet University Press, Washington, DC.

Armstrong, D.F., 1983, "Iconicity, arbitrariness & duality of patterning in signed and spoken language: Perspectives on language evolution", *Sign Language Studies*, 38(1), pp. 51–83.

Aronoff, M., 1994a, "Spelling as culture", in W.C. Watt, ed., *Writing systems and cognition*, pp. 67–86, Springer, Berlin.

Aronoff, M., Berg, K. and Heyer, V., 2016, "Some implications of English spelling for morphological processing", *The Mental Lexicon*, 11(2), pp. 164–185.

Aronoff, M., Meir, I. and Sandler, W., 2005, "The paradox of sign language morphology", *Language*, 81(2), pp. 301–344.

Baayen, R.H. and Renouf, A., 1996, "Chronicling the Times: Productive lexical innovations in an English newspaper", *Language*, 2(1), pp. 69–96.

34 Chinese character grammar

Battison, R., 1978, *Lexical borrowing in American Sign Language*, Linstok Press, Silver Spring, MD.

Bauer, L., 2001, *Morphological productivity*, Cambridge University Press, Cambridge.

Baus, C., Carreiras, M. and Emmorey, K., 2013, "When does iconicity in sign language matter?", *Language and Cognitive Processes*, 28(3), pp. 261–271.

Baxter, W.H. and Sagart, L., 2014, *Old Chinese: A new reconstruction*, Oxford University Press, Oxford.

Bazell, C.E., 1956, "The grapheme", *Litera*, 3, pp. 43–46.

Behr, W., 2006, "Homosomatic juxtaposition and the problem of 'syssymantic' (*huìyì*) characters", in F. Bottéro and R. Djamouri, eds., *Écriture chinoise: données, usages et représentations* [Chinese writing: Data, uses and representations], pp. 75–114, École des hautes études en sciences sociales, Centre de recherches linguistiques sur l'Asie orientale [Graduate School of Social Sciences, East Asian Language Research Center], Paris.

Behr, W., 2010, "In the interstices of representation: Ludic writing and the locus of polysemy in the Chinese sign", in A.J. de Voogt and I.L. Finkel, eds., *The idea of writing: Play and complexity*, pp. 281–314, Brill, Leiden.

Behr, W., 2018, "'Monosyllabism' and some other perennial clichés about the nature, origins and contacts of the Chinese language in Europe", in A. Malinar and S. Müller, eds., *Asia and Europe – Interconnected: Agents, concepts, and things*, pp. 155–209, O. Harrassowitz, Wiesbaden.

Behr, W. and Söderblom-Saarela, M.S., 2018, "Radicals, and why they are called that", University of Zürich and Academia Sinica ms.

Bellugi, U. and Fischer, S., 1972, "A comparison of sign language and spoken language", *Cognition*, 1(2–3), pp. 173–200.

Berent, I., Steriade, D., Lennertz, T. and Vaknin, V., 2007, "What we know about what we have never heard: Evidence from perceptual illusions", *Cognition*, 104(3), pp. 591–630.

Bermúdez-Otero, R. and McMahon, A., 2006, "English phonology and morphology", in B. Aarts and A. McMahon, eds., *The handbook of English linguistics*, pp. 382–410, Blackwell, Oxford.

Bever, T.G., 1975, "Psychologically real grammar emerges because of its role in language acquisition", in D.P. Dato, ed., *Developmental psycholinguistics: Theory and application*, pp. 63–75, Georgetown University Press, Washington, DC.

Bhatt, P.M., 1988, "Graphic systems, phonic systems, and linguistic representations", in D. de Kerckhove and C.J. Lumsden, eds., *The alphabet and the brain*, pp. 106–120, Springer, Berlin.

Bishop, T. and Cook, R., 2007, "A character description language for CJK", *Multilingual*, 18(7), pp. 62–68.

Blevins, J.P., 2004, *Evolutionary phonology: The emergence of sound patterns*, Cambridge University Press, Cambridge.

Blevins, J.P., 2006, "Word-based morphology", *Journal of Linguistics*, 42(3), pp. 531–573.

Bloomfield, L., 1933, *Language*, Holt, New York.

Bohn, H., 1998, *Quantitative Untersuchungen der modernen chinesischen Sprache und Schrift* [Quantitative investigations of modern Chinese language and script], Verlag Dr. Kovač, Hamburg.

Boltz, W.G., 1986, "Early Chinese writing", *World Archaeology*, 17(3), pp. 420–436.

Boltz, W.G., 1994, *The origin and early development of the Chinese writing system*, American Oriental Society, New Haven, CT.

Boltz, W.G., 2006a, "Pictographic myths", in W. Behr and H. Roetz, eds., *Bochumer Jahrbuch zur Ostasienforschung* [Bochum yearbook on East Asian studies], pp. 39–54,

Chinese character grammar 35

Fakultät für Ostasienwissenschaften der Ruhr-Universität Bochum [Faculty of East Asian Studies of the Ruhr University Bochum], Bochum.

Boltz, W.G., 2006b, "Phonographic motivation in the formation of compound Chinese characters: The case of *wŭ* 武", in F. Bottéro and R. Djamouri, eds., *Écriture chinoise: données, usages et représentations* [Chinese writing: Data, uses and representations], pp. 55–73, École des hautes études en sciences sociales, Centre de recherches linguistiques sur l'Asie orientale [Graduate School of Social Sciences, East Asian Language Research Center], Paris.

Boltz, W.G., 2017a, "Ideographic fallacy: Historical and conceptual issues", in R. Sybesma, W. Behr, Y. Gu, Z. Handel, C.T.J. Huang and J. Myers, eds., *Encyclopedia of Chinese language and linguistics*, vol. 2, pp. 404–409, Brill, Leiden.

Boltz, W.G., 2017b, "Origin of the Chinese writing system", in R. Sybesma, W. Behr, Y. Gu, Z. Handel, C.T.J. Huang and J. Myers, eds., *Encyclopedia of Chinese language and linguistics*, vol. 3, pp. 304–316, Brill, Leiden.

Boltz, W.G., 2017c, "Liù shū 六書 (six scripts)", in R. Sybesma, W. Behr, Y. Gu, Z. Handel, C.T.J. Huang and J. Myers, eds., *Encyclopedia of Chinese language and linguistics*, vol. 2, pp. 616–624, Brill, Leiden.

Bottéro, F., 1996, "Review of Boltz (1994)", *Journal of the American Oriental Society*, 116(3), pp. 574–577.

Bottéro, F., 2017, "Chinese writing", in R. Sybesma, W. Behr, Y. Gu, Z. Handel, C.T.J. Huang and J. Myers, eds., *Encyclopedia of Chinese language and linguistics*, vol. 1, pp. 595–605, Brill, Leiden.

Bottéro, F. and Harbsmeier, C., 2008, "The *Shuowen Jiezi* dictionary and the human sciences in China", *Asia Major*, 21(1), pp. 249–271.

Brentari, D., 1998, *A prosodic model of sign language phonology*, MIT Press, Cambridge, MA.

Brentari, D., 2011, "Sign language phonology", in J. Goldsmith, J. Riggle, J. and A.C.L. Yu, eds., *The handbook of phonological theory*, 2nd ed., pp. 691–721, Wiley-Blackwell, Hoboken, NJ.

Burkimsher, P., 2018, "Hakka news: Adding 11 unicode characters", *Medium*, September 12, https://medium.com/@peterburkimsher/hakka-news-adding-11-unicode-characters-320c78807988, accessed 11/17/2018.

Bybee, J.L. and Hopper, P.J. eds., 2001, *Frequency and the emergence of linguistic structure*, John Benjamins, Amsterdam.

Cardona, G., 1994, "Indian linguistics", in G. Lepschy, ed., *History of linguistics: Volume I: The Eastern traditions of linguistics*, pp. 25–60, Longman, London.

Catach, N., 1986, "The grapheme: Its position and its degree of autonomy with respect to the system of the language", in G. Augst, ed., *New trends in graphemics and orthography*, pp. 1–10, Walter de Gruyter, Berlin.

Chan, T.A., 2003, "Character sets and characters: The basis of Chinese language computing", *Journal of the Chinese Language Teachers Association*, 38(2), pp. 87–108.

Chang, S.K., 1987, "Icon semantics: A formal approach to icon system design", *International Journal of Pattern Recognition and Artificial Intelligence*, 1(1), pp. 103–120.

Chang, S.K., Tortora, G., Yu, B. and Guercio, A., 1987, "Icon purity: Toward a formal theory of icons", *International Journal of Pattern Recognition and Artificial Intelligence*, 1(3/4), pp. 377–392.

Chao, Y.R., 1961, "Graphic and phonetic aspects of linguistic and mathematical symbols", in R. Jakobson, ed., *Structure of language and its mathematical aspects*, pp. 69–82, American Mathematical Society, Providence, RI.

36 *Chinese character grammar*

Chao, Y.R., 1968, *Language and symbolic systems*, Cambridge University Press, Cambridge.

Charnavel, I., 2016, *Steps towards a generative theory of dance cognition*, Harvard University ms.

Chen, Y.P., Allport, D.A. and Marshall, J.C., 1996, "What are the functional orthographic units in Chinese word recognition: The stroke or the stroke pattern?", *The Quarterly Journal of Experimental Psychology*, 49(4), pp. 1024–1043.

Chinese Document Processing Lab, 2011, 漢字構形資料庫 [Chinese character configuration database]. http://cdp.sinica.edu.tw/cdphanzi/, accessed 11/17/2018.

Chomsky, N. and Halle, M., 1968, *The sound pattern of English*, Harper and Row, New York.

Chou, Y.M., Hsieh, S.K. and Huang, C.R., 2007, "Hanzi grid", in T. Ishida, S.R. Fussell and P.T.J.M. Vossen, eds., *Intercultural collaboration*, pp. 133–145, Springer, Berlin.

Chu, K. [朱歧祥], 2004, 圖形與文字－殷金文研究 [Figure and text: Research on Shang dynasty bronze inscriptions]. 里仁書局 [Lernbook], Taipei.

Chuang, D.M. [莊德明] and Teng, H.Y. [鄧賢瑛], 2009, 漢字構形資料庫的研發與應用 [Research and development of Chinese characters information database and its application]. Academia Sinica, Taipei, http://cdp.sinica.edu.tw/service/documents/T090904.pdf, accessed 11/17/2018.

Cohen, L., Dehaene, S., Naccache, L., Lehéricy, S., Dehaene-Lambertz, G., Hénaff, M.A. and Michel, F., 2000, "The visual word form area: Spatial and temporal characterization of an initial stage of reading in normal subjects and posterior split-brain patients", *Brain*, 123(2), pp. 291–307.

Cohn, A.C., 2007, "Phonetics in phonology and phonology in phonetics", *Working Papers of the Cornell Phonetics Laboratory*, 16, pp. 1–31.

Cohn, N., Paczynski, M., Jackendoff, R., Holcomb, P.J. and Kuperberg, G.R., 2012, "(Pea) nuts and bolts of visual narrative: Structure and meaning in sequential image comprehension", *Cognitive Psychology*, 65(1), pp. 1–38.

Corballis, M.C., 2002, *From hand to mouth: The origins of language*, Princeton University Press, Princeton, NJ.

Coulmas, F., 1989, *The writing systems of the world*, Blackwell, Oxford.

Coulmas, F., 2003, *Writing systems: An introduction to their linguistic analysis*, Cambridge University Press, Cambridge.

Crystal, D., 2012, *Spell it out: The singular story of English spelling*, Profile Books, London.

Dai, R., Liu, C. and Xiao, B., 2007, "Chinese character recognition: History, status and prospects", *Frontiers of Computer Science in China*, 1(2), pp. 126–136.

Daniels, P.T., 1991, "Is a structural graphemics possible?", *LACUS Forum*, 18, pp. 528–537.

Davidson, K., 2018, "What belongs in the 'logical core' of a language?", *Theoretical Linguistics*, 44(3–4), pp. 227–237.

Deacon, T.W., 1997, *The symbolic species: The co-evolution of language and the brain*, W.W. Norton, New York.

DeFrancis, J., 1989, *Visible speech: The diverse oneness of writing systems*, University of Hawaii Press, Honolulu.

DeFrancis, J., 2002, "The ideographic myth", in M.S. Erbaugh, ed., *Difficult characters: Interdisciplinary studies of Chinese and Japanese writing*, pp. 1–20, National East Asian Languages Resource Center, The Ohio State University, Columbus.

Dehaene, S. and Cohen, L., 2007, "Cultural recycling of cortical maps", *Neuron*, 56(2), pp. 384–398.

Dehaene, S. and Cohen, L., 2011, "The unique role of the visual word form area in reading", *Trends in Cognitive Sciences*, 15(6), pp. 254–262.

Chinese character grammar   37

Demuth, K., 1996, "The prosodic structure of early words", in J.L. Morgan and K. Demuth, eds., *Signal to syntax: Bootstrapping from speech to grammar in early acquisition*, pp. 171–184, Lawrence Erlbaum, Mahwah, NJ.

Di Sciullo, A.M. and Williams, E., 1987, *On the definition of word*, MIT Press, Cambridge, MA.

Downer, G.B., 1963, "Traditional Chinese phonology", *Transactions of the Philological Society*, 62(1), pp. 127–142.

Eccarius, P. and Brentari, D., 2007, "Symmetry and dominance: A cross-linguistic study of signs and classifier constructions", *Lingua*, 117(7), pp. 1169–1201.

Eccarius, P. and Brentari, D., 2010, "A formal analysis of phonological contrast and iconicity in sign language handshapes", *Sign Language & Linguistics*, 13(2), pp. 156–181.

Eden, M., 1961, "On the formalization of handwriting", *Structure of language and its mathematical aspects*, pp. 83–88, American Mathematical Society, Providence, RI.

Emmorey, K., 2001, *Language, cognition, and the brain: Insights from sign language research*, Psychology Press, London.

Emmorey, K., 2014, "Iconicity as structure mapping", *Philosophical Transactions of the Royal Society B*, 369(1651), 20130301, 1–9.

Erbaugh, M., 2017, "Ideographic fallacy: Sociolinguistics and political impact", in R. Sybesma, W. Behr, Y. Gu, Z. Handel, C.T.J. Huang and J. Myers, eds., *Encyclopedia of Chinese language and linguistics*, vol. 2, pp. 409–414, Brill, Leiden.

Fei, J. [费锦昌], 1996, 现代汉字部件探究 [Research on modern Chinese characters]. 语言文字应用 [Applied Linguistics], 2, pp. 20–26.

Feng, S., 2016, "Modern Chinese: Written Chinese", in S.W. Chan, ed., *The Routledge encyclopedia of the Chinese language*, pp. 645–663, Routledge, Abingdon.

Fitch, W.T., 2010, "Three meanings of 'recursion': Key distinctions for biolinguistics", in R.K. Larson, V. Deprez and H. Yamakido, eds., *The evolution of human language: Biolinguistic perspectives*, pp. 73–90, Cambridge University Press, Cambridge.

Fitch, W.T. and Friederici, A.D., 2012, "Artificial grammar learning meets formal language theory: An overview", *Philosophical Transactions of the Royal Society B*, 367(1598), pp. 1933–1955.

Flaherty, M., 2003, "Sign language and Chinese characters on visual-spatial memory: A literature review", *Perceptual and Motor Skills*, 97(3), pp. 797–802.

Fok, A. and Bellugi, U., 1986, "The acquisition of visual spatial script", in H.S.R. Kao, G.P. van Galen and R. Hoosain, eds., *Graphonomics: Contemporary research in handwriting*, pp. 329–355, North-Holland, Amsterdam.

Fok, A., van Hoek, K., Klima, E. and Bellugi, U., 1991, "The interplay between visuospatial language and visuospatial script", in D.S. Martin, ed., *Advances in cognition, education, and deafness*, pp. 38–58, Gallaudet University Press, Washington, DC.

Frishberg, N., 1975, "Arbitrariness and iconicity: Historical change in American Sign Language", *Language*, 51(3), pp. 696–719.

Fujimura, O. and Kagaya, R., 1969, "Structural patterns of Chinese characters", *Proceedings of the 1969 conference on computational linguistics*, pp. 1–17, Association for Computational Linguistics, Stockholm.

Gahl, S., 2008, "*Time* and *thyme* are not homophones: The effect of lemma frequency on word durations in spontaneous speech", *Language*, 84(3), pp. 474–496.

Geisel, T.S., 1955, *On beyond zebra*, Random House, New York.

Glassie, H., 1975, *Folk housing in middle Virginia: A structural analysis of historic artifacts*. University of Tennessee Press, Knoxville.

Goldberg, S.J. and Cohen-Goldberg, A.M., In preparation, "Constraint interaction in the analysis of calligraphic scripts", Tufts University ms, Medford, MA.

38 *Chinese character grammar*

Goodnow, J.J. and Levine, R.A., 1973, "'The grammar of action': Sequence and syntax in children's copying", *Cognitive Psychology*, 4(1), pp. 82–98.

Gu, Y., 2017, "Calligraphy", in R. Sybesma, W. Behr, Y. Gu, Z. Handel, C.T.J. Huang and J. Myers, eds., *Encyclopedia of Chinese language and linguistics*, vol. 1, pp. 331–335, Brill, Leiden.

Guder-Manitius, A., 2009, *Sinographemdidaktik* [Sinographeme didactics], Julius Gross Verlag, Tübingen.

Handel, Z., 2013, "Can a logographic script be simplified? Lessons from the 20th century Chinese writing reform informed by recent psycholinguistic research", *Scripta*, 5, pp. 21–66.

Handel, Z., 2015, "Logography and the classification of writing systems: A response to Unger", *Scripta*, 7, pp. 109–150.

Handel, Z., 2017, "Chinese characters", in R. Sybesma, W. Behr, Y. Gu, Z. Handel, C.T.J. Huang and J. Myers, eds., *Encyclopedia of Chinese language and linguistics*, vol. 1, pp. 435–443, Brill, Leiden.

Handel, Z., 2019, *Sinography: A cross-linguistic study of the borrowing and adaptation of the Chinese script*, Brill, Leiden.

Handel, Z., Forthcoming, "The cognitive role of semantic classifiers in modern Chinese writing as reflected in neogram creation", in I. Zsolnay, ed., *Seen not heard: Composition, iconicity, and the classifier systems of logosyllabic scripts*, The Oriental Institute of the University of Chicago, Chicago.

Harbaugh, R., 1998, *Chinese characters: A genealogy and dictionary*, Han Lu Book and Publishing Co., Taipei.

Harley, H. and Noyer, R., 1999, "Distributed morphology", *Glot International*, 4(4), pp. 3–9.

Harris, R., 1981, *The language myth*, St. Martin's Press, New York.

Harris, R., 1995, *Signs of writing*, Routledge, Abingdon.

Harris, R., 2000, *Rethinking writing*, Continuum, London.

Hatcher, E.P., 1974, "Visual metaphors: A formal analysis of Navajo art", in *American ethnological society monograph no. 58*, West Publishing Co., St. Paul.

Hayes, B., Kirchner, R. and Steriade, D. eds., 2004, *Phonetically based phonology*, Cambridge University Press, Cambridge.

Heinz, J. and Idsardi, W., 2011, "Sentence and word complexity", *Science*, 333(6040), pp. 295–297.

Herforth, D., 2003, "A sketch of Late Zhou Chinese grammar", in G. Thurgood and R.J. LaPolla, eds., *The Sino-Tibetan languages*, pp. 59–71, Routledge, Abingdon.

Hockett, C.F., 1960, "The origin of speech", *Scientific American*, 203(3), pp. 88–96.

Householder, F.W., 1971, "The primacy of writing", in F.W. Householder, ed., *Linguistic speculations*, pp. 244–264, Cambridge University Press, Cambridge.

Hovdhaugen, E., 1982, *Foundations of western linguistics: From the beginning to the end of the first millennium A.D.*, Universitetsforlaget, Oslo.

Hsieh, S.K., 2006, *Hanzi, concept and computation: A preliminary survey of Chinese characters as a knowledge resource in NLP*, Ph.D. thesis, University of Tübingen.

Hsu, T.C. [許逸之], 1991, 中國文字結構說彙 [Chinese character structure]. The Commercial Press, Taipei.

Huang, C.R. and Qi, S., 2017, "Computational linguistics", in R. Sybesma, W. Behr, Y. Gu, Z. Handel, C.T.J. Huang and J. Myers, eds., *Encyclopedia of Chinese language and linguistics*, vol. 1, pp. 652–658, Brill, Leiden.

Huang, C.-R., Wang, H. and Chen, I.-H., 2018, "Characters as basic lexical units and monosyllabicity in Chinese", Hong Kong Polytechnic University and Center for Chinese Linguistics Peking University ms.

Huang, D.K. [黄德宽], 2003, 汉字构形方式的动态分析 [Dynamic analysis of the formation of Chinese characters]. 安徽大学学报(哲学社会科学版) [Journal of Anhui University (Philosophy and Social Sciences)], 27(4), pp. 1–8.

Hue, C.W., 2003, "Number of characters a college student knows", *Journal of Chinese Linguistics*, 31(2), pp. 300–339.

Hunter, L., 1982, "Silence is also language: Hausa attitudes about speech and language", *Anthropological Linguistics*, 24(4), pp. 389–409.

Jackendoff, R. and Audring, J., 2016, "Morphological schemas", *The Mental Lexicon*, 11(3), pp. 467–493.

Jameson, K., 1994, "Empirical methods for evaluating generative semiotic models: An application to the roman majuscules", in W.C. Watt, ed., *Writing systems and cognition: Perspectives from psychology, physiology, linguistics, and semiotics*, pp. 247–291, Springer, Dordrecht.

Jepsen, J.B., De Clerck, G., Lutalo-Kiingi, S. and McGregor, W.B. eds., 2015, *Sign languages of the world: A comparative handbook*, Walter de Gruyter, Berlin.

Jespersen, B. and Reintges, C., 2008, "Tractarian *Sätze*, Egyptian hieroglyphs, and the very idea of script as picture", *The Philosophical Forum*, 39(1), pp. 1–19.

Jobard, G., Crivello, F. and Tzourio-Mazoyer, N., 2003, "Evaluation of the dual route theory of reading: A metanalysis of 35 neuroimaging studies", *Neuroimage*, 20(2), pp. 693–712.

Kawabata, T., 2010, *Kanji database project*, http://kanji-database.sourceforge.net/, accessed 11/17/2018.

Kessler, B. and Treiman, R. 2003, "Is English spelling chaotic? Misconceptions concerning its irregularity", *Reading Psychology*, 24(3–4), pp. 267–289.

Kiparsky, P., 1982, "Lexical morphology and phonology", in Linguistic Society of Korea, ed., *Linguistics in the morning calm: Selected papers from SICOL-1981*, pp. 3–91, Hanshin Publishing Company, Seoul.

Kiparsky, P., 2006, "The amphichronic program vs. evolutionary phonology", *Theoretical Linguistics*, 32(2), pp. 217–236.

Köhler, R., 2008, "The fractal dimension of script: An experiment", in G. Altmann and F. Fan, eds., *Analyses of script: Properties of characters and writing systems*, pp. 115–119, Mouton de Gruyter, Berlin.

Kohrt, M., 1986, "The term 'grapheme' in the history and theory of linguistics", in G. Augst, ed., *New trends in graphemics and orthography*, pp. 80–96, Walter de Gruyter, Berlin.

Kordek, N., 2013, *On some quantitative aspects of the componential structure of Chinese characters*, Wydawnictwo Rys, Poznań.

Korn, S.M., 1978, "The formal analysis of visual systems as exemplified by a study of Abelam (Papua New Guinea) paintings", in M. Greenhalgh and V. Megaw, eds., *Art in society: Studies in style, culture and aesthetics*, pp. 161–173, St. Martin's Press, New York.

Kress, G.R. and Van Leeuwen, T., 1996, *Reading images: The grammar of visual design*, Routledge, Abingdon.

Labov, W., Ash, S., Ravindranath, M., Weldon, T., Baranowski, M. and Nagy, N., 2011, "Properties of the sociolinguistic monitor", *Journal of Sociolinguistics*, 15(4), pp. 431–463.

Ladd, D.R., 2014, *Simultaneous structure in phonology*, Oxford University Press, Oxford.

Lee, H.H., 2016, *A comparative study of the phonology of Taiwan Sign Language and Signed Chinese*, Ph.D. thesis, National Chung Cheng University.

Lerdahl, F. and Jackendoff, R.S., 1985, *A generative theory of tonal music*, MIT Press, Cambridge, MA.

Levitin, D.J., 2006, *This is your brain on music: The science of a human obsession*, Penguin, London.

40 Chinese character grammar

Li, L. [李乐毅], 1996, 简化字源 [The origins of simplified Chinese characters]. Sinolingua, Beijing.

Li, Y., 2017, "Script reform (1940–2002): Context and policies", in R. Sybesma, W. Behr, Y. Gu, Z. Handel, C.T.J. Huang and J. Myers, eds., *Encyclopedia of Chinese language and linguistics*, vol. 3, pp. 668–671, Brill, Leiden.

Lin, Y., 1972, *Lin Yutang's Chinese-English dictionary of modern usage*, The Chinese University of Hong Kong, Hong Kong.

List, J.M., Terhalle, A. and Schulzek, D., 2016, "Traces of embodiment in Chinese character formation", in L. Ströbel, ed., *Sensory motor concepts in language & cognition*, pp. 45–62, Düsseldorf University Press, Düsseldorf.

Liu, I.M. and Wu, J.T., 2017, "Reading characters and words, behavioral studies", in R. Sybesma, W. Behr, Y. Gu, Z. Handel, C.T.J. Huang and J. Myers, eds., *Encyclopedia of Chinese language and linguistics*, vol. 3, pp. 532–536, Brill, Leiden.

Liu, M. [刘曼], 2008, 叠体字的历时考察与认知比较研究 [The diachronic study and cognitive comparison of stacked characters]. Ph.D. thesis, Tsinghua University, Beijing.

Lu, Q., Chan, S.T., Li, Y. and Li, N.L., 2002, "Decomposition for ISO/IEC 10646 ideographic characters", *COLING-02: Proceedings of the 3rd Workshop on Asian Language Resources and International Standardization*, Association for Computational Linguistics, Stroudsburg, PA. Database at http://glyph.iso10646hk.net/, accessed 11/19/2018.

Lu, S. [卢绍昌], 1991, 汉字部件的研究 [Research on the parts of Chinese characters]. 第三届国际汉语教学讨论会论文选 [Selected Papers for the Third International Chinese Teaching Conference].

Lui, H.M., Leung, M.T., Law, S.P. and Fung, R.S.Y., 2010, "A database for investigating the logographeme as a basic unit of writing Chinese", *International Journal of Speech-Language Pathology*, 12(1), pp. 8–18.

Mair, V., 2011, "Polysyllabic characters in Chinese writing", *Language Log*, August 2, http://languagelog.ldc.upenn.edu/nll/?p=3330, accessed 11/17/2018.

Malmqvist, G., 1994, "Chinese linguistics", in G.C. Lepschy, ed., *History of linguistics Volume I: The Eastern traditions of linguistics*, pp. 1–24, Longman, London.

Marr, D., 1982, *Vision: A computational investigation into the human representation and processing of visual information*, W.H. Freeman and Company, New York.

McCandliss, B.D., Cohen, L. and Dehaene, S., 2003, "The visual word form area: Expertise for reading in the fusiform gyrus", *Trends in Cognitive Sciences*, 7(7), pp. 293–299.

McCarthy, J.J. and Prince, A., 1994, "Prosodic morphology", in J. Goldsmith, ed., *The handbook of phonological theory*, pp. 318–366, Blackwell, Oxford.

McCawley, J.D., 1994, "Some graphotactic constraints", in W.C. Watt, ed., *Writing systems and cognition: Perspectives from psychology, physiology, linguistics, and semiotics*, pp. 115–127, Springer, Berlin.

McEnery, T. and Xiao, R., 2016, "Corpus-based study of Chinese", in S.W. Chan, ed., *The Routledge encyclopedia of the Chinese language*, pp. 438–451, Routledge, Abingdon.

Meier, R.P., 1991, "Language acquisition by deaf children", *American Scientist*, 79(1), pp. 60–70.

Ministry of Education of the People's Republic of China, 1997, 信息处理用 GB13000.1 字符集汉字部件规范 [Chinese character component standard of GB 13000.1 character set for information processing]. http://old.moe.gov.cn//publicfiles/business/htmlfiles/moe/s230/201001/75616.html, accessed 11/17/2018.

Ministry of Education of the People's Republic of China, 2009a, 现代常用字部件及部件名称规范 [Specification of common modern Chinese character components and component names]. www.moe.edu.cn/s78/A19/yxs_left/moe_810/s230/201001/t20100115_75696.html, accessed 11/17/2018.

Ministry of Education of the Republic of China, 2011, 標準字與簡化字對照手冊 [Comparative manual of standard and simplified characters]. https://depart.moe.edu.tw/ED2500/News_Content.aspx?n=1DD9A37B3B3857B4&sms=174DD55894170669&s=1DE13940BE5275D9, accessed 11/17/2018.

Moll, R.N., Arbib, M.A. and Kfoury, A.J., 2012, *An introduction to formal language theory*, Springer, Berlin.

Momma, S. and Phillips, C., 2018, "The relationship between parsing and generation", *Annual Review of Linguistics*, 4, pp. 233–254.

Morioka, T., 2008, "CHISE: Character processing based on character ontology", in T. Tokunaga and A. Ortega, eds., *Large-scale knowledge resources: Construction and application*, pp. 148–162, Springer, Berlin.

Mullaney, T.S., 2017, "Typewriter", in R. Sybesma, W. Behr, Y. Gu, Z. Handel, C.T.J. Huang and J. Myers, eds., *Encyclopedia of Chinese language and linguistics*, vol. 4, pp. 459–463, Brill, Leiden.

Munn, N.D., 1973, *Walbiri iconography: Graphic representation and cultural symbolism in a Central Australian society*, Cornell University Press, Ithaca, NY.

Myers, J., 2017a, "Psycholinguistics, overview", in R. Sybesma, W. Behr, Y. Gu, Z. Handel, C.T.J. Huang and J. Myers, eds., *Encyclopedia of Chinese language and linguistics*, vol. 3, pp. 473–484, Brill, Leiden.

Myers, J., 2017b, "Psychological reality of linguistic structure", in R. Sybesma, W. Behr, Y. Gu, Z. Handel, C.T.J. Huang and J. Myers, eds., *Encyclopedia of Chinese language and linguistics*, vol. 3, pp. 484–488, Brill, Leiden.

Myers, J., 2017c, "Acceptability judgments", in M. Aronoff, ed., *Oxford research encyclopedia of linguistics*, Oxford University Press, Oxford, http://linguistics.oxfordre.com/, accessed 11/17/2018.

Myers, J., 2017d, "Sign languages, overview", in R. Sybesma, W. Behr, Y. Gu, Z. Handel, C.T.J. Huang and J. Myers, eds., *Encyclopedia of Chinese language and linguistics*, vol. 4, pp. 88–92, Brill, Leiden.

Myers, J., 2017e, "Words as basic lexical units in Chinese", National Chung Cheng University ms.

Myers, J., Tsay, J.S. and Su, S.F., 2011, "Representation efficiency and transmission efficiency in sign and speech", in J. Chang, ed., *Language and cognition: Festschrift in honor of James H-Y. Tai on his 70th birthday*, pp. 171–199, Crane Publishing, Taipei.

Naka, M., 1998, "Repeated writing facilitates children's memory for pseudocharacters and foreign letters", *Memory & Cognition*, 26(4), pp. 804–809.

Namy, L.L., 2008, "Recognition of iconicity doesn't come for free", *Developmental Science*, 11(6), pp. 841–846.

Namy, L.L., Campbell, A.L. and Tomasello, M., 2004, "The changing role of iconicity in non-verbal symbol learning: A U-shaped trajectory in the acquisition of arbitrary gestures", *Journal of Cognition and Development*, 5(1), pp. 37–57.

Napoli, D.J., Sanders, N. and Wright, R., 2014, "On the linguistic effects of articulatory ease, with a focus on sign languages", *Language*, 90(2), pp. 424–456.

Nash, P.W., 2001, "The abandoning of the long *s* in Britain in 1800", *Journal of the Printing Historical Society (New Series)*, 3, pp. 3–19.

Neeleman, A. and van de Koot, H., 2010, "Theoretical validity and psychological reality of the grammatical code", in M. Everaert, T. Lentz, H. De Mulder, Ø. Nilsen and

42   Chinese character grammar

A. Zondervan, eds., *The linguistics enterprise: From knowledge of language to knowledge in linguistics*, pp. 183–212, John Benjamins, Amsterdam.

Neidle, C., Kegl, J., MacLaughlin, D., Bahan, B. and Lee, R.G., 2001, *The syntax of American Sign Language: Functional categories and hierarchical structure*, MIT Press, Cambridge, MA.

Ninio, A. and Lieblich, A., 1976, "The grammar of action: 'Phrase structure' in children's copying", *Child Development*, 47(3), pp. 846–850.

Novembre, G. and Keller, P.E., 2011, "A grammar of action generates predictions in skilled musicians", *Consciousness and Cognition*, 20(4), pp. 1232–1243.

Novotná, Z., 1962, "Some remarks on the analysis of compound types of Chinese characters", *Archív Orientální*, 30, pp. 597–623.

Ohala, J.J., 1986, "Consumer's guide to evidence in phonology", *Phonology Yearbook*, 3, pp. 3–26.

Pacton, S., Perruchet, P., Fayol, M. and Cleeremans, A., 2001, "Implicit learning out of the lab: The case of orthographic regularities", *Journal of Experimental Psychology: General*, 130(3), pp. 401–426.

PalmerWilcox, S., 1992, *The phonetics of fingerspelling*. John Benjamins, Amsterdam.

Wilkinson, E.P., 2000, "The characters: Evolution and structure", in E.P. Wilkinson, ed., *Chinese history: A manual*, pp. 407–426, Harvard University Asia Center, Cambridge, MA.

Winter, M., 2017, "Kāngxī Zìdiǎn 康熙字典", in R. Sybesma, W. Behr, Y. Gu, Z. Handel, C.T.J. Huang and J. Myers, eds., *Encyclopedia of Chinese language and linguistics*, vol. 2, pp. 481–485, Brill, Leiden.

Wittern, C., 2017, "Encodings, fonts, and input systems", in R. Sybesma, W. Behr, Y. Gu, Z. Handel, C.T.J. Huang and J. Myers, eds., *Encyclopedia of Chinese language and linguistics*, vol. 2, pp. 169–173, Brill, Leiden.

Xiao, D. [晓东], 1994, 现代汉字独体与合体的再认识 [Recognition of simple and combined modern Chinese characters]. 语文建设 [Language Construction], 8, pp. 28–31.

Xu, Z., 2018, "The word status of Chinese adjective-noun combinations", *Linguistics*, 56(1), pp. 207–256.

Yan, H.F., 2005, *Constraint and ranking in language and music*, MA thesis, National Chung Cheng University.

Yau, S.C., 1978, "Element ordering in gestural languages and in archaic Chinese ideograms", *Cahiers de linguistique-Asie orientale*, 3(1), pp. 51–65.

Yau, S.C., 1983, "Temporal order in the composition of Archaic Chinese ideograms", *Journal of Chinese Linguistics*, 11(2), pp. 187–213.

Yin, J.J.H., 2016, "Chinese characters", in S.W. Chan, ed., *The Routledge encyclopedia of the Chinese language*, pp. 51–63, Routledge, Abingdon.

Yip, M., 2002, *Tone*, Cambridge University Press, Cambridge.

Yip, P.C., 2000, *The Chinese lexicon: A comprehensive survey*, Routledge, Abingdon.

Zhang, X., 2016, "Computational linguistics", in S.W. Chan, ed., *The Routledge encyclopedia of the Chinese language*, pp. 420–437, Routledge, Abingdon.

Zhengzhang, S. [郑张尚芳], 2013, 上古音系 (第二版) [Old Chinese phonology, 2nd ed.]. 上海教育出版社 [Shanghai Educational Publishing House], Shanghai.

Zhou, Y.G. [周有光], 1978, 现代汉字中声旁的表音功能问题 [To what degree are the "phonetics" of present-day Chinese characters still phonetic?]. 中国语文 [Chinese Language], 146(3), pp. 172–177.

2 Character morphology

2.1. Introduction

This chapter focuses on CHARACTER MORPHOLOGY: regularities in character structure relating to constituents that may be EXTERNALLY INTERPRETED, that is, have links outside the formal system, either in terms of meaning (the semantic radical) or in terms of pronunciation (the phonetic component).

The method in this and the next chapter follows traditional descriptive and theoretical linguistics in supporting the argument with representative examples of apparent lexical generalizations. For generalizations that are less obvious, I also demonstrate their statistical reliability (which does not necessarily imply productivity or mental activity, issues to be examined in later chapters). The main database used in these two chapters is version 4.0 of the Academia Sinica Balanced Corpus of Modern Chinese (Chen *et al.* 1996), since its 6,607 traditional characters are roughly the number estimated to be known by the typical college-educated reader (Hue 2003). I supplement these with rarer examples, mostly from the 13,058 traditional characters in Tsai (2006), usually to illustrate generalizations with formally simpler characters. I searched for relevant examples with the help of two online resources for traditional characters: the Chinese Character Decomposition page in the Wikimedia Commons (Wikimedia Commons 2017) and the Hong Kong Glyph Specification and Assisting Tools (Lu *et al.* 2002), though without committing to their often quite different decomposition schemes. Traditional classifications of characters as semantic-phonetic (形聲 *xíngshēng*) or as semantic compounds (會意 *huìyì*) came from Wiktionary (2018), supplemented with Handian (2015) and Zaixian hanyu zidian (2018), though they offer unambiguous synchronic classifications for only 5,908 of the traditional characters in my database.

I first discuss the decomposition of characters into what I call character morphemes (Section 2.2). I then argue that the combination of morphemic character constituents can be fruitfully understood in terms of the familiar operations of affixation, compounding, and reduplication (Section 2.3).

2.2. The morphemic decomposition of characters

Prototypically, character morphemes are indivisible constituents that are externally interpreted in meaning or pronunciation, similar to the way that morphemes in spoken

44 *Character morphology*

or signed languages are indivisible constituents interpreted for meaning. Presumably all of the constituents in any given character were interpretable when the character was first coined, but what matters to character grammar is not so much actual history as folk etymology, or more properly, the active (though not necessarily conscious) character knowledge of readers and writers. It is not trivial to establish this knowledge empirically (see Chapters 4, 5, and 6), so for practical purposes I will generally assume the character types and external interpretations as given by my databases.

Character morphemes are clearest in semantic-phonetic characters, by far the most common type, in which a semantic radical is combined with a phonetic component (see Section 1.2.2.1). Unlike semantic radicals, phonetic components are often decomposable, as illustrated with the semantic-phonetic character in (1a), in which the phonetic component is the semantic compound in (1b). The linking of a pronunciation to a decomposable phonetic component is something like semantic opacity in spoken or signed languages, where morphologically complex words have idiosyncratic meanings as wholes (e.g., English *hogwash* 'nonsense'). The basic constituents that make up semantic compound characters are also externally interpreted, hence morphemic. For example, the meaning of the character in (1c) relates to the meaning of its constituents (see Section 4.3.1.1 for a historical addendum on this particular character).

(1) a 梨 *lí* 'pear' = 木 *mù* 'wood, tree' + 利 *lì* 'benefit'
     b 利 *lì* 'benefit' = 禾 *hé* 'grain' + 刂 (刀) *dāo* 'knife'
     c 明 *míng* 'bright' = 日 *rì* 'sun' + 月 *yuè* 'moon'

The external interpretability of a modern character constituent is not an all-or-none affair. Even in semantic-phonetic characters, the interpretation of the semantic radical is often unclear, as illustrated with the semantic radical in (2).

(2) a 女 *nǚ* 'female'
     b 媽 *mā* 'mother'
     c 婚 *hūn* 'marriage'
     d 嫌 *xián* 'suspect'
     e 妖 *yāo* 'demon'
     f 始 *shǐ* 'beginning'

Phonetic components can also be inconsistent in their modern pronunciations, as illustrated in (3), primarily due to regular sound change further obscuring the original character coiners' tolerance of near homophones (see Qiu 2000, pp. 249–252). Thus, the five characters in (3) seem to have had much more similar, though still not identical, pronunciations in Old Chinese (respectively reconstructed by Zhengzhang 2013 as /klaːg/, /klaːg/, /gˑraːgs/, /gˑraːg/, /gˑrag/; the reconstructions of Baxter and Sagart 2014 are also merely near homophones).

(3) a 各 *gè* 'each'
     b 格 *gé* 'pattern'
     c 路 *lù* 'road'

Character morphology   45

    d 络 *luò* 'enmesh'
    e 略 *lüè* 'slightly'

Phonetic components may also sometimes be interpretable semantically as well, as in (4), blurring the line with semantic compounds (see Sections 4.3.1.1 and 4.4.3 for more on this phenomenon, both historically and in modern times).

(4)   a 娶 *qǔ* 'take a wife' = 女 *nǚ* 'female' + 取 *qǔ* 'take'
       b 份 *fèn* 'portion' = 亻(人) *rén* 'person' + 分 *fēn* 'divide'

Constituent interpretation in semantic compounds can be particularly obscure, even to historians (notoriously, Boltz 1994 argues that no characters were ever coined as semantic compounds at all; see Behr 2006; Bottéro 1996; Sampson and Chen 2013 for defenses of the mainstream view). The characters in (5) are often analyzed as semantic compounds in modern regular script, but even if this is true etymologically, it seems doubtful that contemporary readers and writers actively interpret any of the constituents here, any more than many English speakers would care about or even know the etymology of *breakfast*.

(5)   a 好 *hǎo* 'good' = 女 'mother' + 子 'child'
       b 加 *jiā* 'add' = 力 'power' + 口 'mouth'
       c 解 *jiě* 'solve' = 角 'horn' + 刀 'knife' + 牛 'cow'

The degree to which an apparent morpheme is externally interpreted by actual people is an empirical question, but whether external interpretation really matters to defining morphemes is a theoretical question. After all, semantic opacity is common in spoken and signed languages as well, and some linguists have even argued that morphemes can be defined solely by their formal properties; Aronoff (1994b) calls this "morphology by itself." For example, Aronoff (1976) points to formatives like English *ceive*, which has no consistent meaning (*conceive*, *perceive*, *receive*), yet does have consistent phonological alternations (*conception*, *perception*, *reception*; cf. *believe* ~ *belief*, not **beleption*, where * marks apparent ungrammaticality). There is even psycholinguistic evidence from spoken language that morphemes do not have to be interpretable to be mentally activated (e.g., Roelofs and Baayen 2002).

Linguists also know that words are often only partly decomposable. A notorious example is the nose-related formative /sn/ in English words like *snore*, *sneeze*, *snot*, and *sneer*, which, despite its consistent form-meaning correlation, cannot be segmented out as a true morpheme. Similarly, the coinage of *workaholic* depended on extracting *-oholic* from *alcoholic*, leaving the unanalyzed *alc-*; the etymologically correct analysis of *helicopter* is *helico-pter* ('rotating wing'), but speakers are tempted to parse it as *helicopt-er* due to the suffix-like *-er*; surely more than one child has imagined a relationship between the etymologically and morphologically unrelated *pen* and *pencil*; pairs like *cold* ~ *cool* and *hot* ~ *heat* seem simultaneously monomorphemic and morphologically related; and as Ohala (1986) points out, *witticism* is clearly derived from *witty*, but how, exactly?

46 *Character morphology*

In this context, finding incompletely decomposable Chinese characters is hardly surprising. Wang (1983, p. 127) suggests that characters that do not conform to his decomposition scheme "were originally pictographs and ideographs," but the more general principle is simply that lexical grammars often sacrifice synchronic elegance for the sake of diachronic continuity (an older script must still remain legible during the transition to a newer script).

The most morphologically transparent of such characters are fully decomposable, but only contain one constituent familiar enough to have any chance of being interpretable by modern readers, as with the first-listed constituents in the decompositions in (6).

(6) a 麥 *mài* 'wheat' = 來 *lái* 'come' + 夊 *suī* 'go slowly'
     b 賣 *mài* 'sell' = 買 *mǎi* 'buy' + 士 *shì* 'scholar' (< 出 *chū* 'go out')

An amusing example of this kind of character is given in (7), where only extremely close scrutiny shows that the internal component differs subtly from its form as a free character.

(7) 鬪 *dòu* 'struggle' = 鬥 *dòu* 'fight' + 斲 *zhuó* 'chop'

Next most transparent are /sn/-type quasi-morphemes, where one stroke group seems to have an interpretation despite being inseparable from the rest of the character. For example, the characters in (8a) all refer to animals, and though they are iconic as wholes, they all share a row of four dots at the bottom. Rarely, the leftover bits may also appear without the row of dots, as in (8b), and the four-dot stroke group also appears in the apparently morphologically derived animal-related characters in (8c). At the same time, however, the four-dot stroke group is also associated with the completely unrelated meaning of 'fire,' as in (8d), and may also appear in characters that do not seem decomposable in their modern forms at all, as in (8e).

(8) a 魚 *yú* 'fish' 馬 *mǎ* 'horse' 鳥 *niǎo* 'bird' 燕 *yàn* 'swallow' 烏 *wū* 'crow'
     b 島 *dǎo* 'island' = 山 *shān* 'mountain' + 鳥 *niǎo* 'bird' (phonetic)
     c 熊 *xióng* 'bear' = 灬 + 能 *néng* 'can' (originally 'bear')
        羔 *gāo* 'lamb' = 灬 + 羊 *yáng* 'sheep'
     d 熱 *rè* 'hot' = 灬 (火) *huǒ* 'fire' + 埶 *yì* 'art' (phonetic)
     e 無 *wú* 'not' 為 *wèi* 'for'

There are also several character pairs of the *heat-hot* variety, as illustrated in (9), with related forms and interpretations but no generalizable pattern.

(9) a 老 *lǎo* 'old'   考 *kǎo* 'exam' (< 'elderly')
     b 毋 *wú* 'not'   母 *mǔ* 'mother'
     c 小 *xiǎo* 'small' 少 *shǎo* 'few'
     d 心 *xīn* 'heart'   必 *bì* 'obligatory'
     e 刀 *dāo* 'knife'   刃 *rèn* 'blade'   刅 *chuāng* 'injure' (variant of 創)

Character morphology 47

Table 2.1 Iconic character formation

Examples	Possible iconic relationship
叉 *chā* 'fork'	claw shape
蚤 *zǎo* 'flea'	
豕 *shǐ* 'pig'	bulky body and legs
象 *xiàng* 'elephant'	
口 *kǒu* 'mouth'	container
囚 *qiú* 'prisoner'	
臼 *jiù* 'mortar'	grasping container?
臽 *xiàn* 'trap'	
兒 *ér* 'child'	

Other form/meaning correlations, like those in Table 2.1, seem better under-stood in terms of iconicity than morphology (in traditional terms, as 指事 *zhǐshì* 'indicate things' or 象形 *xiàngxíng* 'resemble form' rather than as 形聲 *xíngshēng* 'form and sound' or 會意 *huìyì* 'conjoining meanings,' using the English glosses of Qiu 2000). For example, the boxes in the modern characters 口 and 囚 represent similarly shaped entities (respectively, a mouth and prison containing a person 人), but are otherwise totally unrelated (e.g., they differ in positional preferences; see Section 2.3.1.2).

Somewhere along this continuum are characters that have been reanalyzed into synchronically uninterpretable stroke groups. Examples are given in (10a–b), which share stroke groups with the characters in (10a'–b'), respectively. It is not clear whether to consider such cases as monomorphemic or as opaque compounds, but the same problem arises in spoken and signed languages as well.

(10)   a   能 *néng* 'can' (originally representing a bear)
       a' 公 *gōng* 'public'   胃 *wèi* 'stomach'   北 *běi* 'north'
       b   皇 *huáng* 'magnificent' (originally representing a lit lamp)
       b' 白 *bái* 'white'   王 *wáng* 'king'

2.3. Morphological operations

As I show here, characters can be fruitfully analyzed via operations remarkably similar to affixation (Section 2.3.1), compounding (Section 2.3.2), and reduplica-tion (Section 2.3.3). I then look at how these operations interact (Section 2.3.4).

2.3.1. Affixation

As often in linguistics, the distinction between affix and root is not sharp (see, e.g., Packard 2000 for spoken Mandarin morphology), but the frequent co-occurrence of the formal and functional diagnostics in (11) suggests that something real

48   *Character morphology*

underlies them. Roughly speaking, what makes a morpheme an affix rather than a root is its subordinate role.

(11)   a   Bound
        b   Closed class
        c   Semantically bleached
        d   Fixed in position
        e   May be formally reduced

Consider the English words *greenish* and *greenhouse*. The first word is analyzed as suffixed because *-ish* (a) cannot appear on its own, (b) cannot be easily replaced with a similar morpheme (new affixes are very difficult to coin), (c) has an abstract semantic function rather than a concrete referent (X-*ish* means 'somewhat X'), (d) always appears after the root, and (e) must be unstressed. By contrast, in the compound *greenhouse*, *house* (a) may also be used as a free word; (b) can be replaced with a potentially unlimited number of similar morphemes (nouns like *back*, *belt*, or *card*); (c) has rich semantics; (d) may appear in other positions in other words (e.g., *houseboat*); and (e) receives some stress.

Semantic radicals display all of these affix diagnostics (and again I repeat my request from Chapter 1 that readers set aside the etymological association of 'radical' with 'root'). More accurately, semantic radicals are affix-like, as if the historical development of character morphology was frozen before they could be fully grammaticalized (see Section 2.3.1.4). As with character grammar more generally, what ultimately matters is how actual readers and writers represent character knowledge in their heads, but for convenience, I will assume that a character constituent is a semantic radical if it is indicated as such in modern traditional character dictionaries following the 214-radical *Kangxi* system (Winter 2017) and if the character is classified as a semantic-phonetic character in my sources. Admittedly, this strategy sometimes yields demonstrably wrong results. For example, in my quantitative analyses, I treat the semantic-phonetic character in (12a) as having the radical in (12b) because that is what is given in dictionaries, though the actual semantic component is clearly that in (12c). Nevertheless, relying on traditional dictionaries and databases not only lets us get started, but also makes it easier for others to replicate or modify my analyses. Familiarity with the *Kangxi* system itself has arguably also affected how modern readers and writers conceive of character structure anyway.

(12)   a   到 *dào* 'arrive'
        b   刀 / 刂 *dāo* 'knife'
        c   至 *zhì* 'reach'

I first discuss the first three affix diagnostics (Section 2.3.1.1), then positional fixedness (Section 2.3.1.2) and reduction (Section 2.3.1.3). Finally, I address some related theoretical issues (Section 2.3.1.4).

Character morphology 49

2.3.1.1. Semantic radicals as bound, closed class, and semantically bleached

The first three affix diagnostics are the most obviously true of semantic radicals. Regarding the first, some radicals are never free, like those in (13a), and many others have bound allomorphs, like those in (13b). Yet even radicals that seem to have free forms, like those in (13c), are not actually radicals when free, since as free constituents they are not semantic-phonetic characters.

(13) a 冫   宀   宀   癶   攵 彳
      b 忄(心)   扌(手)   氵(水)   艹(艸)
      c 女   木   金   鳥

Second, the 214 traditional lexicographic radicals are far fewer than the up to 667 character constituents that researchers have identified (see Section 1.2.2.3), let alone the approximately 800 phonetic components estimated by Hoosain (1991), many of which are morphologically complex. The number of mentally active semantic radicals is likely to be far fewer than these 214 lexicographic radicals anyway. Only 192 even appear in the semantic-phonetic characters in my database, and of these, only 39 appear in a set of 172 semantic-phonetic characters coined since the eighteenth century *Kangxi* dictionary, as compiled by Handel (forthcoming), and of these, the four in (14) take up over half of the coinages.

(14) 金 气 口 石

Third, radicals are semantically bleached (to use the term of Sweetser 1988), that is, they have meanings abstracted away from their usage as free forms. For example, Handel (forthcoming) observes that when the constituent in (15a) is used as a semantic radical, as in (15b–c), it preserves only the abstract semantic component of 'money' or 'value' (cowrie shells were used as currency in ancient China).

(15) a 貝 *bèi* 'shell'
      b 賬 *zhàng* 'account'
      c 貨 *huò* 'goods'

The radical in (16a) has a particularly vacuous usage; in addition to indicating meanings literally related to the mouth, as in (16b), it can also indicate nothing more than that the character is pronounced similarly to the phonetic component it contains, as in the function words in (16c–d).

(16) a 口 *kǒu* 'mouth'
      b 吃 *chī* 'eat'   叫 *jiào* 'call'
      c 嗎 *ma* (sentence-final particle)   馬 *mǎ* 'horse'
      d 呢 *ne* (another sentence-final particle)   尼 *ní* 'nun'

50 *Character morphology*

It has also often been noted (e.g., Handel forthcoming; Huang, Yang, and Chen 2013; Huang *et al.* 2013; Wang 1983; Wiebusch 1995) that the semantic function of semantic radicals is to identify a character's semantic class. Though semantic classification is not usually thought of as the primary function of an affix, affixes do indeed classify: *greenish* is in the same semantic class as *youngish* and *fattish*, since all express the vagueness of a physical feature.

However, semantic radicals differ sharply from affixes in that they are not semantic operators. While English X-*ish* implies 'somewhat X,' for any adjective X, similar formulas cannot be given for semantic radicals, since here the X would be the phonetic component, which represents pronunciation rather than meaning. For the same reason, semantic radicals can have no selectional restrictions, the way English -*er* only affixes to human nouns and *un*- to scalar adjectives. Nevertheless, while semantic radicals are not semantic operators, they are still formal operators in that they are added to phonetic components rather than the other way around (at least as perceived synchronically; cf. the historical discussion in Section 4.3.1.1).

2.3.1.2. Radical positions

The fourth affix-like property of semantic radicals is that they have favored positions in characters (as often noted; see, e.g., Hoosain 1991). Their positional preferences are nowhere near as strict as prefixes and suffixes, where the positions are invariant, but this statistical regularity still makes them more affix-like than root-like.

The observations can be quantified in a variety of different ways. Table 2.2 counts the 5,908 characters for which I have character type information, according to character type and lexicographic radical position, illustrated with examples from the Tsai (2006) database. Note that the Tsai database does contain characters with lexicographic radicals simultaneously at the left, bottom, and right (left/bottom/right), like 凵, but none of these characters happens to be included in the databases I used for settling on character types. Note also that the 'other' category includes one-constituent characters like 大, as well as reduplicative structures like 辦, which are not counted in the left/right category with 行 in 術 (see Section 2.3.3.2 for more the splitting of reduplication).

The most obvious pattern in this table is that the top four most common positions for radicals in semantic-phonetic characters involve just one edge, with the left being by far the most common position overall. Positional preferences are much weaker for other types of characters. Two-way chi-squared tests show that in semantic-phonetic characters, single-edge radicals are significantly more common (89 percent vs. 53 percent: $\chi^2(1) = 757, p < .0001$) and radicals without a well-specified edge ('other') are significantly less common (4 percent vs. 41 percent: $\chi^2(1) = 12545, p < .0001$) than in other character types. The table also makes it clear that the left-edge preference is only found in semantic-phonetic characters.

Radical position is also strongly determined by the radicals themselves, another affix-like property; the different positions of English -*er* and *un*- depend on the

Character morphology 51

Table 2.2 Where characters have their radicals

Radical position	Semantic-phonetic	Semantic compound	Other	Examples		
Left	3086	126	3	口	:	嗎
Right	289	60	10	鳥	:	鵝
Top	578	114	44	宀	:	寫
Bottom	410	125	44	皿	:	盒
Left/bottom	140	9	0	廴	:	廷
Left/bottom/right	0	0	0	(凵	:	函)
Left/right	13	0	0	行	:	術
Top/bottom	8	4	0	衣	:	衷
Top/left	133	25	5	厂	:	原
Top/left/bottom	10	2	0	匚	:	匪
Top/left/bottom/right	17	6	5	囗	:	國
Top/left/right	20	5	0	門	:	開
Top/right	16	0	1	勹	:	匍
Other	190	175	235	大	:	大
				目	:	看
				辛	:	辨

affix, not the words in which they appear. Most radicals prefer the left edge, but others prefer the top, right, bottom, or other positions. Table 2.3 counts how many of the 189 radicals in my set of 4,910 semantic-phonetic characters appear in a given position in more than 50 percent of their characters; fewer than 16 percent have no favored position, and the left edge is again the clear favorite. Both character and radical counts also show a slight preference for the top edge over the bottom edge. Two-edge radicals tend to include one or both of these edges too, at the top/left and at the left/bottom. Recall that the bound (and invariantly positioned) radicals in (17) also appear at the left, top, and left/bottom.

(17)　氵　冖　宀　癶　辶

The preference for edge positions is seen in spoken language affixation as well; recall from Section 1.4.1 that sign languages instead prefer simultaneous affixes, showing that the edge bias in characters does not derive from the visual modality. The strong left-edge bias is also affix-like in that languages generally tend to favor one side over the other across all of their affixes: English has many more suffixes than prefixes, for example, whereas Navajo shows the reverse preference (Matthews 1991).

To give a sense of how consistently radicals appear in the same position across characters, as well as how each radical's alternative positions relate to its dominant position, I present the plot in Figure 2.1. Each vertical line represents

Table 2.3 Where radicals prefer to appear in semantic-phonetic characters

Position	Number of radicals
Left	70
Right	21
Top	19
Bottom	13
Left/bottom	6
Left/bottom/right	0
Left/right	1
Top/bottom	0
Top/left	6
Top/left/bottom	0
Top/left/bottom/right	1
Top/left/right	2
Top/right	3
Other	18
No preference	29

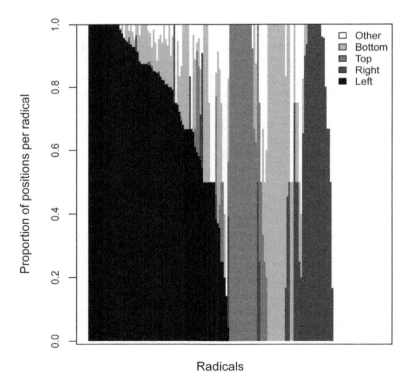

Figure 2.1 Variation in radical position in semantic-phonetic characters

Character morphology   53

a radical, sorted from left to right in terms of the proportion of characters in which the radical appears (at the left, top, bottom, right, or all other positions, at an edge or otherwise). The overall preference for radicals to appear at the left is seen in the large black mass at the left of the figure; the three other blocks represent the top, bottom, and right positions, respectively. The single-shade vertical lines that reach from the bottom of the plot to more than 50 percent towards the top represent radicals with a dominant position. Within a vertical line for a radical, shades are always stacked upward in the order left, top, bottom, right, and other. This arrangement allows us to see that for radicals favoring the left position, the bottom position is the most common alternative (i.e., the black lines are often topped by lines of the lightest shade of gray). I explain this pattern in Section 3.3.1.1.

As with the other radical properties I am reviewing here, such positional regularities merely make radicals affix-like; true affixes, of course, never vary in position at all. Nevertheless, as Wang (1983) shows, one can tame this variation to a great degree by considering competition with the positional preferences of other character constituents. In particular, in a two-constituent character, if one constituent can only appear on a specific edge, it goes there, forcing the other constituent to go on the opposite edge. When neither has a fixed position, the semantic radical will appear on the left by default, and when different types of constituents compete for the same position, the positional preference of the semantic radical has priority (see Wang 1983, pp. 109ff).

For example, in (18a), 力 is a semantic radical that favors the right, so the phonetic component 巠 must appear to the left of it. In (18b), 耳 is a semantic radical that may appear either at the left or the bottom, but the phonetic component 殸 can only appear at the top, forcing 耳 to appear at the bottom (耳 otherwise favors the left, as in 職 *zhí* 'duty'). In (18c–d), 馬 appears on the left when used as a semantic radical but on the right when used as a phonetic component (other constituents of this type include 石 and 全). Finally, the character in (18e) contains a semantic radical that generally favors the left (52 out of the 75 衣 characters in my database, like 被 *bèi* 'quilt'), so the fact that it is pushed to the bottom here suggests that the phonetic component 壯 prefers to appear on the top, yet in (18f) the semantic radical ⁺⁺ obligatorily appears at the top, forcing 壯 to the bottom.

(18) a 勁 *jìng* 'powerful'   = 巠 *jīng*   + 力 'power'
      b 聲 *shēng* 'sound'   = 殸 *kēng*   + 耳 'ear'
      c 駝 *tuó* 'camel'   = 馬 'horse'   + 它 *tā*
      d 媽 *mā* 'mother'   = 女 'female'   + 馬 *mǎ*
      e 裝 *zhuāng* 'baggage'   = 壯 *zhuàng*   + 衣 'clothing'
      f 莊 *zhuāng* 'village'   = 壯 *zhuàng*   + ⁺⁺(艸) 'grass'

Without computational help in searching for characters, Wang (1983) failed to see some problems; the lexicographic radical 力, for example, does not actually

54 *Character morphology*

appear obligatorily on the right, as shown by the examples in (19), where it appears at the bottom or left.

(19) a 勢 *shì* 'power'   努 *nǔ* 'strive'
      b 加 *jiā* 'add'

Nevertheless, Wang's approach to constituent position is worth defending against technical critiques. In particular, Stalph (1989, pp. 45–46) points out that the character in (20a) would create problems if the grammar selected the semantic radical entry in (20b), since then it would compete with the semantic radical in (20c) for the left-side position, with no way to resolve the dilemma. However, Wang could simply reply with another constraint that blocks a character from being composed solely of two semantic radicals, which seems eminently reasonable (and predicted by my analysis of radicals as affixes).

(20) a 媽
      b 馬
      c 女

Wang's observations raise an apparent problem for my own analysis, however. While he notes that semantic radicals take pride of place when there is a conflict for the same position, he also correctly observes that non-radicals can also have favored positions. Is this something we should expect of non-affixes? Well, yes; in spoken languages at least, roots also often have favored locations in a word (psycholinguists quantify this as positional family size; e.g., del Prado Martín, Kostić, and Baayen 2004). For example, the root morpheme *man* appears far more often on the right than on the left in English compounds (e.g., *mailman*, *doorman*), despite counterexamples (e.g., *manpower*, *manhole*). Moreover, such tendencies often seem to derive from pragmatics: there are many ways to be a *man*, making it particularly useful as a compound head (see Section 2.3.2 for similar effects in semantic compound characters). Prosody may also matter: English speakers say *singer-songwriter*, even though the writing precedes the singing, because putting the longer word last improves the rhythm (a pattern that English speakers productively generalize; Pinker and Birdsong 1979). Perhaps the phonetic component 殷 prefers the top edge because of its inverted-U shape, which leaves an opening at the bottom (though in Section 3.3.1.1, we will see that this preference cannot be attributed to character prosody directly). In any case, positional preferences are the strongest and most consistent for semantic radicals, as expected of affix-like constituents.

2.3.1.3. Radical reduction

The final affix-like property of semantic radicals is that they are often formally reduced, disproportionally so in precisely their two most favored radical positions, at the left and top edges.

Two regular reduction processes that apply on the left are what I will call DIAGO-NALIZATION of the lowest horizontal stroke, as in (21a), and DOTTING of the lower right falling stroke, as in (21b) (see also Wang 1983, pp. 140–145).

(21) a 金：鑿～鉛　土：型～地　立：童～站　至：臺～致　牛：犁～物
　　　b 木：桌～村　火：燙～爛　米：粱～精　耒～耗　　　　采～釋

Two other regular processes are SHRINKING of the lower strokes in top-edge radicals, as in (22a), and STRETCHING of the lower right stroke of a left-edge constituent underneath the phonetic component to its right, as in (22b) (see also Wang 1983, pp. 147–148, and pp. 135–140, respectively).

(22) a 雨～電　穴～空　竹～筆　西～覆
　　　b 尤～尬　支～翅　毛～毯　爪～爬　走～起
　　　　風～颱　鼠～鼮　鬼～魅　瓜～瓞　麥～麵

All of these processes involve reduction, both in constituent size and in the distance that the writing instrument has to move to the start of the next constituent; even stretching thins the left-edge constituent (the stretching itself is also consistent with another aspect of character phonology, as discussed in Section 3.4.4). Thus, these processes may be thought of as parallel to the destressing of affixes with free cognates, as in the word *able* /ˈeɪ.bəl/ vs. the suffix -*able* /ə.bl̩/ in English, as well as other cases in which free forms have been grammaticalized into affixes (Hopper and Traugott 2003). I expand on these parallels in Sections 2.3.1.4 and 3.3.1.2.

As regular processes, however, they all also apply to constituents that are not semantic radicals, as illustrated with the phonetic components in (23).

(23) a Diagonalization:　且：宜～助　工：紅～功　重：種～動
　　　b Dotting:　　　　采：採～彩　禾：秌～和
　　　c Shrinking:　　　亦～奕　　尚～當　　高～膏
　　　d Stretching:　　　兀～虺　　兌～虓　　支～翅

Diagonalization and dotting apply as long as there is a constituent to the right, as illustrated in (24). While this means that they are technically not triggered by the left edge, this is the position in which they appear in all but such rare left-branching characters (i.e., characters with the structure [[XX]X]).

(24) a 鴻 *hóng* 'swan species' = 江 *jiāng* + 鳥 'bird'
　　　b 郴 *chēn* (county in Hunan) = 林 *lín* + 阝 (邑) 'district'

Reduction also includes lexically specified alternations that I will call IDIOSYN-CRATIC ALLOMORPHY. Idiosyncratic allomorphy is defined as constituent changes, ad hoc and sometimes quite extreme, that do not follow from one of the four regular processes, though the alternating allomorphs are historically related (i.e., they are not suppletive). An attempt at a complete list of idiosyncratic radical alternations

56 *Character morphology*

in semantic-phonetic characters is given in (25), arranged by position: a. left, b. top, c. bottom, d, right, e. elsewhere. Note that some radicals have more than one idiosyncratic allomorph, and that some also undergo regular reduction processes like diagonalization.

(25)   a 人～們   心：忘～忙 手：掌～拾 水：汞～泊 犬：獎～獨
          玉：瑩～現 示：禁～神 糸：緊～經 羊：羍～羚 肉～腦
          衣：裝～被 足：踅～路 辛：辜～辣 阜～院   食：養～館
    b 彐～彙   爪：爬～爵 网～罵～罕 艸～花
    c 卩：卻～卷 彐～彗 心～慕   木：校～桌 水～泰   火：燈～照
          肉～育
    d 乙～亂   刀：剪～刻 攴～政   邑：鄥～都
    e 辵～過

While it is reasonable to disagree on where to draw the line between idiosyncratic allomorphy and regular reduction in any particular case (see Section 4.4.1 for further observations relating to this), researchers as otherwise different as the grammar-oriented Wang (1983) and the lexicon-oriented Stalph (1989) agree that idiosyncratic allomorphy and regular reduction should be treated differently, respectively as lexically specified and as derived. In my own framework, idiosyncratic allomorphy belongs to character morphology and regular reduction to character phonology.

Further suggesting the morphological nature of idiosyncratic allomorphy is that unlike regular reduction, it is far more pervasive in semantic radicals than in other types of character constituents. In (26), I list some of the examples of modern idiosyncratic allomorphy among the 1,055 etymological phonetic components from Zhengzhang (2003) listed in Wiktionary (2018) (see also Zhengzhang 2013). However, in modern characters, most of the idiosyncratic allomorphy in phonetic components is either unsystematic, as in (26b), or else is borrowed from its role as a semantic radical, as in (26c). Note how the latter point fits with Aronoff's (1976) idea, alluded to Section 2.2, that English *ceive* reveals its morphemic status through its formal properties, not its interpretation.

(26)   a 卯 *mǎo*: 聊 *liáo*   昴 *mǎo* vs. 留 *liú*   貿 *mào*
    b 丰 *fēng*: 蚌 *bàng*   夆 *féng* vs. 奉 *fèng* vs. 邦 *bāng*
    c 示 *shì*: 眂 *shì* vs. 視 *shì*

Idiosyncratic allomorphy in semantic radicals is also more likely in certain positions. Table 2.4 demonstrates this by giving the rates of idiosyncratic allomorphy (and the total counts over which they were computed) by position and character type in the 4,889 characters with single-edge radicals for which I have character type information. All character types (semantic-phonetic, semantic compound, and other) show similar rates of idiosyncratic allomorphy at the left and bottom, but a logistic regression predicting idiosyncratic allomorphy from the interaction of radical position and character type shows that semantic-phonetic characters

Character morphology 57

Table 2.4 Radical position and idiosyncratic allomorphy rate (per number of characters)

Radical position	Semantic-phonetic	Semantic compound	Other
Left	46% (3086)	41% (126)	100% (3)
Right	43% (289)	22% (60)	20% (10)
Top	49% (578)	18% (114)	9% (44)
Bottom	13% (410)	8% (125)	18% (44)

Table 2.5 Radical position and variation in idiosyncratic allomorphy in semantic-phonetic characters

Radical	Position	Full form	Idiosyncratic allomorph (%)	Radical's favored position
刀/刂	Right	1: 切	43: 刻 (98%)	Right
攴/攵	Right	1: 敲	21: 教 (95%)	Right
心/忄	Bottom	48: 忘	3: 恭 (6%)	Left
水/氺	Bottom	1: 汞	1: 泰 (50%)	Left
肉/月	Bottom	1: 胔	10: 背 (91%)	Bottom
火/灬	Bottom	5: 烫	14: 熱 (74%)	Left

Table 2.6 Bottom-edge 火/灬 in semantic-phonetic and compound characters

	Semantic-phonetic			Semantic compound		
	Count	Example	Median frequency	Count	Example	Median frequency
Full	5	烫 *tàng* 'scalding hot'	145	5	焚 *fén* 'burn'	460
Idiosyncratic allomorph	14	熱 *rè* 'hot'	3760	3	焦 *jiāo* 'burned'	109

Note: Token frequencies from Tsai (2006).

show significantly greater idiosyncratic allomorphy rates at the right ($B = -0.83$, $SE = 0.38$, $z = -2.17$, $p = .03$) and at the top ($B = -1.27$, $SE = 0.32$, $z = -4.02$, $p < .0001$) as compared with compounds.

Moreover, single-edge radicals only rarely vary between full and idiosyncratic allomorphs in the same position, and when they do, it is restricted to the right or bottom, never in the canonical radical positions at left and top ('full' being defined within the modern system as usual; historically 刀 derives from something like 刂 rather than the other way around; Qiu 2000, p. 180). Table 2.5 lists all radicals showing such variation in semantic-phonetic characters in my database. Note also that the idiosyncratic variant is generally only preferred if the right or bottom happens to be the radical's overall favored position.

The last two points are illustrated together in Table 2.6, which compares the number of semantic-phonetic and semantic compound characters with the two

58 *Character morphology*

bottom-edge allomorphs of the 'fire' radical (火/灬). Idiosyncratic allomorphy is indeed more common with semantic radical affixation than with compounding, though this may be due to token frequency (see Section 2.3.1.4).

2.3.1.4. Other affix-related issues

The idea that semantic radicals are affix-like raises a number of further issues, the most important of which is what it means to be merely 'affix-like': radicals behave as if they have been frozen in the process of grammaticalization (Hopper and Traugott 2003). The fact that semantic radicals often play abstract classificatory roles even if they do not formally reduce is typical of grammaticalization, where semantic bleaching tends to precede reduction (Booij 2005). Moreover, the more common a linguistic form, the more likely it is to make the next step on the grammaticalization cline (Bybee 2011). This would predict that the higher the token frequency of a character, the more canonical the idiosyncratic allomorphy of its semantic radical (i.e., reducing at the top and left but not at the right and bottom).

Figure 2.2 shows that this prediction is true, though only partly. This plots the results of a logistic regression predicting idiosyncratic allomorphy in semantic radicals (within the 4,363 semantic-phonetic characters with a single-edge radical in my database) from log character token frequency, main character axis (horizontal for left- or right-edge radicals, vertical for top- or bottom-edge radicals), and whether the radical appears on the typical edge along that axis (i.e., left and top vs. right and bottom). The lines show the effects of frequency on idiosyncratic allomorphy, with their 95 percent confidence bands (a measure of analysis reliability). The overall positions of the trend lines reconfirm that idiosyncratic allomorphy rates are higher at the more common edges ($B = -0.48$, $SE = 0.12$, $z = -3.89$, $p < .0001$) and in horizontal-axis characters ($B = 0.26$, $SE = 0.12$, $z = 2.12$, $p = .03$), with an interaction between these two variables ($B = 0.83$, $SE = 0.12$, $z = 6.80$, $p < .0001$), since idiosyncratic allomorphy is disproportionately common at the left edge. The lower plots also show that frequency increases idiosyncratic allomorphy in left-edge radicals (axis = horizontal, edge = common) while decreasing it in right-edge radicals, consistent with the grammaticalization hypothesis. However, the upper plots reveal that vertical-axis characters show the reverse pattern, yielding a three-way interaction among all three variables ($B = -0.06$, $SE = 0.02$, $z = -3.75$, $p < .001$); in fact, across all positions, frequency slightly reduces the probability of idiosyncratic allomorphy ($B = -0.03$, $SE = 0.02$, $z = -2.03$, $p = .04$). In other words, frequency only increases grammaticalization for the default radical position, at the left edge. We will see other differences between the horizontal and vertical axes in Section 2.3.3.2, as well as in Chapters 3, 4, and 5.

Another affix-related issue is the question of circumfixation. The two-part semantic radicals in the characters in (27) look like circumfixes, but are they? Even in spoken languages, circumfixation is rare, because it depends on the

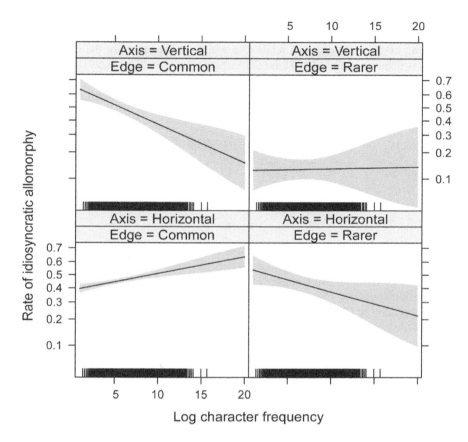

Figure 2.2 The interaction of character token frequency with semantic radical position on idiosyncratic allomorphy rates

cognitively difficult task of coordinating prefixes with suffixes (Dressler and Kilani-Schoch 2016; Harris 2008).

(27) a 門 'door'   關 *guān* 'shut'
     b 行 'walk'   街 *jiē* 'street'
     c 衣 'clothing' 裏 *lǐ* 'inside'

Three observations suggest that character grammar may not have true circumfixation. First, the stroke groups separated in the radicals in (28a) and (29a) can appear without the other, as illustrated by the characters in (28b) and (29b–d). This argument is quite weak, however, and not only because spoken language circumfixes are also composed of independently attested components. Historically, the characters in

60 *Character morphology*

(28b) were actually parsed out of 行 (Qiu 2000, p. 180), in a sort of back-formation, and the constituents illustrated in (29b–d) that appear to make up 衣 do not necessarily share any external interpretation with it, certainly not synchronically. The meaning of 衣 'clothing' does relate to the historical meaning of the character in (29c), which once referred to a kind of outer garment (Qiu 2000, p. 20), but it never related to that of the bound (yet conventionally named) constituent in (29b), often used to represent the top of something or a roof, as illustrated in (29d).

(28) a 行
       b 彳 *chì* 'walk slowly'   亍 *chù* 'stand still'

(29) a 衣
       b 亠 *tóu* (no consistent meaning)
       c 表 *biǎo* 'exterior'
       d 亭 *tíng* 'pavilion'

Secondly, regarding the radical 門, note that it touches not only on the left and right edges, but also the top edge. This is why the constituent it affixes to can never intervene between its two component stroke groups, unlike the examples we have just been discussing. The radical 門 should thus be analyzed the same way as the unitary radical in (30a), and indeed, in the simplified radical in (30b) (where '<' means 'descendent from'), there is a clear top-edge stroke (see Section 4.3.2 for more on the grammar of simplified characters).

(30) a 几   凰
       b 门 < 門

Third and most interestingly, characters with 行, which as a circumfix would have the structure [彳[X]亍], actually seem to have the structure [彳[X亍]]. Evidence for this comes from the observation that constituents in the X position may undergo left-edge idiosyncratic allomorphy, as happens with the constituent in (31a) in the middle of the semantic-phonetic character in (31b), but not when the same constituent appears in middle of the semantic compound in (31c).

(31) a 水 ～ 氵
       b 衍 *yán* 'overflow'
       c 盥 *guàn* 'wash the hands' (hands holding water over a basin)

Finally, if semantic radicals are affix-like, is this affixation derivational or inflectional? Oversimplifying considerably, affixes are inflectional if they trigger or undergo agreement, and derivational otherwise (Anderson 1992). In this context, it is interesting that semantic radicals are the only constituents that can 'agree' with a neighboring character, namely in disyllabic spoken morphemes like that in (32) (see Sproat 2000, pp. 148–154, for many more examples, and Handel 2019, p. 218, fn. 7, for a related insight).

Character morphology 61

(32) a 葡萄 *pútáo* 'grape'
      b 蝴蝶 *húdié* 'butterfly'

2.3.2. Compounding

As Jackendoff (2010) observes, compounding is simply unconstrained concatenation, with even the interpretation left mostly to pragmatics: a *snowman* is a man made of snow, but a *mailman* is a man who delivers mail. Mandarin nominal compounds do not even need to obey the minimal grammatical constraint of right-headedness: 父母 *fùmǔ* (literally 'father-mother') means 'parent,' not 'fatherly mother.' Similarly, semantic compound characters are composed in a far less constrained way than semantic-phonetic characters. These contrasts with affixation motivate the list of diagnostics for identifying root morphemes in (33).

(33) a May be free
      b Open class
      c Not semantically bleached
      d No fixed locations
      e Less formally reduced

Note that diagnostic (a) implies that roots, like affixes, may sometimes be bound. Bound roots are attested in English, as in the afore-mentioned *helicopter*, and in Mandarin, they are quite common (Packard 2000), even in fully transparent compounds like 校長 *xiàozhǎng* 'school principal' (Myers 2007). This allows us to analyze the phonetic component at the top of the semantic-phonetic characters (34) as a root morpheme, despite its bound nature.

(34) 卷 *juàn* 'scroll'   拳 *quán* 'fist'

Compound constituents are less closed class than semantic radicals (see Section 2.3.1.1) and also seem to have less abstract and more pragmatically determined meanings than semantic radicals. Consider, for example, the radical in (35a), which in semantic compounds typically refers to actual mouths, either explicitly as in (35b) or more obscurely as in (35c). Qiu (2000, p. 203) and Boltz (1994, p. 69) offer completely different speculations on how this latter character may have been coined, but both agree that it relates to the notion 'mouth,' and more importantly, this is how modern readers understand it. Never, however, does it take the abstract classificatory role for function words that we saw earlier with semantic-phonetic characters.

(35) a 口 *kǒu* 'mouth'
      b 吠 *fèi* 'bark of a dog'   (cf. 犬 *quǎn* 'dog')
      c 名 *míng* 'name'   (cf. 夕 *xī* 'night')

We have also already seen (in Section 2.3.1.2) that compound constituents do not favor the left edge the way semantic radicals do. For example, in semantic-phonetic

62   *Character morphology*

characters, the constituent 水 'water' shows a very strong preference to affix to the left edge (in its idiosyncratic allomorph 氵), but in semantic compounds it often appears elsewhere, as suggested in (36) (though this is difficult to quantify given that my sources do not take 水 as the lexicographic radical in these characters).

(36)   a   冰 *bīng* 'ice' = 氵 'ice' (bound semantic radical) + 水 'water'
       b   尿 *niào* 'urine' = 尸 'body' + 水 'water'
       c   畓 *duō* 'rice field' = 水 'water' + 田 'field'

Also, unlike semantic radicals, compound constituents are sometimes assigned positions by pragmatics rather than formal principles. This is already suggested by the characters in (36) (water is below the body in 尿 but above the field in 畓), and Qiu (2000, pp. 191–194) lists a number of other examples. A particularly charming minimal pair is shown in (37), with the sun (日) over or under a tree (木).

(37)   a   杲 *gǎo* 'bright'
       b   杳 *yǎo* 'dark'

We may also expect root morphemes to show a lesser tendency to reduce than affixes, due to their receiving greater emphasis (see Section 3.4.4). Unfortunately for the neat picture I have drawn so far, there is no evidence that this is true. The same logistic regression reported in Section 2.3.1.3 as showing differences in position-dependent idiosyncratic allomorphy across character types failed to show an overall effect of character type on idiosyncratic allomorphy, once this position-dependence was taken into account. This is not due to an epidemic of semantic compounds literally becoming semantic-phonetic characters (as we have seen, historical change tends to obscure pronunciation relationships rather than creating new ones). Rather, constituents in canonical semantic radical positions, particularly at the left, seem to be given the idiosyncratic allomorphic treatment regardless of their historical or synchronic function, in another example of 'morphology by itself' (see Section 2.2).

Nevertheless, in another character system based on Chinese orthography there are hints of just such a correlation between constituent form and function. Before the adoption of romanization in the early twentieth century, Vietnamese had been written in Chinese characters for centuries (Nguyễn 1959; Phan 2013), forming a rich orthography (守喃 *chữ nôm*) that boasted many more original coinages than written Cantonese, Japanese, and Korean (see Handel 2019 for much more on such systems, which unfortunately go a bit beyond the scope of the present book). Relevant here are characters in the Vietnamese system that combined a phonetic component with a semantic component, but in a way both functionally and formally more like compounding than like affixation. Consider the examples in (38) (from the online dictionary ChuNom 2015; characters are given in a Song typeface because some are not available in my usual regular typeface). The character in (38a) shows Chinese-like affixation: its meaning has only an abstract relationship with the meaning of the semantic radical for 'hand,' which is realized in its usual left-edge idiosyncratic

Character morphology 63

allomorph. By contrast, the character in (38b) seems to be a compound: its meaning is directly related to that of the 'hand' constituent, and, unlike the native Chinese system, it does not undergo idiosyncratic allomorphy at the left edge. Handel (2019) offers a plausible functional reason why semantic constituents are sometimes used in this way outside the native Chinese system: the borrowing orthography still needs a way to distinguish translation equivalents, whereas within the lexicon of a single language, what expands are taxonomic classes and not synonym sets. Nevertheless, the correlation of function with form here is intriguing.

(38) a 扲 *nghĩ* 'think' = 扌(手) 'hand' + 宁 *nghi*
      b 掓 *tay* 'arm' = 手 'hand' + 西 *tây*

2.3.3. Reduplication

While reduplication is much less productive than radical affixation, it is both more transparent and better defined than compounding. In this section, I sketch out its basic properties (Section 2.3.3.1), then discuss two complexities: splitting (Section 2.3.3.2) and reduction (Section 2.3.3.3).

2.3.3.1. Characteristics of reduplication

In (39), I give a large, representative, but incomplete set of reduplicative forms (including all in the Tsai 2006 database, some of which are rare or alternative forms). In several cases, the base constituent's external interpretation is synchronically doubtful (and some are etymologically holistic as well), but this does not seem to matter for how they behave formally. In particular, note that reduplication comes in three primary shapes (with minor caveats in (39d)): vertical double, horizontal double, and upward-pointing triangle, with the square shape coming in a distant fourth (for other English terms for these shapes, see Boodberg 1957).

(39) a 學 能 多 哥 肉 昌 炎 僵 圭 昍 爻 棗 爱 三 仌
         呂 奸 出 㴱 畕
      b 比 從 林 單 朋 雙 質 麗 替 絲 弱 羽 赫 瑩 蒜
         艸 兢 甡 林 皕 巽 玨 㷊 孖 䊔 奻 屾 豩 雔 砳
         戕 兹 厸 双 吅 炏 幵 弜 皛 炋 竝 蟲 誩 辡 鍂
         駬 驫
      c 品 森 蟲 晶 轟 姦 磊 鑫 聶 淼 蟲 垚 贔 麤 焱
         艸 晶 弄 劦 惢 毳 驫 龘 麤 众 劦 厽 叒 垚 弄
         沝 㙂 犇 畾 犇 譶 飝 龘 飝 鱻
      d 叕 芔 燚 朋

Reduplication is quite distinct from the far rarer mirroring, despite the traditional lumping of these two phenomena together (e.g., Behr 2006; Liu 2008; Wang 1983). Examples of mirroring are shown in (40), involving left/right stroke groups (40a), top/bottom stroke groups (40b), or both (40c). Unlike reduplication, the

64   *Character morphology*

mirrored stroke groups do not appear in other characters and may even overlap, violating a commonly cited criterion for decomposition (see Section 1.2.2.3). I thus consider mirroring merely the historical residue of the iconic origins of many characters rather than a productive morphological process.

(40)   a 發 非 北 興 聯 乖 齊 叟
       b 卡 挬
       c 淵 肅 亞 鼎

This distinction made, there are at least three non-trivial similarities between character reduplication and reduplication in spoken and signed languages. First, the semantics of reduplication is similar across these systems (see in particular the analysis in Behr 2006, pp. 99–102). For example, the characters in (41a) involve plurality or abundance, those in (41b) involve intensity, and that in (41c) involves attenuation. These are the very same meanings that reduplication represents in spoken and signed languages (see, e.g., Hurch 2005).

(41)   a 多 *duō* 'many'   品 *pǐn* 'all sorts'   蟲 *chóng* 'insects'
       b 晶 *jīng* 'glittering'   炎 *yán* 'blazing'
       c 弱 *ruò* 'weak'

Second, reduplication in spoken and signed languages only comes in a restricted set of forms (McCarthy and Prince 1998; Sandler and Lillo-Martin 2006). The same is true in modern Chinese characters (though less so in older scripts; see Section 4.3.1.1). Lines of triply or quadruply copied stroke groups are quite rare, usually consisting of just one stroke each, as in (42a), and if more complex, either seem to be analogically derived, as in (42b), or essentially bound synchronically, as in (42c–d). Even two-by-two squares are of vanishing rarity, aside from the example in (42e), often used as a phonetic element.

(42)   a 三 影 巢 巡 馬 黑
       b 川 州
       c 侖 (cf. 會 冊)
       d 靈 (cf. 需 雨 巫)
       e 叕

Third, reduplication in spoken and signed languages consists of filling content (the base constituent) into an abstract template (Berent and Dupuis 2018; Berent, Dupuis, and Brentari 2014; McCarthy and Prince 1998). The same analysis turns out to work for character constituent reduplication, as we will see in Sections 3.3.2 and 5.3.2.

2.3.3.2. *Reduplication and splitting*

Complicating the formal analysis of reduplicative structures in characters is the fact that they can sometimes be split, which is unusual in spoken or signed languages (cf. Shaw 2005). In the case of two-by-two squares, splitting is actually the

Character morphology 65

norm, as illustrated in (43), suggesting that they are derived in the modern grammar via vertical doubling applied to horizontal doubling or vice versa (regardless of how they may have originally been coined).

(43) a 爽 爾 傘 㗊 蘦
　　　b 齒 繼 器 罬

The idea that the two-by-two reduplication shape is synchronically derived rather than basic is further supported by the fact that constituents that appear in this shape also appear in doubled reduplication, as illustrated in (44). This generalization does not hold for other reduplication shapes; (45) lists some examples containing constituents that only seem to reduplicate in one way.

(44) a 叕 茻 焱 朤
　　　b 双 艸 炎 朋

(45) a 哥 多
　　　b 比 弱 羽
　　　c 轟 惢

Consistent with the above analysis, non-identical one-dimensional reduplicative structures can also be combined together, as in (46a), including via splitting, as in (46b).

(46) a 琵 翌 蠶
　　　b 椕

Splitting never happens with vertical doubling or triangular reduplication. While the character in (47a) seems to be a split inverted triangle reduplicating the constituent in (47b), it actually contains the same phonetic component as in (47c–d). This lack of splitting, along with the constituents noted above that only permit triangular reduplication, challenges the otherwise tempting alternative analysis of triangular reduplication as horizontal doubling topped by a single constituent (assumed by the Character Description Language of Bishop and Cook 2007).

(47) a 熒 *yíng* 'fluorescent'
　　　b 火 *huǒ* 'fire'
　　　c 營 *yíng* 'camp'
　　　d 塋 *yíng* 'grave'

However, splitting is attested in horizontally doubled reduplication, as shown in (48). I return to this point in the next section and further in Section 3.3.2.

(48) a 絲 ：變
　　　b 辡 ：辦 辯 瓣 辮
　　　c 玨 ：斑

d 弜：弼
e 奻：㛂
f 雔：雦

2.3.3.3. Reduplication and reduction

Unlike semantic radical affixation, the constituents in a reduplicative structure do not undergo idiosyncratic allomorphy, as shown in (49).

(49) a 火：炎 (cf. 灬：熱)
b 水：沝 (cf. 氵：江)
c 手：掱 (cf. 扌：拾)
d 人：從 (cf. 亻：們)

This generalization suggests that at least some cases of split horizontal doubling are not reduplication but semantic radical affixation, since they do show idiosyncratic allomorphy, as in (50).

(50) 獄 *yù* 'prison' = 犬 (犭) 'dog' + 言 'speech' + 犬 'dog' (cf. 犭：獨)

Other apparent cases of idiosyncratic allomorphy in reduplication may be amenable to the same analysis, as indicated in (51a). Alternatively, the examples in (51b–c) may show that some idiosyncratic allomorphs can themselves be reduplicated, as if the system can sometimes treat them as basic rather than derived (though see Section 3.3.2 for arguments that reduplication does not actually involve the concatenation implied here). As a reminder, not all apparent doubling represents synchronic reduplication; the character in (51d) is an even more implausible candidate (see Sections 3.4.6 and 3.5, respectively, for the limited productivity of hooking and the restriction on such processes in reduplication).

(51) a 絲 = 糹 + 糸 (cf. 糸：緊～經)
b 變 = 糹 + 言 + 糹
c 玨 = 王 + 王 (cf. 玉：瑩～現; note also the variant form 珏)
d 竹 (cf. 亇)

In contrast to the virtual absence of idiosyncratic allomorphy in reduplication, reduplicated constituents readily undergo regular reduction processes like diagonalization, as in (52a), and dotting, as in (52b).

(52) a 玨 孖 比
b 林 炏 沝

Regular reduction also applies in the lower left constituent in triangular reduplication, as seen with diagonalization in (53a) and dotting in (53b). Again, idiosyncratic allomorphy does not occur for constituents that have idiosyncratic left-edge allomorphs, as in (53c–d); the character in (53e) seems better analyzed as vertical reduplication within a semantic compound (see Section 2.3.4 for more on the interactions between morphological operations).

(53) a 鑫 孨 犇
      b 焱 森
      c 众 (not 彳)
      d 淼 (not 氵)
      e 渁 (variant of 淵 *yuān* 'gush forth')

2.3.4. Morphological interactions

In spoken and signed languages, morphological operations tend to interact in asymmetrical ways, depending on their relative productivity. For example, while English can compound derived words (e.g., *singer-songwriter*), it does not do so readily with inflected words (e.g., **rats-eater*; Alegre and Gordon 1996). This pattern is consistent with inflection being more productive than compounding, which in turn is more productive than derivational affixation.

Given that radical affixation is by far the most productive morphological operation in Chinese characters, we expect that it should be able to apply to the output of reduplication and compounding, but not the other way around. Compounding appears in many more characters than reduplication, so we also expect compounding to be able to contain reduplicative structures, but not the other way around.

There is no doubt that semantic radical affixation readily applies to compounded and reduplicated constituents, as in (54) and (55), respectively.

(54) a 份 *fèn* 'portion' = 亻(人) 'person' + 分 *fēn* 'divide'
         分 *fēn* 'divide' = 八 'separate' + 刀 'knife'
      b 想 *xiǎng* 'think' = 相 *xiāng* 'evaluate' + 心 'heart'
         相 *xiāng* 'evaluate' = 木 'tree' + 目 'eye'

(55) a 琳 *lín* 'beautiful jade' = 玉 'jade' + 林 *lín* 'forest'
         林 *lín* 'forest' = 木 'tree' (reduplicated)
      b 歌 *gē* 'song' = 哥 *gē* 'brother' + 欠 'blow'
         哥 *gē* 'brother' = 可 *kě* (reduplicated)

By contrast, it is intrinsically impossible for semantic compounds to contain semantic-phonetic constituents. Reduplication of constituents created via semantic radical affixation is also strongly disfavored, making (56) a rare exception (and arguably this is a case of language play, where grammatical generalizations may be violated for effect; see Section 4.4.3).

(56) 靐 *duì* 'cloudy' = 雲 *yún* 'cloud'
      雲 *yún* 'cloud' = 雨 'rain' + 云 *yún*

68 *Character morphology*

Reduplication can technically apply to semantic-phonetic characters as well, but only when the modern structure is opaque. Etymologically speaking, the base constituent of (57a), seen in (57b), shares the same phonetic component as the character in (57c), but since modern readers are unlikely to recognize it as such, they probably do not have to mark this character as an exception to their synchronic mental grammar.

(57) a 哥 *gē* 'brother'
      b 可 *kě* 'can' = 口 'mouth' + 丂 *kǎo* (phonetic)
      c 考 *kǎo* 'examine'

In the same way, reduplication seems incapable of applying to constituents formed via compounding. Semantic compounds commonly contain reduplicated structures, however, as illustrated in (58).

(58) a 雙 *shuāng* 'pair' (hand holding two birds)
      b 區 *qū* 'district'   (many mouths [people] in an area)

Curiously, however, some lexicographic radicals themselves contain reduplicative structures, as in (59a), or compound-like structures, as in (59b).

(59) a 羽 竹 麻 艸/艹
      b 音 癶 邑 穴 彡 鼓 龍

Morphologically decomposable affixes seem odd, especially given that one of the diagnostics I cited is that affixes are closed class. Nevertheless, they are attested in spoken languages as well. For example, even though English *-ation* is decomposable into the verbal suffix *-ate* (*hyphen* ~ *hyphenate*) and the nominal suffix *-ion* (*delete* ~ *deletion*), it also nominalizes many verbs as a whole (e.g., *alter* ~ *alteration, starve* ~ *starvation, compile* ~ *compilation*; note the absence of *alterate, *starvate, *compilate).

2.4. Summary

This chapter has shown that Chinese characters can generally be decomposed into constituents that are interpretable in meaning or pronunciation, similar to the way words in spoken and signed languages can ultimately be decomposed into morphemes interpreted in meaning. Also similar are the cases of less than fully transparent interpretations and less than complete decomposition expected with lexical grammars.

We have also seen that semantic radicals in semantic-phonetic characters share a number of diagnostics with affixes: they are closed class, bound, semantically bleached, and have favored positions and a predilection towards reduction. Also, like spoken languages, they favor edges but not circumfixation, may show inflection-like agreement, and reduce both via lexicalized idiosyncratic allomorphy,

Character morphology 69

which generally only affects this particular morphological class, and regular processes, which apply to all constituent types. However, semantic radicals also differ from affixes in important ways: their positional preferences are merely statistical rather than fixed, they do not act as operators deriving interpretations from the bases they affix to, and once position is taken into account, idiosyncratic allomorphy applies just as readily in semantic compounds. Nevertheless, there is some evidence, from semantic bleaching and lexical frequency effects, that semantic radicals may have been frozen on their way towards full grammaticalization.

Compounding and reduplication behave quite differently from semantic radical affixation, but quite like their counterparts in spoken and signed languages. The position and interpretation of the constituents in semantic compounds is more pragmatically determined than formally specified. Reduplication has a different interpretation from compounding since the reduplication itself is typically meaningful, with a narrow range of interpretations similar to those found in spoken and signed languages. Reduplication is nevertheless not merely iconic because only a very restricted number of formal patterns are permitted. While regular reduction is common in reduplication, idiosyncratic allomorphy is generally blocked, suggesting again that reduction differs from idiosyncratic allomorphy and that reduplication differs from affixation and compounding.

There are apparent exceptions to this ban on idiosyncratic allomorphy in reduplication, however, and other anomalies as well: reduplicated structures may sometimes be split and constituents derived via semantic radical affixation may sometimes be reduplicated, even though the former process is far more productive. Such details suggest that the borders between affixation, compounding, and reduplication are not absolutely sharp, just as in spoken and signed languages.

In Chapter 3, I continue my grammatical analysis by exploring the much less well-trod domain of character regularities irrelevant to character interpretation: character phonology.

References

Alegre, M.A. and Gordon, P., 1996, "Red rats eater exposes recursion in children's word formation", *Cognition*, 60(1), pp. 65–82.
Anderson, S.R., 1992, *A-morphous morphology*, Cambridge University Press, Cambridge.
Aronoff, M., 1976, *Word formation in generative grammar*, MIT Press, Cambridge, MA.
Aronoff, M., 1994b, *Morphology by itself: Stems and inflectional classes*, MIT Press, Cambridge, MA.
Baxter, W.H. and Sagart, L., 2014, *Old Chinese: A new reconstruction*, Oxford University Press, Oxford.
Behr, W., 2006, "Homosomatic juxtaposition and the problem of 'syssymantic' (*huìyì*) characters", in F. Bottéro and R. Djamouri, eds., *Écriture chinoise: données, usages et représentations* [Chinese writing: Data, uses and representations], pp. 75–114, École des hautes études en sciences sociales, Centre de recherches linguistiques sur l'Asie orientale [Graduate School of Social Sciences, East Asian Language Research Center], Paris.
Berent, I. and Dupuis, A., 2018, "The unbounded productivity of (sign) language", *The Mental Lexicon*, 12(3), pp. 309–341.

70 *Character morphology*

Berent, I., Dupuis, A. and Brentari, D., 2014, "Phonological reduplication in sign language: Rules rule", *Frontiers in Psychology*, 5, Article 560.

Bishop, T. and Cook, R., 2007, "A character description language for CJK", *Multilingual*, 18(7), pp. 62–68.

Boltz, W.G., 1994, *The origin and early development of the Chinese writing system*, American Oriental Society, New Haven, CT.

Boodberg, P.A., 1957, "The Chinese script: An essay on nomenclature (the first hecaton)", *Bulletin of the Institute of History and Philology*, 29, pp. 113–120.

Booij, G., 2005, "Compounding and derivation: Evidence for construction morphology", in W.U. Dressler, D. Kastovsky, O.E. Pfeiffer and F. Rainer, eds., *Morphology and its demarcations*, pp. 109–132, John Benjamins, Amsterdam.

Bottéro, F., 1996, "Review of Boltz (1994)", *Journal of the American Oriental Society*, 116(3), pp. 574–577.

Bybee, J.L., 2011, "Usage-based theory and grammaticalization", in B. Heine and H. Narrog, eds., *The Oxford handbook of grammaticalization*, pp. 69–78, Oxford University Press, Oxford.

Chen, K.J., Huang, C.R., Chang, L.P. and Hsu, H.L., 1996, "Sinica corpus: Design methodology for balanced corpora", *Proceedings of the 11th Pacific Asia Conference on Language, Information and Computation (PACLIC 11)*, pp. 167–176.

ChuNom, 2015, *ChuNom.org*, www.chunom.org, accessed 11/17/2018.

del Prado Martín, F.M., Kostić, A. and Baayen, R.H., 2004, "Putting the bits together: An information theoretical perspective on morphological processing", *Cognition*, 94(1), pp. 1–18.

Dressler, W.U. and Kilani-Schoch, M., 2016, "Natural morphology", in A. Hippisley and G. Stump, eds., *The Cambridge handbook of morphology*, pp. 356–389, Cambridge University Press, Cambridge.

Handel, Z., 2019, *Sinography: A cross-linguistic study of the borrowing and adaptation of the Chinese script*, Brill, Leiden.

Handel, Z., Forthcoming, "The cognitive role of semantic classifiers in modern Chinese writing as reflected in neogram creation", in I. Zsolnay, ed., *Seen not heard: Composition, iconicity, and the classifier systems of logosyllabic scripts*, The Oriental Institute of the University of Chicago, Chicago.

Handian [汉典], 2015, 汉典 [Chinese dictionary]. www.zdic.net/, accessed 11/17/2018.

Harris, A.C., 2008, "On the explanation of typologically unusual structures", in J. Good, ed., *Linguistic universals and language change*, pp. 54–76, Oxford University Press, Oxford.

Hoosain, R., 1991, *Psycholinguistic implications for linguistic relativity: A case study of Chinese*, Lawrence Erlbaum, Hillsdale, NJ.

Hopper, P.J. and Traugott, E.C., 2003, *Grammaticalization*, Cambridge University Press, Cambridge.

Huang, C.R. [黄居仁], Hong, J.F. [洪嘉馡], Chen, S.Y. [陈圣怡] and Chou, Y.M. [周亚民], 2013, 汉字所表达的知识系统:意符为基本概念导向的事件结构 [Exploring event structures in Hanzi radicals: An ontology-based approach]. 当代语言学 [Contemporary Linguistics], 15(3), pp. 294–311.

Huang, C.R., Yang, Y.J. and Chen, S.Y., 2013, "Radicals as ontologies: Concept derivation and knowledge representation of four-hoofed mammals as semantic symbols", in G. Cao, H. Chappell, R. Djamouri and T. Wiebusch, eds., *Breaking down the barriers: Interdisciplinary studies in Chinese linguistics and beyond: A festschrift for Professor Alain Peyraube*, pp. 1117–1133, Institute of Linguistics, Academia Sinica, Taipei.

Character morphology 71

Hue, C.W., 2003, "Number of characters a college student knows", *Journal of Chinese Linguistics*, 31(2), pp. 300–339.

Hurch, B. ed., 2005, *Studies on reduplication*, Walter de Gruyter, Berlin.

Jackendoff, R., 2010, "The ecology of English noun-noun compounds", in R. Jackendoff, ed., *Meaning and the lexicon*, pp. 413–451, Oxford University Press, Oxford.

Liu, M. [刘曼], 2008, 叠体字的历时考察与认知比较研究 [The diachronic study and cognitive comparison of stacked characters]. Ph.D. thesis, Tsinghua University, Beijing.

Lu, Q., Chan, S.T., Li, Y. and Li, N.L., 2002, "Decomposition for ISO/IEC 10646 ideographic characters", *COLING-02: Proceedings of the 3rd Workshop on Asian Language Resources and International Standardization*, Association for Computational Linguistics, Stroudsburg, PA. Database at http://glyph.iso10646hk.net/, accessed 11/19/2018.

Matthews, P.H., 1991, *Morphology*, 2nd ed., Cambridge University Press, Cambridge.

McCarthy, J.J. and Prince, A., 1998, "Prosodic morphology", in A. Spencer and A.M. Zwicky, eds., *The handbook of morphology*, pp. 283–305, Blackwell, Oxford.

Myers, J., 2007, "Generative morphology as psycholinguistics", in G. Jarema and G. Libben, eds., *The mental lexicon: Core perspectives*, pp. 105–128, Elsevier, Amsterdam.

Nguyễn, Đ.H., 1959, "Chữ Nôm the demotic system of writing in Vietnam", *Journal of the American Oriental Society*, 79(4), pp. 270–274.

Ohala, J.J., 1986, "Consumer's guide to evidence in phonology", *Phonology Yearbook*, 3, pp. 3–26.

Packard, J.L., 2000, *The morphology of Chinese: A linguistic and cognitive approach*, Cambridge University Press, Cambridge.

Phan, J.D., 2013, *Lacquered words: The evolution of Vietnamese under Sinitic influences from the 1st century BCE through the 17th century CE*, Ph.D. thesis, Cornell University, Ithaca.

Pinker, S. and Birdsong, D., 1979, "Speakers' sensitivity to rules of frozen word order", *Journal of Verbal Learning and Verbal Behavior*, 18(4), pp. 497–508.

Qiu, X., 2000, *Chinese writing*, compiled and translated from Chinese by G.L. Mattos and J. Norman, The Society for the Study of Early China and The Institute of East Asian Studies, University of California, Berkeley.

Roelofs, A. and Baayen, H., 2002, "Morphology by itself in planning the production of spoken words", *Psychonomic Bulletin & Review*, 9(1), pp. 132–138.

Sampson, G. and Chen, Z., 2013, "The reality of compound ideographs", *Journal of Chinese Linguistics*, 41(2), pp. 255–272.

Sandler, W. and Lillo-Martin, D., 2006, *Sign language and linguistic universals*, Cambridge University Press, Cambridge.

Shaw, P.A., 2005, "Non-adjacency in reduplication", in B. Hurch, ed., *Studies on reduplication*, pp. 161–210, Walter de Gruyter, Berlin.

Sproat, R., 2000, *A computational theory of writing systems*, Cambridge University Press, Cambridge.

Stalph, J., 1989, *Grundlagen einer Grammatik der sinojapanischen Schrift* [Foundations of a grammar of the Sino-Japanese script], Harrasowitz Verlag, Wiesbaden.

Sweetser, E.E., 1988, "Grammaticalization and semantic bleaching", in K. Lambrecht, S. Axmaker, A. Jaisser and H. Singmaster, eds., *Proceedings of the Fourteenth Annual Meeting of the Berkeley Linguistics Society*, pp. 389–405, Berkeley Linguistics Society, Berkeley.

Tsai, C.H., 2006, *Frequency and stroke counts of Chinese characters*, http://technology.chtsai.org/charfreq/, accessed 11/17/2018.

Wang, J.C.S., 1983, *Toward a generative grammar of Chinese character structure and stroke order*, Ph.D. thesis, University of Wisconsin, Madison.

72 Character morphology

Wiebusch, T., 1995, "Quantification and qualification: Two competing functions of numeral classifiers in the light of the radical system of the Chinese script", *Journal of Chinese Linguistics*, 23(2), pp. 1–41.

Wikimedia Commons, 2017, *Chinese character decomposition*, https://commons.wikimedia.org/wiki/Commons:Chinese_characters_decomposition, accessed 11/17/2018.

Wiktionary, 2018, *Wikitionary*, www.wiktionary.org/, accessed 11/17/2018.

Winter, M., 2017, "Kāngxī Zìdiǎn 康熙字典", in R. Sybesma, W. Behr, Y. Gu, Z. Handel, C.T.J. Huang and J. Myers, eds., *Encyclopedia of Chinese language and linguistics*, vol. 2, pp. 481–485, Brill, Leiden.

Zaixian hanyu zidian [在线汉语字典], 2018, 在线汉语字典 [Online Chinese dictionary]. http://xh.5156edu.com/, accessed 11/17/2018.

Zhengzhang, S. [郑张尚芳], 2003, 上古音系 [Old Chinese phonology]. 上海教育出版社 [Shanghai Educational Publishing House], Shanghai.

Zhengzhang, S. [郑张尚芳], 2013, 上古音系(第二版) [Old Chinese phonology, 2nd ed.]. 上海教育出版社 [Shanghai Educational Publishing House], Shanghai.

3 Character phonology and phonetics

3.1. Introduction

This chapter focuses on CHARACTER PHONOLOGY, which relates to formal patterns that do not affect external interpretation, and CHARACTER PHONETICS, which relates to the perception and production of characters. These topics have received much less attention than character morphology, presumably because they are irrelevant to the function of orthography as encoding spoken language, but as will be seen, there are great empirical and theoretical riches here. After a brief introduction to the notion of character phonology (Section 3.2), I examine the generalizations in overall character form that I call CHARACTER PROSODY (Section 3.3), turn to regularities in strokes and stroke groups (Section 3.4), then address the role of the lexicon in character phonology (Section 3.5), and finally discuss character phonetics, including stroke order (Section 3.6). This sequence allows me to build on the morphological analysis given in the previous chapter, and it also highlights the dependence of many lower-level generalizations on higher-level constraints.

3.2. The nature of character phonology

Claiming that Chinese characters have a formal phonology is essentially the same as claiming that they show duality of patterning (see Section 1.3.1.4). Reflecting the controversial nature of orthographic linguistics more generally, Ladd (2014) cites two studies on language evolution that dismiss this claim out of hand (Carstairs-McCarthy 1999; Hewes 1973), and two studies on Chinese orthography that take it for granted, though they disagree on where to locate the meaningless half of the duality: Hansell (2003) sees it in strokes and Coulmas (1989) sees it in stroke groups. Note the meaningless strokes shared by the characters in (1a) and the stroke groups, synchronically uninterpreted for pronunciation or meaning, shared by the characters in (1b). While the latter may be better analyzed as opaque morphology (like *hogwash*; see Section 2.2), the distinction between the stroke and constituent levels certainly seems like duality of patterning (see also Sections 4.2.1 and 4.3.1.2).

(1) a 一 十 大 川 木
    b 能 公 八 胃 田 北

74 *Character phonology and phonetics*

As Ladd (2014) observes, stroke groups rarely share completely identical strokes, and there is no consensus on the inventory of character constituents (see Section 1.2.2.3). Yet he still sees something akin to phonology in several aspects of character structure, including the semantic radical alternations discussed in Chapter 2 (Section 2.3.1.3), the hierarchy of strokes comprising constituents comprising characters, and the fact that invented characters can differ in their intuitive well-formedness (a point I return to in Chapter 5). In my scheme, his first two observations relate to character morphology as well, since interpreted constituents land in the other half of the patterning duality, but otherwise I agree with his strategy: when looking for phonology, look beyond phonemics alone.

Even in spoken and signed languages, phonology is not concerned solely with lists of phonemes or handshapes but also includes holistic structural patterns (prosody), restrictions on morphemic and phonemic inventories (phonotactic constraints and feature co-occurrence constraints), and context-dependent changes (morphophonemic alternations and allophonic variation). We have already seen in Chapter 2 that Chinese characters show similar patterns, and in this chapter, we will see many more.

Character phonology, if it really exists, should be psychologically real and involve amodal representations. Regarding the first point, character form was likely shaped, at least in part, by scholarly or even aesthetic decisions made by individual writers for individual characters, but these decisions swam in a current of unconscious cognitive forces. After all, even highly conventionalized art forms like Tang dynasty poetry obey the same phonological regularities active in ordinary speech (e.g., Duanmu 2004). It may be true that any specific character form may have survived because a sufficient number of influential writers thought that it 'looked better' than a rejected alternative, but this is too ad hoc and question-begging to serve as a genuine explanation for the system as a whole.

Regarding the second point, it is hard to get objective empirical evidence about the amodal mental representations underlying character phonology (though see Chapters 4, 5, and 6), so in this chapter I focus on the physical input that readers induce them from, namely printed characters. Most of the patterns I discuss are robust across typefaces (though see Section 4.4.1); they may show more variation in everyday handwriting, but this is unfortunately much more difficult to study (though see Sections 3.6.2.2, 4.4.2, 5.2.2.1, and 5.2.3.2). The amodality of character phonology is also suggested by the finding that stroke order is more sensitive to visual character form than the other way around (see Section 3.6.2), presumably because form, but not order, is essential in both reading and writing.

3.3. Character prosody

In spoken and signed languages, phonological representations are comprised of both content and structure. In spoken languages, phonological content involves elements like features, phonemes, and tones, and in signed languages, elements like handshapes, locations, and movements. Prosodic structure indicates how

Character phonology and phonetics   75

these elements group together in rimes, syllables, metrical feet, prosodic words, and prosodic phrases (Nespor and Vogel 1986).

Though abstract, prosodic structure has far-reaching effects. Take metrical feet, for example (Hayes 1995). The English foot can be schematized as the prosodic TEMPLATE [SW], representing two syllables, the first the HEAD, which is STRONG (receiving prominence), and the second WEAK (unstressed). This template applies to both *máma* and *flóunder*, despite their segmental differences, and even to monosyllabic *cát*, by leaving the weak SLOT unfilled. Application of the template depends in part on WEIGHT, so that HEAVY syllables (containing a long vowel or final consonant), as opposed to LIGHT syllables ((C)V), must correspond with template heads, which is why the final syllable in *kàngaróo*, with its long vowel, is stressed ([SW][S]). Template application also depends on lexically specified exceptional stress, which is why the final syllable is stressed in exceptional *batón* but not in regular *bútton*. Different levels of stress are captured by the iteration of prosodic templates; the first syllable of *kàngaróo* receives secondary stress because the prosodic word as a whole has final stress, that is, is right-headed ([[SW]$_w$[S]$_s$]), putting primary stress on the final syllable. A secondary stress usually cannot be adjacent to the primary one: *elícit ~ elìcitátion* preserves the stem's original stress position even after suffixation changes the location of main stress, but *refórm ~ rèformátion* does not (cf. **refòrmátion*), in order to avoid STRESS CLASH. Parallels to all of these phenomena will be seen in Chinese characters.

Prosody is associated not just with stress (marked in amplitude, length, and/or pitch) but also with vowel quality (e.g., in American English, the stressed vowel in *átom* is [æ] while its unstressed counterpart in *atómic* is [ə]) and consonantal allophones (e.g., American English flapping before unstressed syllables: *á[ɾ]om ~ a[tʰ]ómic*). It is also linked to morphology (Inkelas 2014; Kager, van der Hulst, and Zonneveld 1999). In English, nouns and adjectives often have primary stress on the third-to-last syllable, shifting even after suffixation (e.g., *órigin, original, originálity*), but certain suffixes are ignored (e.g., the stress in *Américanizing* implies the parsing [*Américan*]*izing*). Morphology can even be indicated through prosody alone. Diyari, for example, has disyllabic feet with initial prominence, that is, that are left-headed (McCarthy and Prince 1994), as shown by the stress pattern in (2) (after their (31), p. 350). Exactly the same prosodic unit is used in partial reduplication, as shown in (3) (after their (29), p. 350). We will see character parallels for all of these phenomena as well.

(2) a káɳa   ('man')
     b pínadu   ('old man')
     c ŋándawàlka   ('to close')

(3) a wíla-wíla   (reduplicant + 'woman')
     b kánku-kánku   (reduplicant + 'boy')
     c kúḻku-kúḻkuɳa   (reduplicant + 'jump')
     d tⁱílpa-tⁱílparku   (reduplicant + 'bird species')
     e ŋánka-ŋánkaṉṯi   (reduplicant + 'catfish')

76   *Character phonology and phonetics*

By CHARACTER PROSODY, then, I mean the structure which may interact with character morphology and within which lower-level content, like strokes and stroke groups, is realized. I argue that the full prosodic template has the shape shown in (4a), where S stands for strong (the unique head position) and W stands for weak (all nonhead positions in the remainder of the constituent). Reductions of this template via the dropping of one or both of the weak slots are shown in (4b–d). I assume that the template is given as-is by the phonology, though in Section 3.6.1 I discuss the forces in character phonetics that may have motivated its shape.

$$(4) \quad \text{a} \quad \begin{bmatrix} & \text{W} \\ \text{W} & \text{S} \end{bmatrix}$$

$$\text{b} \quad \begin{bmatrix} \text{W} \\ \text{S} \end{bmatrix}$$

c   [W   S]
d   [S]

This section argues for this template by reexamining two morphological generalizations from the previous chapter, namely the tendency for semantic radicals to appear and reduce at the left and top (Section 3.3.1) and formal constraints on reduplication (Section 3.3.2). In later sections, I provide other types evidence for the templatic analysis.

3.3.1. The prosody of semantic radicals

In this section, I argue that the weak slots at the left and top in the prosodic template explain why these positions are favored by light constituents like affixes (Section 3.3.1.1) and why reduction is favored there as well (Section 3.3.1.2).

3.3.1.1. Radical position

The relationship that I claim to hold between semantic radical affixation and prosodic structure is illustrated in (5), which posits an association of recursive morphology with recursive prosody, with semantic radicals in weak positions. This sort of association is also found in spoken and signed phonology, though usually not within lexical items (Nespor and Vogel 1986).

$$(5) \quad \text{a} \quad 甫 \text{ [S]} \qquad 浦 \text{ [W \quad S]} \qquad 蒲 \begin{bmatrix} & \text{W} \\ [\text{W} & \text{S}]_s \end{bmatrix}$$

$$\text{b} \quad 鳥 \text{ [S]} \qquad 寫 \begin{bmatrix} \text{W} \\ \text{S} \end{bmatrix} \qquad 瀉 \begin{bmatrix} \text{W} & \begin{bmatrix} \text{W} \\ \text{S} \end{bmatrix}_s \end{bmatrix}$$

This scheme implies that characters with semantic radicals in the strong positions at the right or bottom would have to be treated as lexical exceptions

Character phonology and phonetics 77

(including those containing the top-edge phonetic component 殳 mentioned in Section 2.3.1.2). It's not clear how this exceptionality should be formalized; alternative analyses of the characters in (6a), which have reduced semantic radicals at the right and bottom, are given in (6b) (reversed prosodic templates) and (6c) (extra-templatic material); see Pater (2000, 2009) for discussions of such issues in spoken language phonology. In any case, the surface patterns here would be the same under either analysis.

(6)　a　刻　　　　熱

　　b　[S　W]　$\begin{bmatrix} S \\ W \end{bmatrix}$

　　c　[S]　W　$\begin{matrix} [S] \\ W \end{matrix}$

Top/left radicals, like those in (7a), may perhaps be analyzed with the full triangular template, as shown in (7b); in Section 2.3.1.2, we saw that this type is among the most common, after single-edge radicals. Left/bottom radicals are also quite common, though; I return to these shortly.

(7)　a　厭　居　底　扉　痛　處

　　b　$\begin{bmatrix} & W & \\ W & & S \end{bmatrix}$

A prediction of the prosodic approach to character structure is that radical position and radical dimensions should be related, similar to the way syllable weight affects stress patterns. Table 3.1 lists the favored single-edge positions for all lexicographic radicals that have one (regardless of character type), along with the dominant axis of the full form of the radical itself. Dominant axis was determined by counting the maximum number of strokes that would be intersected by an imaginary line along each axis; for example, 言 is vertical because a vertical line

Table 3.1 Effect of semantic radical dimensions on position

Favored position	Dominant axis		
	Horizontal	*Vertical*	*None*
Left	人山巾心木水火肉 血赤齒	冫土女弓彳手方日月犬玉白目矛 矢立糸羊耒耳至舌舟角言谷豕豸 貝足身車酉金長阜青革韋音食香 馬骨魚黑鼻	口歹爿片牛 田石示禾 米缶虫衣鹵 鬥龠
Right	欠	彡戈攴斗殳瓦皮色見邑隶隹頁鳥	刀力卩斤羽
Top	宀爪父癶穴竹网艸雨麻	亠士彐老自髟鹿鼓龍	大宀西
Bottom	儿八廾皿肉	曰黽鼎	厶夂寸

would intersect it in maximally six strokes, whereas a horizontal line would intersect it in at most two strokes (see Peust 2006 for a related measure of orthographic complexity). The question is whether there is a relationship between radical position and 'weight,' where tall and thin radicals are light along the horizontal axis but heavy along the vertical axis, and vice versa for wide/flat radicals.

As Table 3.1 shows, there is indeed a strong tendency for radicals in the weak left-edge position to be tall and thin rather than wide and flat (47 radicals vs. 1: $\chi^2(1) = 22.3, p < .0001$), though right-edge radicals also tend to be tall and thin (14 vs. 1: $\chi^2(1) = 11.3, p < .001$). There is no clear tendency for top-edge radicals to be wide and flat rather than tall and thin (10 vs. 9 radicals), nor a dimension contrast in bottom-edge radicals (5 flat, 3 tall). However, these results depend on my particular quantification of radical dimensions, which has some counterintuitive properties; ⼍, ⼇, and ⼧ are classified as having horizontal, vertical, and no dominant axis, respectively. Unfortunately, using absolute dimensions would be problematic, since it would be hard to define objectively and risks conflating character phonology with character phonetics. Nevertheless, even my crude measure suggests that radical weight has some influence on position, by favoring light radicals at the weak left edge.

Strong positions may also attract heavy radicals under certain circumstances. Recall from Section 2.3.1.2 that left-edge-dominant radicals take the bottom edge as their most common alternative position. The majority of left-edge radicals are tall and thin, since these dimensions make them light along the horizontal axis, but they also mean that they are heavy along the vertical axis, making the bottom edge an attractive alternative position. This logic is illustrated in Figure 3.1 with the tall thin radical in (8a), which has 271 left-edge characters in Tsai (2006), like that in (8b), 18 bottom-edge characters like that in (8c), and no right- or top-edge characters.

(8)   a   言
       b   說
       c   警

Constituent weight may also help explain the greater preference of semantic radicals for the left edge than for the top, despite both being weak positions. Radicals tend to have a dominant vertical axis, perhaps due to some sort of orthographic universal (Roman letters also tend to be tall and thin). Character prosody

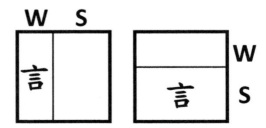

Figure 3.1 The role of semantic radical dimensions in alternative positions

Character phonology and phonetics 79

then favors placing them on the left, where they are light along the horizontal axis. Admittedly, the analysis here raises a chicken-or-egg problem, but the same is true in spoken and signed languages: does English prefer suffixation because it has left-headed stress while Navajo prefers prefixing because it is stressless (McDonough 2003), or does the causality run the other way around?

3.3.1.2. Radical reduction

The canonical locations for semantic radical reduction, whether regular or idiosyncratic, are also in the two weak positions, at the left and top (see Section 2.3.1.3). The role of position in idiosyncratic allomorphy is demonstrated elegantly with the minimal pairs in (9), where each is composed of the same modern constituents, but where allomorphy only appears at the left edge. Not all of these are semantic-phonetic characters (nor in the rest of this chapter), but as we saw in Section 2.3.2, idiosyncratic allomorphy is not restricted to this character type.

(9) a 忄：忙　～　心：忘
    b 扌：拾　～　手：拿
    c 氵：泊　～　水：泉

Though idiosyncratic allomorphy is a morphological operation, it still interacts with phonology. In particular, when it changes radical dimensions, it changes radical weight. Table 3.2 shows all of the single-edge radicals that have Unicode symbols, cross-classifying them by position and (non)change in dominant axis, according to the same line-intersection method used earlier. For example, the idiosyncratic allomorphic change in (10) makes the radical more vertical because the ratio of vertical to horizontal intersections is 3/3 (1) in 示 but 4/3 (1.3) in 礻.

(10)　示→礻

The most common of these changes is to give radicals a dominant vertical axis when they appear on the left, though the numbers are too small for statistical testing. The pattern is even stronger if absolute dimensions could be taken into account in an objective way (e.g., if 心→忄 were counted as extension along the vertical axis); in this case, widening top-edge radicals would also be counted as quite common.

Regular reduction also seems to be prosodically motivated, occurring only in nonhead positions. As we have seen, shrinking only applies at the (weak) top edge (11a), while diagonalization (11b) and dotting (11c) only apply when there is material to the right, which means that they never occur at the (strong) right edge.

(11)　a　雨～電　　　穴～空　　　竹～筆
     b　土：型～地　金：鑒～鉛　立：童～站　至：臺～致　止：歷～此
     c　木：築～相　夫：扶～規　火：燙～煩　米：粱～精　矢：候～短

80 *Character phonology and phonetics*

Table 3.2 Effect of idiosyncratic allomorphy on radical dimensions

| | Change in dominant axis | | |
Position	Horizontal	Vertical	None
Left	心→忄	水→氵	犬→犭
	手→扌	人→亻	糸→糸
	阜→阝	示→礻	木→朩*
		衣→衤	
		肉→月	
Right	乙→乚	邑→阝	
	刀→刂		
	攴→攵		
Top	目→罒	艸→艹	爪→爫
	网→罒		
	网→罓		
Bottom	攴→攵	卩→巴	水→氺
	火→灬		
	心→忄		

Note: The constituent marked * has no hook in actual characters, but Unicode lacks this symbol (see also Section 4.4.1).

The regular process of stretching, whether it applies to a falling diagonal stroke at the bottom of the constituent (12a), a falling diagonal at the right edge (12b), or a rightward curved and hooked stroke (12c), conforms to the prosodic template in two ways. Not only does it target constituents on the (weak) left edge, but the stretched stroke lengthens along the (strong) bottom edge; as we will see in Section 3.4.4, character phonology includes an independently motivated regular process that lengthens the lowest stroke in a constituent.

(12) a 走～起   支～遫   麥～麵
       b 爪～爬   瓜～瓞
       c 鼠～鼺   毛～毬   風～颱   鬼～魅

Thus, left/bottom radicals are arguably as prosodically well formed as top/left radicals, where both portions appear in weak positions (see Section 3.3.1.1). A possible templatic analysis of such radicals is illustrated in (13), treating them essentially as left-edged, but with some sort of additional level of prosodic but non-morphological structure.

(13) a 起

       b $\left[\text{W} \quad \left\{ \begin{matrix} \text{W} \\ \text{S} \end{matrix} \right\} \right]$

Character phonology and phonetics 81

The most productive of the four regular reduction processes seems to be diagonalization, as reflected in the wide variety of situations in which it appears. It targets bottom-edge horizontal strokes with free end points (14a), bottom-edge horizontal strokes in bound stroke groups (14b), the lowest horizontal portion of a complex stroke (14c), the lowest but non-bottom-edge stroke in certain constituents, some obligatorily (14d) and some optionally (14e) (cf. the lack of change in (14f)), and the lowest stroke in some idiosyncratic allomorphs (14g).

(14) a 且：宜～助　工：紅～功　重：種～動　圭：佳～卦　壴：嘉～鼓
      b 對　斲　段　印
      c 九：氿～鳩
      d 牛：牽～物　子：好～孔
      e 舟：珩～般
      f 木：休～校　車：輦～較　十：汁～博
      g 足：踅～路　手：拿～拾　羊～羯

Regarding the last point, stretching may also be lexicalized within idiosyncratic allomorphy, as in (15).

(15) 辵：道　爻：建

Using the formalism of 1970s-era generative phonology, Wang (1983, p. 152) attempts to merge all four regular processes into a single monstrously nested and alpha-riddled rule, but it seems more insightful to see their shared motivation as lying in prosody, as already discussed, and in character phonetics, as discussed in Section 3.6.1.

Evidence that these processes have a life beyond the memorized characters in which they appear comes from a surprising place: Korean Hangul (한글). Even though this system is alphabetic (with a famously transparent visual relationship with its letters' pronunciations; see, e.g., Sampson 1985), it was invented and developed by writers intimately familiar with Chinese characters (Ledyard 1966). One result is that Hangul letters undergo both diagonalization and dotting, as can be seen by comparing those in (16) with the Chinese characters in (17) (see Section 3.4.4 for more on Hangul and Section 4.3.2.1 for more on the second character in (17b), which replaces the indicated traditional character in the simplified character system).

(16) a ㅗ *o*　ㅘ *wa*　ㅙ *wae*　ㅚ *oe*
      b ㅅ *s*　ㅆ *ss*

(17) a 土　地
      b 人　从　(＜從)

3.3.2. Reduplication

As we saw in Section 2.3.3, virtually all reduplication in Chinese characters involves vertical doubling (18a), horizontal doubling (18b), or an upward-pointing

82 *Character phonology and phonetics*

triangle (18c). Squares (18d) are much rarer and are derivable from the first two patterns, as shown in Section 2.3.3.2; the even rarer linear tripling (18e) only occurs within synchronically non-decomposable constituents. These patterns clearly conform to the posited triangular prosodic template and its horizontal and vertical reductions, though unlike reduplication in spoken and signed languages, the character template shapes total reduplication (entire constituents copied as wholes), not partial reduplication (as in Diyari).

(18) a 吕
      b 吅
      c 品
      d 㸚
      e 畾

To make this more precise, Table 3.3 counts the 110 reduplication structures listed in Section 2.3.3.1 (virtually all from the 13,058-character database in Tsai 2006). The relative paucity of vertical reduplication may be another consequence of the tendency for character constituents to be taller than wide (see Section 3.3.1.1), so that vertical reduplication risks putting a heavy constituent in the weak top position.

Templates have an interesting technical implication. Recall that spoken and signed phonology and morphology are 'regular,' in the sense of the mathematical theory of formal languages (Section 1.4.3.2), and that Sproat (2000) argued that orthographic systems are also always regular (Section 1.5.1). Without templates, however, the analysis of (19a) would have to be as in (19b) (recall that in Sproat's notation, A $\rightarrow$ B means "A concatenates to the left of B"). This implies that we would have to block the ungrammatical (*) tripling in (19c) via counting, which regular grammars cannot do. Sproat (2000, pp. 52–53) acknowledges the counting problem posed by the unrestricted copying that marked pluralization in Old Kingdom Egyptian hieroglyphs, but also notes that by the Middle Kingdom orthographic reduplication had disappeared. Reduplication remains attested in modern Chinese characters, as in spoken and signed languages, but fortunately for Sproat's hypothesis, it is restricted (much more so than in earlier Chinese scripts; see Section 4.3.1.1). This makes possible another solution to the counting

Table 3.3 Frequencies of character reduplicative templates

Shape	Count (%)
Vertical	20 (18%)
Horizontal	47 (43%)
Triangular	39 (35%)
Square	4 (4%)

Character phonology and phonetics 83

problem: fixed-shape templates could be concatenated with base components via a template-linking operator (|). This is illustrated in (19d), where [ws] represents an empty horizontal template (see Bird and Ellison 1994 for more on the formalization of templates in regular grammars).

(19) a 林
  b 木 → 木
  c *木 → 木 → 木
  d 木|[ws]

As expected from a templatic that accounts for both reduplication and reduction, reduplication also shows dotting (20a) and diagonalization (20b–c), though top-edge shrinking is less extreme in (20d) than in semantic radicals like those in (21a) (note that the upper copy preserves the hooked vertical stroke of (21b) rather than reducing to the hooked horizontal stroke of (21c)).

(20) a 林　炏　枞　㷼
  b 玨　竝　鈝　孖
  c 比　䃶　競　麤
  d 棗

(21) a 雨～電
  b 冂
  c 冖

Triangular reduplication also shows dotting (22a–b) and diagonalization (22c–d), though the lack of diagonalization in (22e) reminds us that even regular processes need not be obligatory in a lexical grammar. The topmost constituent also behaves oddly from the perspective of my prosodic template; while it sometimes reduces in size as expected for its weak position, as in (22a) and (22c), it may also widen, as in (22b) and (22d), though this still does not increase its weight along the vertical axis. These details also vary across typefaces (see Section 4.4.1).

(22) a 森　淼　焱
  b 众
  c 垚　孨　犇
  d 㐷
  e 垚　轟

I end this section by returning to a problem noted in Section 2.3.3.2: the splitting of horizontal reduplication, as in (23). If reduplication results from mapping to a template, how can the template be split?

(23) a 玨　斑
  b 辡　辦

84   *Character phonology and phonetics*

A solution is suggested by examples like those in (24a–c), in which the constituent doing the splitting is an idiosyncratic allomorph of 刀 'knife' (even more reduced than its usual variant 刂). This stroke group otherwise only appears on the left, as in the character in (24d), and as we will see in Section 3.4.5, vertical stroke curving is restricted to a constituent's left edge as well. A non-reduced constituent anomalously splits a reduplicative structure in (24e), but we already saw in Section 2.3.3.3 that this particular constituent is also anomalous in other ways, in particular undergoing idiosyncratic reduction within reduplication in (24f).

(24)   a   辡：辨 (< 辬)
       b   玨：班
       c   畐：皕 (cf. 畐)
       d   帰 (variant of 歸; cf. the simplified form 归)
       e   糸：辮 (cf. 幺)
       f   糸：絲

Just as with the argument against circumfixation given in Section 2.3.1.4, these observations suggest that split reduplication may (usually) have the structure [X[Y[X]]], not [X[Y]X]. This outcome happens to obey two independently motivated constraints (as in Optimality Theory; McCarthy 2003), where one requires that all template slots must be filled and the other favors right-branching structures like [X[Y[Z]]]. I provide further evidence for this analysis in Section 4.3.2.1.

3.4. Strokes

While morphology and prosody provide character structure, strokes and stroke groups provide the content. In this section, I first look at feature-like generalizations relating to the stroke inventory (Section 3.4.1) and phonotactic-like constraints on stroke combinations (Section 3.4.2), then turn to dot variations (Section 3.4.3), stroke lengthening (Section 3.4.4), curving (Section 3.4.5), and hooking (Section 3.4.6).

3.4.1. Stroke parameters

One way to see sense in the inventory of character strokes is to classify them in terms of simple parameters or features. Simple strokes follow a cardinal axis (horizontal or vertical) or a diagonal, either the MAIN DIAGONAL between the upper left and lower right (\), or the COUNTERDIAGONAL between the lower left and upper right (/). All strokes are written rightward, downward, or both (following the main diagonal, as dots do by default), except for counterdiagonal strokes, where a compromise is struck by splitting into two types, one written rightward (but upward) and the other downward (but leftward). Note that the necessity of referring to both visual form (axis) and articulatory implementation (direction)

Character phonology and phonetics 85

Table 3.4 Parameters for the simplest character strokes

Stroke	Axis	Direction	Examples
﹨	None	(default)	太
一	Horizontal	(default)	十
｜	Vertical	(default)	十
﹨	Main diagonal	(default)	木
⟋ ノ	Counterdiagonal	Leftward falling	千 才
⟋	Counterdiagonal	Rightward rising	子

Note: Stroke images from https://commons.wikimedia.org/wiki/Category:CJK_strokes (by user 'Cangjie6'), licensed under the Creative Commons CC0 1.0 Universal Public Domain Dedication.

Table 3.5 Some other simple character strokes

Stroke	Axis	Curving	Hooking	Examples
）	Vertical	Yes	No	川
亅	Vertical	No	Leftward	丁
㇄	Vertical	No	Rightward	艮
⟍	Horizontal	No	Downward	宀
㇂	Main diagonal	Yes	Upward	戈
）	Vertical	Yes	Leftward	犭

Note: Stroke images from https://commons.wikimedia.org/wiki/Category:CJK_strokes (by user 'Cangjie6'), licensed under the Creative Commons CC0 1.0 Universal Public Domain Dedication.

suggests that stroke parameters are amodal (see Section 1.3.1.4 on the abstractness of grammar). Table 3.4 describes some simple strokes by means of these parameters.

As shown in Table 3.5, simple strokes can differ in two other parameters: curving and hooking. Curving in vertical strokes is strongly favored in certain contexts (see Section 3.4.5). Hooks may appear at the end of vertical, horizontal, and falling diagonal strokes, again with some degree of predictability (see Section 3.4.6).

Complex strokes are produced without lifting the writing instrument but contain sharp changes in axis, as if they chain simple strokes in sequence. Possible decompositions for a few of them are listed in Table 3.6. The current Unicode standard recognizes 36 stroke symbols, 21 of which contain more than

86 *Character phonology and phonetics*

Table 3.6 Some complex strokes

Complex stroke	Simple components	Examples
㇆	一 𠃌	刀
㇗	丿 一	公
㇜	㇀ ㇁	阝
㇆	丨 一 丿	弓
㇋	一 丨 一 丿	乃

Note: Stroke images from https://commons.wikimedia.org/wiki/Category:CJK_strokes (by user 'Cangjie6'), licensed under the Creative Commons CC0 1.0 Universal Public Domain Dedication.

one segment longer than a hook (Unicode Consortium 2018); I return to the problem of distinguishing hooks from chained simple strokes in Section 3.4.6. Though not implausible, these analyses, as always, are merely hypotheses about mental character grammar in need of testing. One strike against them is that they do not correspond in any simple way with traditional stroke counts (e.g., for indexing in character dictionaries). However, metalinguistic awareness need not reflect normal language processing; speakers, and signers also often have trouble counting phonological elements. In this regard, it is worth noting that traditional stroke counts have surprisingly little effect on character processing (see Sections 5.2.2.1 and 5.2.3.2).

The challenges for a phonological analysis of strokes are the same as for phonemes and distinctive features in spoken phonology, and the potential solutions are the same as well. As Ladd (2014) points out (see Section 3.2), canonical strokes are not identical across characters; for example, the leftward falling counterdiagonal (撇 *piě* 'throw away') stroke varies in angle, length, and curving in the constituents in (25). Yet predictable phonetic variation is what phonological systems are all about (see Sections 3.4.3, 3.4.5, and 3.4.6).

(25) 千   午   才

Not all logically possible parameter combinations or stroke chains are common or even attested, but spoken languages also often have marginal phonemes (e.g., English /ʒ/ is restricted to French and Latin borrowings like *garage* and *vision*), and in any case, constraints on inventories are themselves phonological generalizations (see Section 3.4.2). Orthographic parameters may not be universal, but they could still be derivable through the interaction of innate phonetic and cognitive forces on a system-by-system basis, as has been argued for spoken languages (e.g., Mielke 2008).

Minimal pairs are much rarer in characters than in spoken phonology; some of the very few instances of lexically contrastive strokes are shown in (26). However, this is only to be expected of a system with so many degrees of freedom;

Character phonology and phonetics 87

minimal pairs are also rare in sign language phonology (e.g., Liddell and Johnson 1989). Moreover, even when stroke parameters are not contrastive, they may still be distinctive, that is, unpredictable and thus memorized as part of the lexical representation.

(26) a 子 孑 孓
     b 犬 尤
     c 用 甩
     d 天 夭

Stroke parameters are also like phonological features in that they participate in phonological processes. In English, for example, voicing not only distinguishes morphemes like *rice* [s] and *rise* [z], but also assimilates in words like *bits* [s] and *bids* [z]. In a similar way, the difference between a horizontal stroke and a rightward counterdiagonal stroke is not only lexically distinctive (27a), but also employed in diagonalization (27b) (see Wang 1983 for a feature-based formalization of stroke-changing rules). Other implications of this observation are discussed in Section 3.5.

(27) a 子 vs. 孑
     b 好～孔

Unlike character-level prosody, stroke-level patterns are not always reflected robustly in handwriting; in particular, many writers neutralize curved and leftward-hooked strokes with plain vertical strokes. As readers, however, the same people encounter these features quite frequently in print, and in Section 5.3.3, I will report experiments showing that stroke patterns are productively generalized in reading. Since stroke type neutralization clearly benefits ease of articulation and is not obligatory (i.e., when writing carefully), it seems to reflect modality-specific character phonetics rather than character phonology.

3.4.2. Stroke groups

Stroke groups differ not only in the strokes that compose them, but also in how these strokes interact, whether by touching at an endpoint, crossing, or hovering nearby. Minimal pairs are rare as usual, but some involving stroke position are shown in (28).

(28) a 太 犬
     b 本 未

Some (near) minimal sets involving stroke contact are shown in (29).

(29) a 人 入
     b 己 已 巳

88 *Character phonology and phonetics*

c　丁　寸
d　上　下
e　夕　夂
f　田　由　甲　申　由　甲

Similar to phonotactic constraints in spoken and signed languages, strokes seem to favor particular positions. For example, counterdiagonals favor the top and/or left while main diagonals favor the bottom right, as illustrated in (30a) and (30b), respectively. Non-contacting dots at the top prefer to appear on the right (30c). Articulatory explanations may be imagined for such patterns (e.g., that it is somehow easier for a left-to-right series of strokes to end in a dot than to begin with one), but the patterns still seem to be conventionalized (for more on the role of character phonetics in shaping character phonology, see Section 3.6.1).

(30)　a　才　生　千
　　　　b　木　尺
　　　　c　犬　友　戈　弋　尤　求　甫

Certain stroke interactions are favored as well. A pair of strokes can interact in five ways: they can make no contact, cross, chain the end of one stroke to the start of another, start a stroke from contact with another, end a stroke at contact with another, or make contact at both ends. Table 3.7 illustrates these interactions with all 76 two- and three-stroke characters in the Tsai (2006) database (three-stroke characters may appear in more than category).

As can be seen, the most common stroke interaction initiates a stroke at the point where it makes contact with another stroke; that is, 下-type (一 first) characters are more common than 上-type characters (一 last), and 片-type characters (vertical stroke first) are more common than 爿-type characters (vertical stroke last). In spoken languages, the coordination of gestures is also initiated at syllable onsets (e.g., Browman and Goldstein 1988), suggesting that this stroke contact generalization ultimately has an articulatory explanation. Nevertheless, it must be phonologized amodally as well: both 人 and 入 conform to it (and in both, the

Table 3.7 Stroke interactions in two- and three-stroke characters

Contact	Examples
None	小三二八凡川幺寸又刁乞弋勺亍彳与儿
Cross	大也子力女十才士七九千土干于丸丈寸叉巾弋孑孓也尤廾乂屮毛
Chain	了子弓丫孑孓
Start at contact	大人上下工又己才入口久千刀凡亡乃丁干于丌夕几卜刃巾乞巳匕尸万勺亍彳尤口与毛厂匚
End at contact	上之工已己山士口土乇么夕弓刃巳丫尸口屮凵

Character phonology and phonetics 89

counterdiagonal is written before the main diagonal), even though in the latter the point of contact is not the initiation point for the second stroke (see Section 3.6 for the relationship between character phonology and phonetics, with particular regard to stroke order).

Non-contacting strokes are mostly restricted to dots or parallel strokes, as illustrated by the (single-constituent?) forms in (31a) and (31b), respectively. Both options are illustrated in (31c), albeit with contact. Non-parallel, non-contacting strokes are illustrated in (31d), though in Section 3.4.3 we will see that some may not count as true exceptions.

(31) a 以 小 心 太 火 永 亦 母 凡 玉 丹 瓦 斗 寸 叉
         犬 求 弋 勺 犮 丼
      b 三 二 言 元 豆 川 谷 旦 幺 云 乞 亥 亍 彳 亓
         气 与 儿 艹 彡
      c 下 上
      d 只 八 六 示 父 米 京 刁 糸

This last pattern is reminiscent of the complementary filling in of features via assimilation or via defaults, which, as noted in Section 1.4.1, is also common in both spoken and signed languages. In the case of non-contacting strokes, the axis parameter is either filled in by assimilating with that of an adjacent stroke or by being realized as the simplest possible stroke, the dot with its default axis.

3.4.3. Dots

The remainder of my phonological analysis will address the shape of various stroke types, starting with dots. We have already seen that some dots are derived from long strokes, as in the dotting reduction in (32a). Other strokes are arguably derived from dots as well, such as the short diagonals at the bottom of the constituents (32b–c); analyzing these as dots removes them as exceptions to the axis assimilation generalization (see Section 3.4.2). Their somewhat increased length can be accounted for by an independent process (see Section 3.4.4). Indeed, the character in (32c) is sometimes written with long bottom strokes like those in (32d) (see Section 4.4.2 for more on individual variation in character form).

(32) a 木～根
      b 只 六 示 京 糸
      c 米
      d 木

By default, dots fill in their axis parameter with the main diagonal, as exemplified in (33a); the unconditioned nature of this default is shown by the punctuation mark in (33b). Thus, even though dots only appear as literal circles in particularly

90 *Character phonology and phonetics*

playful calligraphic styles and typefaces, they do not need to be lexically specified for axis.

(33) a 宀 亡 太 寸 州 尤
　　　 b 、

Dot axis appears to be lexically contrastive in the pair (34), but the contrast may actually be coded in a different way: while the central dot in (34a) seems like a 'true' dot, perhaps that in (34b) is actually lexically specified as a short stroke, with its axis assimilating to the stroke above it.

(34) a 戍 *shù* 'defend borders'
　　　 b 戌 *xū* 'eleventh of twelve earthly branches'

Though dots may fall along other axes, they do so quite predictably (see Wang 1983, p. 156, for a small subset of the patterns noted here). Counterdiagonal dots virtually never appear unless there is at least one other dot along the main diagonal, with their axes arranged to intersect with the center of the stroke group, creating partial symmetry vertically or horizontally. I illustrate this descriptive generalization in (35) using my regular traditional typeface, though see Section 4.4.1 for discussion of cross-typeface variation in these and other patterns. The generalization holds straightforwardly for all of the dots at constituent edges in (35a–i), though in (35a, d–e) the other dots retain their default axis, and for (35g), the generalization must be applied within each of the stroke groups comprising this otherwise non-composable constituent. The axes of the dots in (35j–k) do not intersect in the center, though their directions are still complementary.

(35) a 清 冰
　　　 b 首 曾 平 火 兆 會
　　　 c 當
　　　 d 受
　　　 e 黑 馬 魚 杰 只 亦
　　　 f 礻
　　　 g 飛
　　　 h 兆 雨 米 泰 函 率
　　　 i 業
　　　 j 胃 勻
　　　 k 小 心

Dot axis patterns have no obvious parallels in spoken or signed phonology, except abstractly: like a particularly subtle form of allophonic variation, they seem to be only marginally phonologized from their phonetic origins (see also Section 3.6.1).

Character phonology and phonetics 91

3.4.4. Prominence of strokes and stroke groups

As with other properties of character phonology, stroke size is lexically contrastive in only a few minimal pairs, listed in (36).

(36) a 口 *kǒu* 'mouth'   vs.   囗 (semantic radical for enclosed spaces)
     b 日 *rì* 'sun'   vs.   曰 *yuē* 'say'
     c 土 *tǔ* 'soil'   vs.   士 *shì* 'gentleman'
     d 未 *wèi* 'not yet'   vs.   末 *mò* 'final'

Otherwise size is highly predictable: the bottommost and rightmost strokes are almost always larger than the rest. In other words, strokes in prosodically strong positions receive PROMINENCE, similar to stress in spoken languages. The role of the prosodic template is made clear by size differences in reduplication, as seen in the vertically doubled constituents in (37a) and the horizontally doubled constituents in (37b).

(37) a 昌　呂　圭　燚　多　炎　哥
     b 玨　林　比　炊　㮾

Prominence also applies within unitary constituents, enlarging the bottommost of vertically stacked stroke groups (38a) or individual strokes (38b), as well as the rightmost of horizontally arrayed strokes (38c). The constituent in (38d) displays these prominence asymmetries along both axes.

(38) a 呂　串　官　虽　弗　龟　飛
     b 二　三　土　工　干　于　王　丰　手　彡
     c 川　州　介
     d 井

Formally, the overall arrangement of prominence conforms to the one-dimensional reductions of the idealized prosodic template, as illustrated in (39) and (40).

(39) a 三
     b $\begin{bmatrix} W \\ S \end{bmatrix}$

(40) a 川
     b [W S]

Further examples of prominence targeting the lowest horizontal stroke or stroke group are shown in (41).

(41) a 玉　車　里　羊　立　平　牛　革　共　五　互　青　豆　亏
       爰　看　毛　示　告　晋　並　其　耳　㽙　長　舍　金　夫
       未　末　失　先　春　黑

92 *Character phonology and phonetics*

    b 大：奧～奇
    c 田：富～畢
    d 田：由～甲

Bottommost prominence also helps explain the stretching of the lower semantic radical strokes in (42a) (see Section 3.3.1.2), and the enlargement of the lower dots in (42b) (see Section 3.4.3).

(42)   a 走～起　支～婺　毛～毯
      b 六　只

Stroke lengthening is only allowed if doing so does not require changing the stroke interaction type (e.g., from touching to crossing), as suggested by its absence in (43), where the bottommost horizontal stroke is not enlarged because it makes or almost makes contact at its end points.

(43)   口　月　本　承

Since character prosody is constrained by morphological structure, bottommost and rightmost prominence are defined within individual constituents, as illustrated in (44). The first example in (44a) is worth highlighting: it is an obsolete variant of 四 *sì* 'four' that has been reanalyzed as vertical doubling rather than quadrupling, since the former is favored by the prosodic template (see Sections 3.3.2 and 4.3.1.1 for historical changes in reduplication within Chinese characters).

(44)   a 三　圭　墨
      b 順　刑

These observations make prominence a potential diagnostic for constituenthood, independently of external interpretation (recall the discussion of "morphology by itself" of Aronoff 1994b, in several places in Chapter 2). For example, the characters in (45) contain a prominent horizontal stroke in a location other than at the bottom, but this stroke is bottommost within the possible constituent indicated in parentheses.

(45)   a 畫　聿　(聿)
      b 幸　(土)
      c 辛　(立)
      d 糞　舉　(业)
      e 言　(亠)
      f 事　(亠聿)

Other exceptions to bottommost prominence seem to be closely related to each other. The starting point is the constituent in (46a), which, if it were contained within the characters in (46b), would explain the anomalous location of prominence. The characters in (46c) share 千 with (46b), those in (46d) share the horizontally doubled 十 with (46c), and the character in (46e) also shows horizontal (and vertical) doubling, but of 人. Given the piecemeal nature of these generalizations, they seem to involve ad hoc analogy rather than phonology proper.

(46) a 千
　　 b 重　垂　熏　秉
　　 c 垂　乘
　　 d 華　畢
　　 e 華

The few other exceptions to bottommost prominence in (47a) simply have to be stipulated, in contrast to their regular counterparts in (47b). Exceptional stress is also common in spoken languages, of course, including with lexical contrast (e.g., English *ínsìght* vs. *incíte*).

(47) a 士　末　壬
　　 b 土　未　王

These exceptions help illustrate another regularity, however. Similar to stress clash (see the introduction to Section 3.3), if a stroke adjacent to the bottommost stroke receives exceptional prominence, the bottommost stroke is not lengthened, as shown in (48a). By contrast, when there are intervening strokes, as in (48b), both strokes are lengthened, the exceptional one more than the bottommost one. The same may hold of (48c), since 口 seems to be prominent relative to the two strokes just above it.

(48) a 士　末　壬　華　畢　華
　　 b 聿　幸　重　垂　熏　垂　事　秉
　　 c 言

Since there seems to be secondary prominence at the top in (49a) and at the left in (49b), it is tempting to posit templates that iterate within constituents, similar to the analysis of the two levels of stress in *kàngaróo* (e.g., 川 would be analyzed as $[[S]_w[WS]_s]$).

(49) a 三　王　玉　丢
　　 b 川　州　卅

Unfortunately, such an analysis cannot work. Not only would iterative templates falsely predict 'rhythmic' prominence within constituents, but as we will see in Section 3.4.5, left-edge curving only occurs in prosodically weak positions (ruling out [[S][WS]] as an analysis of 川). The slight lengthening in top-edge strokes may instead relate to the inconsistent widening of the topmost constituents in triangular reduplication (see Section 3.3.2), while curving may be too hard

94   *Character phonology and phonetics*

to write or see when shortened too much; both phenomena would then seem to belong more to character phonetics than character phonology.

Finally, prominence is another aspect of Chinese character phonology that has been borrowed into the otherwise very different Korean Hangul alphabetic system (see also Section 3.3.1.2): strokes are enlarged at the bottom of Hangul letters, whether horizontal (50a) or vertical (50b–c). The horizontal axis is treated in a less Chinese-like manner, with rightmost prominence for vertical strokes (51a) but leftmost prominence for horizontal strokes (51b–c). There is more that could be said about the influence of Chinese character phonology on neighboring orthographies, including Tangut script (Miyake 2017), but unfortunately they go a bit beyond the scope of this book (see also comments on the orthographic morphology of Vietnamese characters in Section 2.3.2).

(50) a ㅍ *p*
      b ㅗ *o*   ㅜ *u*
      c ㅛ *yo*   ㅠ *yu*

(51) a ㅐ *ae*   ㅒ *yae*   ㅔ *e*   ㅖ *ye*
      b ㅏ *a*   ㅓ *eo*
      c ㅑ *ya*   ㅕ *yeo*

3.4.5. Curving

Curving is traditionally treated as an intrinsic feature of the leftward falling stroke, thus putting the counterdiagonal strokes in (52a–c) into the same class as the curved vertical stroke in (52d).

(52) a 木 必
      b 生 千
      c 大
      d 川

I prefer instead to analyze the falling counterdiagonal strokes in 木, 必, 生, and 千 as intrinsically diagonal, with their precise curving and axis determined by regular processes: less curved if short (see Section 3.4.4), more vertical for left-edge strokes, and more horizontal for top-edge strokes (making them lighter in both of these prosodically weak positions). By contrast, I consider the leftmost strokes in 大 and 川 as intrinsically vertical, curved not due to lexical specification but because they are at the constituent's left edge.

Many more examples of this regular CURVING process are shown in (53) (again, keep in mind that I am describing curving as it appears in this particular typeface; other styles show somewhat different patterns, as discussed in Section 4.4.1). It targets a left-edge vertical stroke when adjacent to other vertical strokes (53a), when adjacent to a vertical left-hooked stroke (53b), when adjacent to complex

Character phonology and phonetics   95

strokes containing a vertical portion (53c), and, generally speaking, when to the left of any other material (53d).

(53) a 川 州 卅 介 �升 非 拜 弗 飛 爪 瓜 帶
      b 月 有 丹 舟 周 角 用 亦
      c 片 爿 肅
      d 大 九 乃 刀 力 虎 戶 底 右 厷 及 看 虎

By contrast, vertical strokes are never curved in the center (54a) or on the right (54b).

(54) a 十 中 木 不 丫 羊 半 平 下 串 甲 申 車 革 辛
        聿 年 市 午 丰 乍
      b 耳 斗

The left-edge requirement is abstract, as shown by the near-minimal pair in (55): the vertical stroke in (55a) is conceptualized as central, as shown by its combining with a stroke group below it, whereas that in (55b) is conceptualized as being at the left, since other stroke groups combine with it on its lower right.

(55) a 肀～書
      b 尹～君

This restriction to the left, combined with the necessity for there to be material on the right, makes curving yet another example of a process that applies within a prosodically weak position, defined by its opposition to a strong position, as in the templatic analysis in (56).

(56) a 川
      b [W   S]

The pairs in (57) show that curving is impossible if the lower end of the stroke makes contact or chains to another, similar to the blocking of lengthening in contacting strokes (see Section 3.4.6).

(57) a 斤   丘
      b 廾   廿
      c 月   目
      d 几   口
      e 非   韭

Like prominence, the edge where curving applies is defined within and not across constituents. This is why there is curving at the left edge of the right-side constituents in (58a) and why in (58b) there is curving of the long vertical stroke

96　*Character phonology and phonetics*

on the left edge, like (58c), but not of the short vertical stroke in the constituent-internal stroke group to its right, unlike (58d).

(58)　a　悱　佛　聯　所
　　　b　肅　淵
　　　c　片
　　　d　爿

For the same reason, the leftmost stroke in left-edge semantic radicals remains straight if there is no constituent-internal material to its right (59a), unlike when such material is present constituent-internally (59b).

(59)　a　個　博　帽　很　情　校　牲　神　稱　精　耗　耶　被　校　陳　鞋
　　　b　牆　版　確　於　服　短　船　觸　靜

The same is generally true for reduplication, as shown by the lack of curving in (60).

(60)　a　林
　　　b　森　犇　轟

However, a small set of lexically marked constituents are curved at the left edge of the entire character, whether they are affixed (61a), compounded (61b), or reduplicated (61c).

(61)　a　辛：辣～辟　　羊：羚～群
　　　b　邦　朔
　　　c　辡　拜　艸　芔

Even within constituents, the leftmost vertical stroke is not always curved, as in the less than fully decomposable characters in (62a). Such examples suggest that curving is disfavored if the leftmost vertical stroke is part of a separable stroke group, as if their prosodic structure were as in (62b).

(62)　a　門　鬥　叚　行　竹　段
　　　b　[S] [S]

However, the (near) minimal pairs in (63) suggest that curving has some true lexical exceptions as well.

(63)　a　卅　廿
　　　b　角　甬
　　　c　周　同

There is still an interesting generalization lurking here, though. As first noticed by Wang (1983, pp. 203–206), the curved 周 seems 'taller' than the non-curved

Character phonology and phonetics 97

Table 3.8 The relationship between curving and constituent dimensions

	Dominant axis		
Stroke shape	Horizontal	Vertical	None
Curved		月甩周(有舟角)	丹用
Straight	冊同岡(巾內向兩肉市肖)	(再甬高商喬)	同罔(冉束)

同, and that is indeed true according to my intersection metric (maximally five intersections along the vertical axis in 周 but only four in 同). Wang does not test this observation further nor does he explain it, but it turns out to be empirically generalizable, and it has a natural explanation in character prosody.

First, recall from Section 3.3.1.2 that the idiosyncratic allomorph for the wide radical in (64a) is the narrow constituent in (64b), and now observe that narrowing is associated with curving (this allomorph differs across styles, though not in ways that affect the argument here; see Sections 4.3.1.2 and 4.4.1). Next consider Table 3.8, which contains a representative (perhaps exhaustive) sample of 27 constituents containing the stroke group in (64c) (including the curved variant), cross-classified into left-stroke curving and dominant axis.

(64)   a   肉
       b   月
       c   冂

Notably missing are curved wide constituents, and indeed, a Fisher exact test (akin to a two-way chi-squared test, but for very small samples) finds a significant interaction between stroke shape (curved vs. straight) and dominant axis (horizontal vs. all others) ($p = .01$). Further evidence comes from comparing the constituents (in parentheses) that have material above 冂, which tends to flatten/widen it, against those without; almost all with topping material have straight left-edge strokes (14/17), while many of the rest have curved strokes (5/10).

Yet another way to see the relevance of constituent dimensions to left-stroke curving is to examine where these constituents tend to take their semantic radicals (an idea suggested to me by Yu-Hsuan Lin). Constituents conceived of as wide should tend to appear in characters that have a main vertical axis, that is, with semantic radicals at the top or bottom to keep the overall character square, whereas constituents conceived of as tall should tend to appear in characters with a main horizontal axis. Consequently, curved left strokes should be more common in constituents that favor radicals to their left or right. This claim is correct for the near-minimal pair in (65) and (66): despite having identical dimensions, the constituent with the straight left stroke appears more often with more top/bottom radicals in the Tsai (2006) database than the constituent with the curved left stroke (three vs. none).

(65) a 甬 with left/right radicals: 俑 埇 蛹 誦 踊 恿 捅 桶 涌
    b 甬 with top/bottom radicals: 勇 恿 箶

(66) a 角 with left/right radicals: 哨 埆 捔 桷 确 斛
    b 角 with top/bottom radicals: none

Figure 3.2 shows that the claim applies much more generally. This so-called mosaic plot is based on all 224 characters in the Tsai (2006) database containing only the 27 constituents presented earlier in Table 3.8, plus a single-edge radical. While the plot shows that there are proportionally more characters with straight-stroke constituents and with a main horizontal axis, there is also an interaction between these two factors: curved constituents favor radicals at the left or right more than at the top or bottom. This interaction is not only significant by a two-way chi-squared test ($\chi^2(1) = 4.4$, $p < .05$), but also by a mixed-effect logistic regression analysis ($B = -1.37$, $SE = 0.63$, $z = -2.17$, $p < .05$) taking into account random variation in radical-specific position preferences.

Now that Wang's empirical generalization has been established, how can we explain it? In spoken and signed languages, temporal duration is an aspect of prosody, with longer constituents containing a greater number of prosodic units (see, e.g., Hayes 1995). In the case of character prosody, a wider constituent could be analyzed as containing two prosodic templates rather than one. This would place the leftmost stroke of a wider constituent within its own separate prosodic template, which would necessarily consist solely of a strong position. Since curving only applies in weak positions, the stroke would therefore

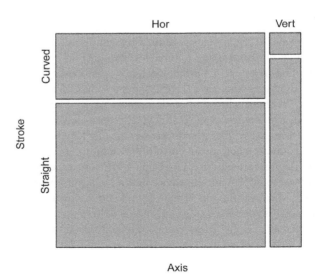

Figure 3.2 The interaction of left-edge stroke shape and main character axis

Character phonology and phonetics 99

remain straight. For example, the narrow constituent in (67a) would be associated with the single template in (67b), putting the curved stroke in a weak position, whereas the wide constituent in (68a) would be associated with two templates, each with an obligatory strong head, as in (68b), putting the left edge straight stroke in a strong position (see Section 4.4.1 for more on this particular character).

(67) a 月
      b [W   S]

(68) a 冊
      b [S] [S]

There are technical challenges with implementing this idea, in particular in determining where the morpheme-internal prosodic boundary lies (recall my rejection of constituent-internal template boundaries at the end of Section 3.4.4). There are also empirical problems, including constituents, like those in (69a), that are wider than tall by the line-intersection diagnostic, yet still show left-stroke curving. A more arcane issue is illustrated in (69b), where the constituents on the left are curved and those on the right are idiosyncratically reduced (from 刀 and 邑, respectively), even though it should be prosodically impossible for a character to have weak positions on both sides. Perhaps such cases simply represent yet more of the exceptionality inevitable in lexical grammars.

(69) a 廾   川   州   卅   爪
      b 判   邦

3.4.6. Hooking

Hooks, or at least what seem to be hooks (recall the caveats in Section 3.4.1), appear on a variety of strokes in a variety of forms. They point into the curve in concave strokes (70a–b), downward on horizontal strokes (70c), and either rightward or leftward on vertical strokes (70d–e).

(70) a 犭   豸   豕
      b 乚   心   戈
      c 冖   疋   也
      d 衣   艮   切
      e 丁   寸   司

Each type of hook requires its own separate analysis. Convex strokes (as opposed to merely curved strokes or chained straight strokes) seem to be obligatorily hooked, at least in standard typefaces (see also Wang 1983, p. 208). By contrast, hooked horizontal strokes behave as if they were actually complex strokes

100 *Character phonology and phonetics*

ending in a short straight stroke, since unlike 'true' hooks they can be quite long and may even be chained to another stroke, as in (71).

(71)　了 阝

This 'hook' is also derivationally related to straight strokes via shrinking, as in (72).

(72)　a　雨～電
　　　b　尚～當

For the same reasons, some rightward-pointing hooks also actually seem to be short strokes: those in (73a) make contact with another stroke and those in (73b) are derivable via diagonalization.

(73)　a　丩　卯　瓜　(cf. 云)
　　　b　七～切　匕～比　奋～鶴　以鼠

All other rightward hooks appear in a curiously specific environment: immediately to the left of crossed strokes, whether long (74a) or short (74b). The ad hoc specificity of this pattern suggests analogy, rather than a general grammatical process. It also weakens the argument in Wang (1983, pp. 208–209) that rightward hooks result from stroke order (putatively due to flicking the brush pen towards the top right in preparation for the next stroke), since they are not found without the crossed stroke environment, as illustrated by the hookless leftmost strokes in (74c) (see Section 3.6 for more on stroke order).

(74)　a　氏　民
　　　b　長　艮　良　衣　喪　辰　派
　　　c　川　門

Also consistent with analogy is the observation that in characters formed with the crossed right-edge constituent in (75a), rightward hooking is superseded by the more productive process of left-edge curving if any material intervenes, as in (75b). Even if nothing intervenes, hooking is still not obligatory, as shown by the minimal pair in (75c).

(75)　a　戈
　　　b　成　戚　戍　戌　戎　戒
　　　c　戉 *yuè* '(kind of) battle axe'　vs.　戊 *wù* 'fifth heavenly stem'

The leftward-pointing hook on vertical strokes seems to be a true hook, since it cannot make contact, as suggested by the minimal pairs in (76).

(76)　a　丁　工
　　　b　月　目

Character phonology and phonetics   101

Leftward hooking also seems to be lexically distinctive, as suggested by the near-minimal pairs in (77).

(77)   a 于 干
       b 丁 下
       c 事 聿
       d 乎 平

Nevertheless, even this hook type is partially predictable. Not only does it never appear on the left edge of a constituent (complementary to rightward hooking and curving), but as noted by Wang (1983, pp. 206–210), it also tends to appear on strokes that make contact at the top and in constituents with left/right asymmetry. Both generalizations are trivially obeyed in the complex stroke in (78a) (this Unicode symbol is not available in my usual example typeface); a variety of constituents containing it are listed in (78b).

(78)   a ⺄
       b 刀 司 月 母 身 考 弗 馬 永

Wang's generalizations also apply statistically in simple vertical strokes, as shown in Table 3.9. The top half of the table contains a reasonably thorough sample of constituents (mostly from Lu *et al.* 2002) with vertical strokes ending in leftward hooks, cross-classified by top contact and asymmetry; curving and hooking (both presumed to be derived) are ignored when determining symmetry. The bottom half of the table applies the same classification to simple vertical strokes without hooks. In order to show all constituents in the same typeface, some are illustrated with complex characters containing them (e.g., the constituent on the right of 姊).

As can be seen, there are more hooked strokes with than without top contact (22 vs. 10) and in asymmetrical than in symmetrical constituents (26 vs. 6), whereas non-hooked strokes show neither tendency (38 vs. 54 and 46 vs. 46, respectively). Indeed, according to a logistic regression analysis on this sample, hooking is significantly more likely with top contact ($B = 0.74$, $SE = 0.31$, $z = 2.37$, $p < .05$) and

Table 3.9 The effect of asymmetry and top contact on leftward hooking

		Asymmetrical	*Symmetrical*
Hooked	Top contact	了可子手竹乎爭承予牙亨矛 糸孑孓亇爭	亦丁京于丁
	No top contact	事才水求寸事刂扌隶	小
Not hooked	Top contact	不下年雨第千眾拜午耳斥斤 乍禾釆彳乘亻挿礻	而果平市示甲雨幸冊辛干羊 革丌并丫半帚
	No top contact	引制飛牛布升姊州庸斗卜傘 甫弗爪丰求韋丬耒丩刁丰帚 术中	中本車十東非未半介木申東 未米井川串淵卌巾柬廾屮弗 卝尘忄柿

102　*Character phonology and phonetics*

asymmetry ($B = 0.85$, $SE = 0.31$, $z = 2.72$, $p < .01$), with no significant interaction between these two factors ($p > .3$).

One way to explain the relevance of top contact and asymmetry is that these two properties make constituents visually more similar to the complex hooked stroke ⌐; leftward hooking would thereby be another example of analogy, rather than phonology proper. Nevertheless, it may be relevant that top contact is favored over bottom contact in stroke interactions more generally (see Section 3.4.2), and asymmetric contexts may favor hooking because hooking itself enhances the asymmetry.

3.5. Lexical phonology

"All grammars leak," as Sapir (1921, p. 38) famously observed; lexical grammars particularly so. It is no surprise, then, that all of the phonological generalizations observed in Chinese characters have exceptions, even the most productive ones (e.g., reduplication shapes and bottommost stroke prominence). Some generalizations have so many exceptions that the regularity is hard to see without statistical analysis (e.g., leftward hooking). The productivity of the rest fall somewhere in between (e.g., curving). This means that, even if these generalizations are mentally active, readers and writers must still memorize the exceptions.

Wang (1983, p. 90) emphasizes the same point:

> Since the total number of characters a person knows at any given time forms a finite set, and their shape and structure are largely determined by convention, it would be counter-intuitive to assume that these characters are generated anew from character formatives each time they are used. And, in fact, it is in principle impossible to construct an algorithm that can generate only and all the characters that a person knows.

Nevertheless, even lexical phonology obeys generalizations at a higher level of description, as indicated by the co-occurring properties listed in (79) (see, e.g., Hargus and Kaisse 1993; Kiparsky 1982).

(79)　a　Has lexical exceptions
　　　　b　Does not create novel structures
　　　　c　Is sensitive to morphology

For example, the [i] ~ [ɛ] alternation in the third-to-last syllable in many English words (e.g., *obscene ~ obscenity*) not only has lexical exceptions (e.g., [i] ~ [i] in *obese ~ obesity*), but it also involves a lexical contrast (/i/ vs. /ɛ/ as in *bead* vs. *bed*) and is sensitive to morphology ([i] not [ɛ] with a different type of suffix in *weariness* and in monomorphemic *stevedore*).

Character phonology has these three properties as well. As just noted, all of the patterns have lexical exceptions. All stroke-level patterns also replace one existing stroke category with another, rather than creating a novel stroke (a property technically called structure preservation). For example, while dotting, diagonalization, shrinking, and prominence are predictable in (80), the same stroke distinctions are lexically specified in (81).

(80) a 木～根
      b 子～孩
      c 雨～電
      d 日～昌

(81) a 木 *mù* 'wood'   vs.   米 *mǐ* 'uncooked rice'
      b 子 *zǐ* 'child'   vs.   孑 *jié* 'remaining'
      c 雨 *yǔ* 'rain'   vs.   宀 *mián* (semantic radical for roofed structures)
      d 日 *rì* 'sun'   vs   曰 *yuē* 'say'

Character phonology also interacts with character morphology. Many of the stroke-level patterns we have discussed, including prominence, regular curving, and axis assimilation, apply within but not across constituents, just as third-to-last stress only applies stem-internally in [*Américan*]*ìzing*, ignoring the suffixes -*ize* and -*ing*. By contrast, other patterns do take neighboring constituents into account, including constituent-specific curving (see the end of Section 3.4.5) and regular reduction (diagonalization, dotting, shrinking, stretching). It may be relevant that these patterns are most often seen with semantic radicals, which, uniquely, may also undergo idiosyncratic allomorphy. The effect of morpheme type on phonology here is reminiscent of fact that -*al* and -*ity* are not ignored in the shifting third-to-last stress in *órigin*, *original*, and *originálity*.

The two kinds of curving processes, one more lexicalized than the other, has parallels in spoken languages as well. For example, in English (Borowsky 1990), the more lexicalized version of nasal place assimilation is obligatory morpheme-internally (*lamp* vs. **lanp*) and with certain prefixes (*impossible* vs. **inpossible*), whereas the less lexicalized version applies (optionally) with other types of prefixes (*u*[n]*popular ~ u*[m]*popular*) and across word boundaries (*te*[n] *boys ~ te*[m] *boys*). Curving and nasal place assimilation differ importantly, however, in that for the latter, the less lexicalized variant applies in the larger domain (phrases), while in character phonology constituent-internal curving is the more general variant.

3.6. Character phonetics

The traditional distinction between phonology and phonetics has proven to be trickier than once thought (Cohn 2007; Ohala 1990). For example, some familiar phonological rules have turned out to be phonetically gradient (Port and Leary 2005), and languages have been found to differ not just in phonological systems but in articulatory detail as well (Gick *et al.* 2004). We will see that the line between character phonology and character phonetics is also somewhat blurred. However, it still seems fair to characterize phonology as more mental and categorical and phonetics as more physical and gradient. In the case of character phonetics, the (psycho)physics involves both visual biases and hand physiology.

104 *Character phonology and phonetics*

A complete analysis of character phonetics would also have to take the writing instrument into account (ink brushes have very different physical properties from carving knives, ballpoint pens, and chalk), though motor control systems are remarkably flexible in adapting to external forces while still aiming at the intended targets, including in speech (Saltzman and Munhall 1989).

While phonetics lies at the periphery of grammar, it still has a role to play in phonological explanation. Nevertheless, I argue that the influence of character phonetics on character phonology is mostly restricted to diachronic change (Section 3.6.1). I then look at stroke order (Section 3.6.2), arguing that because it is intrinsically gradient and physical, it should be treated as an aspect of character phonetics, not character phonology.

3.6.1. Phonetic motivation in character phonology

Character phonology is neither gradient nor physical. As observed in Section 3.5, stroke alternations output precisely the same strokes that must be memorized as part of the lexical representation of other characters. The positional restrictions are not gradient either: only strokes precisely at constituent edges are lengthened or curved; strokes do not get gradually longer or more curved the closer they are to an edge. Character phonology is also not mere physics: the generalizations, as well as their lexical exceptions, must be learned, rather than emerging spontaneously from articulatory and visual constraints, and they interact with the learned and even more abstract system of character morphology.

Similarly, while there have been attempts to reduce prosodic structure to phonetics in spoken language (e.g., Gordon 2002a; Steriade 1999), the correlates of prosody have a way of taking on a life of their own, and the same is true in character phonology. The prosodic template in Chinese characters is associated with too many distinct categorical processes to ascribe them all directly to gradient character phonetics, including those relating to semantic radical position, idiosyncratic reduction, reduplication, and the stroke modifications of dotting, diagonalization, shrinking, stretching, lengthening, and curving.

Nevertheless, it is obvious that, just as with spoken and signed phonology, character phonology has been shaped by character phonetics. For speech and sign, it continues to be debated whether this only happens diachronically (Blevins 2004) or whether an individual's phonological knowledge also incorporates phonetic information (Hayes 1999). However, for character phonology, which has remained mostly unchanged for centuries and is even reflected in mechanical typefaces, only a diachronic explanation is plausible.

The influence of character phonetics on character phonology can be seen in many areas. For example, the shape of the character prosodic template seems to derive ultimately from the direction with which constituents and strokes are written, top to bottom and left to right, which puts the final gestures at the bottom right. Increased articulatory effort at the completion of gestures is realized as final lengthening in both spoken (Beckman and Edwards 1990) and signed languages (Sandler 1993), and in writing, final strokes receive greater pressure (Wann and

Character phonology and phonetics 105

Nimmo-Smith 1991). Since the detailed mechanics of writing need not leave a visible trace, Cohen-Goldberg (2017) concludes that all final emphasis phenomena, including in speech and signing, arise through automatic physiological forces. However, in Chinese characters the last-written strokes are typically visibly larger (e.g., 宝), and similar phenomena are observable in other writing systems (e.g., the slightly larger lower loops in <B> and <8> and the larger word-final Greek /s/ allograph <ς> as compared with non-final <σ>; word-final allographs are generally also larger in Arabic script: Coulmas 1989, p. 153). Bottom prominence, also reflected in the bottom-heaviness of the triangular template, may be motivated visually as well, via the same optical illusion underlying the traditional enlargement of the base of architectural columns to make them seem of consistent width (Luckiesh 1965).

The rightward/downward writing direction, which applies between and within strokes, is also motivated by articulation. The hand of a right-handed writer hovers over the lower right corner of the writing surface, so the easiest maneuver is to pull the writing instrument towards this position (for other observations on the role of hand position and physiology on writing, see Watt 2015). Consistent with this idea, Goodnow and Levine (1973) observed that their American participants, including children, also started at the upper left when copying simple figures, then drew each stroke rightward and/or downward. Individual Roman letters are generally written rightward/downward as well, so that the Chinese character in (82a) and the letter in (82b) are produced with exactly the same stroke direction and stroke order. These simple observations also highlight another distinction between character phonology and phonetics: even though the asymmetries in the character prosodic template mainly benefit right-handed writers, left-handed writers, not to mention printers, are still obliged to conform to it.

(82) a 丁
      b **T**

Other aspects of character phonology seem to have a visual motivation. For example, triangular reduplication shows left/right symmetry (see Section 3.3.2), and symmetry also matters in dot axis (see Section 3.4.3) and leftward hooking (see Section 3.4.6). The preference for left/right symmetry is an orthographic universal (Morin 2018) and presumably derives from the fact that the visual system is better at detecting it than top/bottom symmetry (Wenderoth 1994). Yet mirroring is rare and unsystematic (see Section 2.3.3.1), dot axis is variable and rarely fully symmetrical, and curving and hooking necessarily ruin any symmetry that would otherwise appear. These observations suggest that symmetry is not an independent productive principle of character phonology but rather an aspect of character phonetics that has operated opportunistically across character history. The only place where it has become deeply entrenched is in the prosodic template, where triangular reduplication shows obligatory left/right symmetry.

In another visual constraint, Changizi *et al.* (2006) show that Chinese characters prefer having fewer angles and that this preference is also an orthographic

106 *Character phonology and phonetics*

universal, ultimately derived from the visual processing of natural scenes. Morin (2018) also observes that orthographic systems favor cardinal axes (horizontal and vertical) and rarely mix them with oblique axes, arguing that this separation benefits legibility; it may also be one of the factors that favoring what I described as the assimilation of Chinese stroke axes (see Section 3.4.2).

Perceptual and articulatory constraints can also interact. For example, wrist rotation makes it easier to produce curved than straight strokes, particularly at the left edge, yet the straight stroke is still the default, appearing far more frequently in Chinese and other orthographic systems. This implies that visual constraints may trump articulatory ones. Changizi and Shimojo (2005) even argue that this should usually be the case in orthography, since any given form is written only once, but may be read many times.

As a final example of phonetic forces in orthography, recall that when strokes make contact at a point without crossing, it is usually at the initial point (e.g., the topmost point for a vertical stroke or the leftmost point for a horizontal stroke). Ninio and Lieblich (1976) also observed this bias in children's drawings. Specifically, when they asked 34-year-old Israeli children to copy an upside down T figure (⊥), 16 reproduced it in two strokes, all but three of whom drew the horizontal stroke first so that they could begin drawing the vertical stroke upward from the point of contact. An additional eight flipped it upside down (⊤) or sideways (⊦) so that they could obey the contact bias while also obeying the downward and rightward constraints on stroke direction. The remaining six children split the horizontal stroke into two separate strokes, but still always started them at the point of contact. A possible reason for this stroke contact bias is that it helps coordinate manual gestures with visual cues (or at least with the mental images of upcoming strokes). As noted in Section 3.4.2, it is also reminiscent of the gestural coordination at the beginning of spoken syllables (Browman and Goldstein 1988).

3.6.2. Stroke order

Stroke order looms large in traditional discussions of Chinese characters, but here I show that it depends on higher levels of character structure, rather than being a synchronic driving force (Section 3.6.2.1). I then show that stroke order is intrinsically gradient and physical (Section 3.6.2.2), hence an aspect of character phonetics.

3.6.2.1. The synchronic irrelevance of stroke order

Stroke order is one of the most widely discussed aspect of Chinese characters, especially in pedagogical settings (see Wan 2017; Zhang 2014, and citations therein). Even Wang (1983), who otherwise takes a highly nontraditional approach to characters, considers stroke order important enough to highlight in his title (*Toward a generative grammar of Chinese character structure and stroke order*). In fact, he places stroke order operations in the center of his sequentially

Character phonology and phonetics   107

structured grammar, after operations that combine constituents (what I call character morphology) and before operations that adjust constituent form (what I call character phonology); several of the latter make direct reference to stroke order.

However, even if character phonology has been diachronically shaped by stroke order, it is possible, and indeed preferable, to give elegant descriptions of phonological patterns in modern characters without reference to stroke order at all. For example, Wang (1983, pp. 208–209) is correct that rightward hooks on vertical strokes always have material to the right that is written immediately afterwards in the standard stroke order, but we saw in Section 3.4.6 that the actual triggering environment is defined visually: the material to the right is always crossed.

Leftward hooking has an even more tenuous relationship with stroke order. Wang (1983, p. 208) observes that the hook points towards the next-written strokes in the constituents in (83a), and further examples are listed in (83b). Yet he still has to give a purely structural analysis for the many leftward hooks that are written last, like those in (83c) (see Section 3.4.6 for contextual triggers that have nothing to do with stroke order).

(83) a 小 水 寸
      b 才 牙 矛 扌
      c 了 可 事 手 乎 爭 予 亇 争 事 刂

The reduction processes in left-edge constituents are likely to be motivated by stroke order, but again only diachronically: dotting (84a) and diagonalization (84b) both serve to reduce the distance between the endpoint of the affected stroke and the onset of following stroke, to its upper right.

(84) a 木～村
      b 土～地

Nevertheless, there are number of clues that the patterns have been phonologized: both replace one lexical stroke with another rather than creating a new stroke type (see Section 3.5), both are obligatory across all standard typefaces, and both have conditioning environments that are learnable directly from the final written forms, making stroke order superfluous. Compare the presence of diagonalization in (85a) with its absence in (85b). Even without knowing that the changed horizontal strokes are always written last in (85a) while the unchanged horizontal strokes in (85b) are not, it is possible to describe the pattern purely structurally, as applying to horizontal strokes at the bottom edge.

(85) a 土～地 金～鉛 立～站 至～致 止～此 且～助 工～功 重～動
      b 車～較 十～博 木～校 辛～辣 革～鞋

The few cases where diagonalization targets non-bottom-edge horizontal strokes merely help confirm that a synchronic stroke order analysis would miss the point. In some styles (as in the typeface here), diagonalization applies in the

108 *Character phonology and phonetics*

constituent in (86a) despite the fact that its horizontal stroke is not the last-written one. The diagonalized complex stroke at the bottom of the constituent in (86b) is not written last either, and the diagonalized stroke in (86c) is not last in Japanese kanji stroke order conventions.

(86)   a   舟～般
      b   山～峰
      c   耳～聰

Even more striking are cases where stroke order clearly depends on diagonalization rather than the other way around. The stroke that is diagonalized in (87a) is both the lowest 'horizontal' stroke and also the last-written one within the left-edge allomorph 牜. However, the final stroke in the unreduced form 牛 is the long vertical stroke; it is only when reduced that the stroke order is reversed. A similar switch occurs in the idiosyncratic 手～扌 alternation in (87b) (in Section 4.3.2.2, we will see that this stratagem has been productively extended in simplified characters).

(87)   a   牛～物 (牜)
      b   手～拾 (扌)

In short, there are good reasons to put stroke order not just after character morphology, as in Wang's (1983) grammar, but after character phonology as well, and to ascribe its apparent influences on phonology to history, just as with phonetic influences more generally.

3.6.2.2. Stroke order as phonetics

Stroke order is phonetics because it is both gradient and physical. Gradience is seen in the considerable variation in stroke order observed across teaching traditions and individual writers (discussed later in this section). This variation is partly due to the fact that stroke order leaves few visible traces, a fact noted with dismay by Chinese teachers, since it hides deviations from prescriptive norms (Zhang 2014). The logic of Cohen-Goldberg (2017) (see Section 3.6.1) would thus imply that stroke order is subject more to internal physiological forces (i.e., phonetics) than to learned conventions (i.e., phonology). Indeed, writers seem to be quite capable of working out efficient stroke orders on their own. As Yin (2016, p. 59) puts it: "Sometimes, after years of writing, people find that one way of writing is easier than another, even though it does not comply with the stroke order rules." Of course, an overly idiosyncratic stroke order may reduce the legibility of rapidly written characters, where sequentially produced strokes tend to merge, but rapid writing, like rapid speech or signing, is likely to pose comprehension challenges even if the reader shares the writer's ordering conventions.

One set of conventional rules is given in (88), based on that in Zhang, Li, and Lun (2015, p. 1434), with each illustrated with a maximally simple example (an

Character phonology and phonetics 109

additional convention, discussed later, is that a constituent tends to be completed before the next one is begun).

(88) a First horizontal, then vertical: 十
      b First leftward diagonal, then rightward diagonal: 人
      c First top, then bottom: 二
      d First left, then right: 川
      e First outside, then inside: 同
      f First center, then sides: 小
      g Bottom of box last: 目
      h Left/bottom radicals last: 近
      i Left/bottom stroke last: 匹
      j Vertical before upward/rightward counterdiagonal: 牡
      k Dot last: 犬

All such rule lists quickly run into problems, however. For example, the character in (89a) is often used as a tally marker, making its stroke order, shown in (89b), particularly salient. However, deriving even this highly familiar order from the conventional rules is not at all straightforward. If the 'first horizontal, then vertical' rule is taken literally, all three horizontal strokes should be written before the two vertical ones, which is clearly wrong. Similarly, if we took the 'first left, then right' rule literally, the short vertical stroke would be incorrectly ordered before the long vertical one. Things get even more complex when the other rules and stroke groups are considered, since they often contradict each other; for example, 'first outside, then inside' conflicts with 'first left, then right,' and both conflict with 'first center, then sides.'

(89) a 正
      b 一 丁 干 正 正

In his struggle to find the underlying logic behind such rules, Wang (1983, pp. 169–201) starts with a reasonable idea: focus on the starting and ending points rather than the strokes themselves. Unfortunately, the rest of his approach is far less insightful. Consider the ordering of the long horizontal stroke as first in (90a) but last in (90b). In the first character, the starting point of the vertical stroke is higher than that of the horizontal stroke, but its ending point is lower than that of the other stroke, canceling out its priority, so that the greater leftness of the starting point of the horizontal stroke triggers its being written first. In the second character, the starting point of the vertical stroke is higher than that of the long horizontal stroke, but both strokes end at the same height, thus giving an overall advantage to the vertical stroke. The starting point of the horizontal stroke is still to the left of that of the vertical stroke, but Wang's algorithm treats the vertical point as twice as important, so the vertical stroke is still written earlier.

(90) a 十
      b 上

110 *Character phonology and phonetics*

As complex as his algorithm already is for these maximally simple cases, Wang (1983, pp. 187–199) is forced to add six further provisions to it. For example, complex strokes must be decomposed into simple strokes when determining end points or else the end of the complex stroke in (91a) would be treated as just as low as that of the simple stroke, the counterdiagonal in (91b) is first because for diagonals only the ending points matter and not the starting points, and so on for an additional four provisions (some with subprovisions). Wang then ends his long discussion with the acknowledgment that "the exact nature and cause of variant stroke orders are still imperfectly understood" (p. 201).

(91) a 力
      b 人

A phonetic approach to stroke order seems far more promising since it builds on the independently necessary forces of articulation and perception. The articulatory influence is easiest to recognize here. For example, the most basic of the conventional stroke order rules simply encode the universal rightward and downward directions of right-handed writers (see Section 3.6.1).

Articulation also provides a simple framework for how strokes interact, as can be seen by returning to the example of 正. As shown in Figure 3.3, we can derive the standard stroke order simply by minimizing the total path distance of the writing instrument. Any other stroke order would require a longer path; writing the short vertical stroke last, for example, would require a long hop from the end of the bottommost horizontal stroke. Lin (2014) has the same insight, but cannot resist turning it into a one-size-fits-all prescriptive principle, missing the more fundamental point of Yin (2016), noted earlier, that writers, like speakers and signers, ultimately need to find their own articulatory way.

The phonetic approach to stroke order also helps explain where variation can occur. One situation is when competing articulatory constraints are equally applicable. The 'first horizontal, then vertical' rule, for example, is no better at minimizing the total path distance in (92a) than the 'first top, then bottom' convention

Figure 3.3 Writing path for standard stroke order in 正

Figure 3.4 Writing paths for standard stroke orders in 十 and †

used for the Roman letters like (92b), as illustrated in Figure 3.4. This arbitrary cross-system difference is akin to arbitrary but consistent differences in phonetic detail across spoken or signed languages (e.g., Gick *et al.* 2004).

(92) a 十
       b †

We can even track the learning of such arbitrary conventions in time. In their study of line drawing habits, Goodnow and Levine (1973) observed that when copying a cross (+), American children initially had no strong preference for which stroke to draw first, but as they got older, they gradually switched to the Western convention of drawing the vertical stroke (top of +) before the horizontal one (left of +); see Figure 3.5 (based on part of their Figure 2, p. 88).

The Chinese horizontal-before-vertical convention is not followed strictly even within Chinese. According to Zhang and Cheung (2013), the standard stroke orders taught in the People's Republic of China and in Taiwan differ for at least 32 character constituents that are otherwise identical between the two systems. For example, in Taiwan, the crossed horizontal and vertical strokes in (93) are written in accordance with 'first horizontal, then vertical,' but in the PRC, this order is reversed, instead conforming to the Western stroke order convention.

(93) 里 黑 冉 重

The same variation is seen across individuals trained within the same teaching tradition. Katayama, Uchida, and Sakoe (2009) analyzed the stroke orders in 3 million handwritten kanji tokens from 283 Japanese writers, collected via trackpads by Nakagawa and Matsumoto (2004). Among other things, Katayama *et al.* observe that about 15 percent of the time the central vertical stroke in the character in (94) is written before the two horizontal strokes that cross it, thereby violating the 'first horizontal, then vertical' rule prescriptively required here.

(94) 用

112 *Character phonology and phonetics*

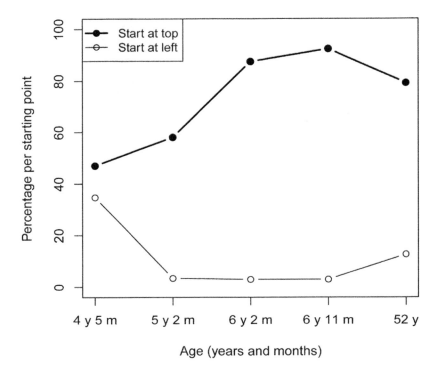

Figure 3.5 The learning of the Western stroke order convention for +
Source: Based on Figure 2 in Goodnow and Levine (1973, p. 88).

The result is a conflict between 'first horizontal, then vertical' and 'first left, then right,' as reflected in the order variation in horizontal and vertical strokes sharing the same upper left starting point. For the characters in (95a), Taiwanese conventions order the left vertical stroke first, whereas the PRC conventions order the top horizontal stroke first. Wang (1983, p. 194) reports similar variation in the left-stroke group in the constituent in (95b), this time across individual writers of traditional characters. Wang also observes that the stroke order variation on the left in (95b) is not seen in (95c), where the hooked vertical stroke is always written after the 日-like stroke group at its top. Interestingly, this orders it just before the crossed strokes to its right, making this look like another case where stroke order (vertical last) is driven by stroke configuration (rightward hooking), rather than the other way around (see also Section 3.6.2.1).

(95) a 皮 镸
     b 門
     c 艮

Character phonology and phonetics 113

Stroke order variation can also result from competition between articulatory and visual constraints. Visual symmetry is presumably responsible for the 'first center, then sides' rule that applies in (96a). However, this conflicts with the articulatorily motivated 'first left, then right' rule. Based on the contrasting stroke orders listed in Zhang and Cheung (2013), the PRC conventions also apply the visually motivated center-first rule to the idiosyncratic allomorph of 心 in (96b), with the vertical stroke first, whereas the Taiwanese conventions follow the articulatorily motivated left-to-right ordering for all three strokes.

(96)　a　小
　　　　b　忄

Further highlighting the different ways to resolve the same constraint conflict, in the vertically arranged dots in (97) it is now the prescriptive PRC conventions that follow the articulatorily motivated 'first top, then bottom' rule (writing the top dot, then the horizontal stroke, then the bottom dot), whereas the prescriptive Taiwanese conventions visually pair the dots (writing the horizontal stroke, then the top dot, then the bottom dot).

(97)　母 舟

A visual/articulatory conflict may also be responsible for the stroke order variation in (98). The PRC follows the 'dots last' rule here, which seems to be visually motivated, since dots have only a minimal effect on the overall appearance of a constituent, regardless of their location. However, dots are also strokes, and strokes tend to be written from left to right and top to bottom, which is the articulatorily motivated convention followed in Taiwan for this constituent.

(98)　戈

Another type of variation apparently resulting from articulatory/visual conflicts is that shown in (99a). According to both PRC and Taiwanese conventions, the complex hooked stroke 乛 is supposed to be written before the counterdiagonal, but it seems that many writers prefer to write the counterdiagonal first, in accordance with 'first left, then right.' These individual alternatives are codified for (99b), which obeys 'first left, then right' in Taiwan but not in the PRC. The motivation for those who write the more complex stroke first may be visual, since it takes up more area than the simple stroke, and thus does more to affect the overall layout of the character. A similar motivation may underlie the otherwise anomalous horizontal-last stroke order for (99c) that is standard across teaching conventions.

(99)　a　方
　　　　b　乃
　　　　c　女

114   *Character phonology and phonetics*

The 'first outside, then inside,' 'bottom of box last,' and 'left/bottom stroke last' rules may also be motivated by a combination of visual and articulatory forces. The orders they assign to the constituents in (100) seem designed to lay out the visual frame before filling in the details, then finishing at the bottom as articulation prefers.

(100) a 同
       b 目
       c 匹

Given the permeable boundary between phonetics and phonology, however, I must admit that stroke order is not pure physics. We have already seen that it may be differently conventionalized across teaching traditions. More surprisingly, it also shows limited sensitivity to character morphology. This is already seen in the simple fact that in multi-constituent characters, one constituent is generally completed before the next is started. Order variation can thus arise when the decomposition of a stroke group is ambiguous. For example, stroke order for the constituent in (101a) follows 'first left, then right' for some writers, while others write the diagonal stroke first or last, as if (104a) contains the constituent in (101b).

(101) a 必
       b 心

A conventional way to defend the border between phonology and phonetics despite such evidence would be to posit that morphology actually affects prosody, and it is prosody, not morphology itself, that phonetics is sensitive to (Selkirk 1986). This solution is not fully satisfying with examples like 必, let alone in spoken languages. For example, Steriade (2000), following Withgott (1982), points to American English words like *mílitàrism*, in which [tʰ] is permitted to have the lexically non-contrastive feature of aspiration, normally disallowed in unstressed syllables, out of faithfulness to the morphologically related *mílitàry*, where the syllable containing [tʰ] is stressed. It really looks like phonetics may sometimes see morphology directly.

Wang (1983, p. 139) describes another stroke order pattern apparently requiring a similar border skirmish. The radicals in (102a) are written last, in accordance with 'left/bottom radicals last,' but despite having a superficially similar form, the radicals in (102b) are not written last. The explanation, Wang points out, is that the latter radicals are derived from the constituents in (102c) via the regular stroke stretching process, so that 'underlyingly' they are left-edge radicals, not left/bottom radicals. This contrast implies that constituent ordering (which I ascribe to phonetics) is determined before stretching (which I ascribe to phonology). It does not help to note that the second radical in (102a) is, at least etymologically, derived by stretching as well, as indicated in (102d), since as we have seen, idiosyncratic allomorphs behave quite differently from regularly derived ones. I think that I

Character phonology and phonetics 115

simply must admit that this particular aspect of stroke order, unlike any of the many other aspects we have discussed, has truly been phonologized.

(102) a 建　道
　　　b 趕　麵　颱　魅
　　　c 走　麥　風　鬼
　　　d 辵～道

3.7. Summary

This chapter has shown that Chinese characters have duality of patterning, that is, phonological regularities unrelated to how the character is interpreted. Central to character phonology is character prosody, which I express via a structural template that helps explain a wide range of superficially very different generalizations: the most favored positions for semantic radicals, the effect of radical shape on radical position and vice versa, the locations for idiosyncratic allomorphy and regular reduction, reduplication shapes, the enlargement of strokes and stroke groups, the rightward stretching of the bottommost stroke in some left-edge radicals, and the location of the curved vertical stroke and why constituent width matters to it. Like prosodic structure in spoken and signed languages, the prosodic template in characters is sensitive to morphology, shows a binary asymmetry between weak and strong positions, accounts for both prominence and reduplication, and shows phenomena similar to weight and stress clash. Unlike lexical prosody in spoken and signed languages, however, the character template also shows symmetry, is recursively applied, does not iterate within morphological constituents, shapes total rather than partial reduplication, and tolerates the splitting of reduplicated structures.

Character phonology is also seen in the restricted inventory of simple strokes, which can be parameterized by axis (vertical, horizontal, main diagonal, counterdiagonal), direction (distinctive only for the counterdiagonal), curving, and hooking, with dots taking the default values (no lexically specified axis). Complex strokes are chains of simple strokes; apparent hooks that can participate in a stroke chain are actually short strokes. Stroke interactions are also highly restricted; besides chaining, a stroke can have no contact, cross another, end at contact, or start at contact, with the last the most common. Non-contacting strokes are almost always either dots or full strokes parallel to an adjacent stroke, due to feature filling via defaults or assimilation. Dot axis can also be modified under complex circumstances with no obvious similarity with spoken and signed languages, particularly in the role played by symmetry. Full strokes also undergo shape alternations, via processes like dotting, diagonalization, shrinking, and stretching (highly regular), curving (less regular), and hooking (least regular).

Like lexical phonology in spoken and signed languages, character phonology has lexical exceptions, manipulates lexically distinctive structures rather than creating new ones, and interacts with morphology. Stroke patterns that are restricted to apply within constituents can also help reveal otherwise obscure constituent

116 *Character phonology and phonetics*

boundaries. Curving comes in two variants, one more lexicalized (left-edge radicals) and one less lexicalized (constituent-internal).

Though character phonology involves abstract and categorical representations, it is also similar to spoken and signed phonology in being motivated by character phonetics: manual articulation and visual perception. Stroke direction, the prosodic template, and left-edge curving may all derive ultimately from the physiology of right-handed writers, while the preference for horizontal and vertical strokes and the symmetry seen in dot rows and triangular reduplication seem to relate to visual biases. Stroke order, which is mostly invisible to learners, is also constrained partly by articulation and partly by vision, and where the constraints compete or are indecisive, variant stroke orders appear.

Like other aspects of character phonetics, stroke order has certainly shaped character phonology, including dotting and diagonalization, which shorten the path from one constituent to the next, and hooking, which often points towards the stroke to be written next, but these influences must be diachronic: not only has character phonology remained the same for centuries, even in printing and left-handed writing, but processes like diagonalization can apply to non-final strokes, or even require reversing the usual stroke order. Nevertheless, stroke order is also sometimes sensitive to character morphology, most notably in the ordering of left/bottom constituents, suggesting that, again as in spoken and signed languages, the boundary between phonetics and phonology is not sharp.

As noted at the outset of this chapter, character phonology has received much less attention than character morphology, so I hope my brief survey will help inspire further research in this area. In the following two chapters, I demonstrate productivity in both domains of character grammar, starting in Chapter 4 with corpus-based evidence.

References

Aronoff, M., 1994b, *Morphology by itself: Stems and inflectional classes*, MIT Press, Cambridge, MA.

Beckman, M.E. and Edwards, J., 1990, "Lengthening and shortening and the nature of prosodic constituency", in J. Kingston and M.E. Beckman, eds., *Papers in laboratory phonology I: Between the grammar and the physics of speech*, pp. 152–178, Cambridge University Press, Cambridge.

Bird, S. and Ellison, T.M., 1994, "One-level phonology: Autosegmental representations and rules as finite automata", *Computational Linguistics*, 20(1), pp. 55–90.

Blevins, J., 2004, *Evolutionary phonology: The emergence of sound patterns*, Cambridge University Press, Cambridge.

Borowsky, T., 1990, *Topics in the lexical phonology of English*, Garland Publishing, New York.

Browman, C.P. and Goldstein, L., 1988, "Some notes on syllable structure in articulatory phonology", *Phonetica*, 45(2–4), pp. 140–155.

Carstairs-McCarthy, A., 1999, *The origins of complex language: An inquiry into the evolutionary beginnings of sentences, syllables, and truth*, Oxford University Press, Oxford.

Changizi, M.A. and Shimojo, S., 2005, "Character complexity and redundancy in writing systems over human history", *Proceedings of the Royal Society of London B: Biological Sciences*, 272(1560), pp. 267–275.

Changizi, M.A., Zhang, Q., Ye, H. and Shimojo, S., 2006, "The structures of letters and symbols throughout human history are selected to match those found in objects in natural scenes", *The American Naturalist*, 167(5), pp. E117–E139.

Cohen-Goldberg, A.M., 2017, "Informative differences: An argument for a comparative approach to written, spoken, and signed language research", in S. Plane, C. Bazerman, F. Rondelli, C. Donahue, A.N. Applebee, C. Boré, P. Carlino, M.M. Larruy, P. Rogers and D. Russell, eds., *Research on writing: Multiple perspectives*, pp. 457–476, The WAC Clearinghouse and CREM, Fort Collins, CO.

Cohn, A.C., 2007, "Phonetics in phonology and phonology in phonetics", *Working Papers of the Cornell Phonetics Laboratory*, 16, pp. 1–31.

Coulmas, F., 1989, *The writing systems of the world*, Blackwell, Oxford.

Duanmu, S., 2004, "A corpus study of Chinese regulated verse: Phrasal stress and the analysis of variability", *Phonology*, 21(1), pp. 43–89.

Gick, B., Wilson, I., Koch, K. and Cook, C., 2004, "Language-specific articulatory settings: Evidence from inter-utterance rest position", *Phonetica*, 61(4), pp. 220–233.

Goodnow, J.J. and Levine, R.A., 1973, "'The grammar of action': Sequence and syntax in children's copying", *Cognitive Psychology*, 4(1), pp. 82–98.

Gordon, M., 2002a, "A phonetically driven account of syllable weight", *Language*, 78(1), pp. 51–80.

Hansell, M., 2003, "Chinese writing", in G. Thurgood and R.J. LaPolla, eds., *The Sino-Tibetan languages*, pp. 156–165, Routledge, Abingdon.

Hargus, S. and Kaisse, E.M. eds., 1993, *Studies in lexical phonology*, Academic Press, Cambridge, MA.

Hayes, B.P., 1995, *Metrical stress theory: Principles and case studies*, University of Chicago Press, Chicago.

Hayes, B.P., 1999, "Phonetically driven phonology: The role of Optimality Theory and inductive grounding", in M. Darnell, E.A. Moravcsik, M. Noonan, F.J. Newmeyer and K. Wheatley, eds., *Functionalism and formalism in linguistics, vol. 1: General papers*, pp. 243–285, John Benjamins, Amsterdam.

Hewes, G.W., 1973, "Primate communication and the gestural origin of language", *Current Anthropology*, 14(1/2), pp. 5–24.

Inkelas, S., 2014, *The interplay of morphology and phonology*, Oxford University Press, Oxford.

Kager, R., van der Hulst, H. and Zonneveld, W., eds., 1999, *The prosody-morphology interface*, Cambridge University Press, Cambridge.

Katayama, Y., Uchida, S. and Sakoe, H., 2009, "Stochastic model of stroke order variation", *10th International Conference on Document Analysis and Recognition*, pp. 803–807, IEEE.

Kiparsky, P., 1982, "Lexical morphology and phonology", in Linguistic Society of Korea, ed., *Linguistics in the morning calm: Selected papers from SICOL-1981*, pp. 3–91, Hanshin Publishing Company, Seoul.

Ladd, D.R., 2014, *Simultaneous structure in phonology*, Oxford University Press, Oxford.

Ledyard, G.I., 1966, *The Korean language reform of 1446: The origin, background, and early history of the Korean alphabet*, Ph.D. thesis, University of California, Berkeley.

Liddell, S.K. and Johnson, R.E., 1989, "American Sign Language: The phonological base", *Sign Language Studies*, 64(1), pp. 195–277.

118 *Character phonology and phonetics*

Lin, G.S. [林桂生], 2014, 汉字笔顺规范的理论是路径法 [Chinese character stroke order theory is the path method]. 黄冈师范学院学报 [Journal of Huanggang Normal University], 34(1), pp. 91–96.

Lu, Q., Chan, S.T., Li, Y. and Li, N.L., 2002, "Decomposition for ISO/IEC 10646 ideographic characters", *COLING-02: Proceedings of the 3rd Workshop on Asian Language Resources and International Standardization*, Association for Computational Linguistics, Stroudsburg, PA. Database at http://glyph.iso10646hk.net/, accessed 11/19/2018.

Luckiesh, M., 1965, *Visual illusions: Their causes, characteristics and applications*, Dover Publications, New York.

McCarthy, J.J., ed., 2003, *Optimality theory in phonology: A reader*, Blackwell, Oxford.

McCarthy, J.J. and Prince, A.S., 1994, "The emergence of the unmarked: Optimality in prosodic morphology", in M. Gonzàlez, ed., *NELS 24: Proceedings of the North East Linguistic Society*, vol. 2, pp. 333–379, University of Massachusetts, Amherst.

McDonough, J.M., 2003, *The Navajo sound system*, Kluwer Academic Publishers, Dordrecht.

Mielke, J., 2008, *The emergence of distinctive features*, Oxford University Press, Oxford.

Miyake, M., 2017, "Tangut language", in R. Sybesma, W. Behr, Y. Gu, Z. Handel, C.T.J. Huang and J. Myers, eds., *Encyclopedia of Chinese language and linguistics*, vol. 4, pp. 267–274, Brill, Leiden.

Morin, O., 2018, "Spontaneous emergence of legibility in writing systems: The case of orientation anisotropy", *Cognitive Science*, 42(2), pp. 664–677.

Nakagawa, M. and Matsumoto, K., 2004, "Collection of on-line handwritten Japanese character pattern databases and their analyses", *Document Analysis and Recognition*, 7(1), pp. 69–81.

Nespor, M. and Vogel, I., 1986, *Prosodic phonology*, Foris Publications, Dordrecht.

Ninio, A. and Lieblich, A., 1976, "The grammar of action: 'Phrase structure' in children's copying", *Child Development*, 47(3), pp. 846–850.

Ohala, J.J., 1990, "There is no interface between phonology and phonetics: A personal view", *Journal of Phonetics*, 18(2), pp. 153–172.

Pater, J., 2000, "Non-uniformity in English secondary stress: The role of ranked and lexically specific constraints", *Phonology*, 17(2), pp. 237–274.

Pater, J., 2009, "Morpheme-specific phonology: Constraint indexation and inconsistency resolution", in S. Parker, ed., *Phonological argumentation: Essays on evidence and motivation*, pp. 123–154, Equinox, London.

Peust, C., 2006, "Script complexity revisited", *Glottometrics*, 12, pp. 11–15.

Port, R.F. and Leary, A.P., 2005, "Against formal phonology", *Language*, 81(4), pp. 927–964.

Saltzman, E.L. and Munhall, K.G., 1989, "A dynamical approach to gestural patterning in speech production", *Ecological Psychology*, 1(4), pp. 333–382.

Sampson, G., 1985, *Writing systems*, Stanford University Press, Stanford.

Sandler, W., 1993, "A sonority cycle in American Sign Language", *Phonology*, 10(2), pp. 243–279.

Sapir, E., 1921, *Language: An introduction to the study of speech*, Harcourt, Brace and Company, New York.

Selkirk, E., 1986, "On derived domains in sentence phonology", in C. Ewen and J. Anderson, eds., *Phonology yearbook* 3, pp. 371–405, Cambridge University Press, Cambridge.

Sproat, R., 2000, *A computational theory of writing systems*, Cambridge University Press, Cambridge.

Steriade, D., 1999, "Alternatives to syllable-based accounts of consonantal phonotactics", UCLA ms.

Character phonology and phonetics   119

Steriade, D., 2000, "Paradigm uniformity and the phonetics-phonology boundary", in M.B. Broe and J.B. Pierrehumbert, eds., *Papers in laboratory phonology V: Acquisition and the lexicon*, pp. 313–334, Cambridge University Press, Cambridge.

Tsai, C.H., 2006, *Frequency and stroke counts of Chinese characters*, http://technology.chtsai.org/charfreq/, accessed 11/17/2018.

Unicode Consortium, 2018, *CJK Strokes*, www.unicode.org/charts/PDF/U31C0.pdf, accessed 11/17/2018.

Wan, Y., 2017, "Stroke order", in R. Sybesma, W. Behr, Y. Gu, Z. Handel, C.T.J. Huang and J. Myers, eds., *Encyclopedia of Chinese language and linguistics*, vol. 4, pp. 212–214, Brill, Leiden.

Wang, J.C.S., 1983, *Toward a generative grammar of Chinese character structure and stroke order*, Ph.D. thesis, University of Wisconsin, Madison.

Wann, J. and Nimmo-Smith, I., 1991, "The control of pen pressure in handwriting: A subtle point", *Human Movement Science*, 10(2–3), pp. 223–246.

Watt, W.C., 2015, "What is the proper characterization of the alphabet? VII: Sleight of hand", *Semiotica*, 2015(207), pp. 65–88.

Wenderoth, P., 1994, "The salience of vertical symmetry", *Perception*, 23(2), pp. 221–236.

Withgott, M.M., 1982, *Segmental evidence for phonological constituents*, Ph.D. thesis, University of Texas, Austin.

Yin, J.J.H., 2016, "Chinese characters", in S.W. Chan, ed., *The Routledge encyclopedia of the Chinese language*, pp. 51–63, Routledge, Abingdon.

Zhang, H., 2014, "A review of stroke order in *hanzi* handwriting", *Language Learning in Higher Education*, 4(2), pp. 423–440.

Zhang, X. [張小衡] and Cheung, W.K. [張煥淇], 2013, 兩岸漢字規範筆順比較 [A Mainland-Taiwan comparative study on standard stroke order of Chinese characters]. 中國語文通訊 [Newsletter of Chinese Language], 92(1), pp. 17–26.

Zhang, X. [張小衡], Li, X. [李笑通] and Lun, C. [蘭蓀], 2015, 一二三漢英大詞典 [YES-CEDICT Chinese dictionary], *The Journal of Modernization of Chinese Language Education (HK Office)*, 4(1), appendix, http://hdl.handle.net/10397/64049, accessed 12/6/2017.

4 Corpus-based evidence for character grammar

4.1. Introduction

If the character grammar sketched in the previous two chapters is psychologically real and productive, it should be revealed in how people actually use characters. In this chapter, I consider how people coin and modify them, as reflected in text corpora and character databases derived from them; the next chapter examines experiments on how characters are recognized and processed.

I start by taking a second look at the body of existing traditional characters, but rather than merely testing if the patterns are statistically different from chance, as I did in earlier chapters, I now test for quantitative signs of productivity (Section 4.2). I then survey the ancient small seal script and modern simplified characters, to try to see how character grammar came together and whether it remains relevant in the system most commonly used today (Section 4.3). Finally, I look for evidence for character grammar in conventionalized stylistic variation, recent character coinages, slips of the pen, and artistic creations (Section 4.4).

4.2. Productivity in traditional characters

The method used in the previous two chapters was, in essence, qualitative corpus analysis, with an occasional statistical test to show that a pattern was no accident. Yet if the patterns arose through mentally active processes, there should be quantitative clues of more specific kinds. Here, I explore some of these: the statistical distribution of character components (Section 4.2.1), estimates of potential character coinage (Section 4.2.2), and the effect of the number of exceptions on pattern learnability (Section 4.2.3).

4.2.1. Quantifying character decomposition

Many aspects of Chinese characters can be quantified, including token frequency (how often a lexical item appears in a corpus) and type frequency (how many items of a given type appear in the lexical inventory); see Kordek (2013) for a thorough survey and many original analyses. Here, I discuss just three that potentially provide evidence for the nature of character decomposition.

Corpus-based evidence for character grammar 121

Perhaps the best-known result in quantitative linguistics is Zipf's law (Baayen 2001; Zipf 1935, also known as the Zipf-Mandelbrot law due to extra parameters proposed by Mandelbrot 1953): if one sorts units from highest to lowest token frequency, assigning them the ranks one, two, three, and so on, the frequencies tend to be inversely proportional to the ranks, forming a straight line in a logarithmic plot. Zipf's law has been tested in Chinese as well (Schindelin 2017a). While it works relatively well for multicharacter words, the fit is worse when tested on individual characters (Ha *et al.* 2003; Xiao 2008). Xiao (2008) ascribes this to the fact that standardized characters, by definition, form an essentially closed set, making the rarest characters more common than Zipf's law would predict. This result reminds us that no writing system is as productive as the lexicons of spoken and signed languages (see Section 1.4.3.1 on other fundamental limitations of orthography). However, Uttal (2003) points out that Zipf's law, like many mathematical laws, arises in a wide variety of natural contexts beyond language, including city populations and volcanic eruptions. He thus denies that it reveals anything in particular about language or cognition per se.

A second widely studied principle of quantitative linguistics is Menzerath's law (also called the Menzerath-Altmann law; Altmann and Schwibbe 1989; Menzerath 1954), which states that the more constituents there are within a linguistic form, the simpler each constituent is. This law also applies to Chinese character structure (Schindelin 2017b), with Prün (1994) and Bohn (1998) demonstrating that the more constituents contained in a Japanese kanji or simplified Chinese character, respectively, the fewer strokes each constituent contains. Bohn also showed that the more strokes there are in a constituent, the fewer the within-stroke direction changes (i.e., the fewer the simple strokes within each complex stroke). The applicability of Menzerath's law to characters suggests that strokes and character constituents are genuine linguistic units, or else they would not be able to take part in the law's trade-off between the number and complexity of units (a point made explicitly by Prün 1994, p. 150). In other words, the people who coined and modified characters over the centuries did so in a way that distinguished between the stroke level (in character phonology) and the constituent level (in character morphology), providing further support for duality of patterning within characters (see Section 3.2).

The final quantitative approach that I consider is network modeling (see Stalph 1989 and Kordek 2013 for related approaches). Fujiwara, Suzuki, and Morioka (2004) and Li and Zhou (2007) independently modeled the combinability of semantic radicals and phonetic components in Japanese kanji and simplified characters, respectively, as networks that link characters sharing a constituent. Both studies found that these networks have a 'small world' structure, whereby most characters are linked to very few other characters but distributed sufficiently evenly for it to be possible to travel from any character to another along a very small number of links (with mean paths of 2.0 and 3.2 links for kanji and simplified characters, respectively).

While small worlds are found in many systems (most famously in the 'six degrees of separation' of social networks: Barabási 2003), the evenness of the character distribution is grammatically suggestive, since it implies that existing

122 *Corpus-based evidence for character grammar*

characters were coined via a general-purpose constituent-combining operation, rather than via ad hoc analogy from specific characters. Consistent with this, Li and Zhou (2007) found that the statistical properties of artificial lexicons created by randomly combining semantic radicals and phonetic components were virtually identical to those of the actual character set.

This observation is intriguingly similar to one made by Yang (2013) regarding child syntax. While it may appear from child language corpora that children tend to favor certain word combinations over others, as if they are merely emitting multi-word lexical units rather than applying grammar productively, Yang shows that this is an illusion caused by Zipfian word frequency skew. Once this skew is taken into account, children are seen to combine their words as freely as their very small vocabularies allow them to do. In a similar way, the set of actual Chinese characters appears as if it has arisen through the virtually unfettered combination of constituents, as expected if character morphology is truly productive.

4.2.2. *Quantifying character coinage*

If a lexical process is productive, not only should the class it generates be large (high type frequency), but many class members should be rare (low token frequency) or even unique in a corpus (hapax legomena), as if coined on the fly. Of course, lexical items can be rare for other reasons as well, such as if they have become obsolete or if their practical usage is restricted. For example, in his study of semantic-phonetic characters coined since the eighteenth century (see Section 2.3.1.1), Handel (forthcoming) observes that a disproportionate number relate to Western science, including 11 percent in his sample with the historically rare semantic radical shown in (1a), used in the names of gaseous elements like that in (1b).

(1)   a 气 *qì* 'steam'
       b 氧 *yǎng* 'oxygen'

Nevertheless, lexical items that are rare for reasons other than productivity should tend to be unsystematic, rather than falling into morphologically well-defined classes. Building on this idea, Baayen and Renouf (1996) propose quantifying the productivity of a morphological class as the proportion of its hapax legomena relative to all hapax legomena in the lexicon. This can be expressed formally as in (2) (their (2), p. 73), where $V_N(1,c)$ represents the vocabulary size of hapax legomena in lexical class c and h_N represents the total number of hapax legomena across all classes in the set of N lexical items.

$$(2) \quad \wp^{*}_{N_c} = \frac{V_N(1,c)}{h_N}$$

This formula can be used to estimate the relative productivity of semantic-phonetic characters, as compared with semantic compounds and other character

Corpus-based evidence for character grammar 123

Table 4.1 Estimated productivity for character types

Character type	Productivity	Character count	Proportion in sample
Semantic-phonetic	.86	3,804	.81
Semantic compound	.10	550	.12
Other	.04	317	.07

types. I conducted the following analyses on the 4,671 characters in the Academia Sinica corpus (Chen *et al.* 1996) for which I had character type information from Wiktionary (2018), supplemented with Handian (2015) and Zaixian hanyu zidian (2018). Since this sample size is close to the estimated character vocabulary of educated readers (Hue 2003), productivity scores derived from it are interpretable as the probability that the very next character seen by an ordinary adult reader will be unfamiliar for each of these character types.

Table 4.1 reports the productivity score for each character type, along with its associated number of characters ($V_N(c)$) and ratio out of all characters in the sample ($V_N(c)/N_c$). Note that the productivity score for semantic-phonetic characters is slightly higher than the proportion of such characters in the sample: these characters are not merely the most common type, but also the most likely to yield potential novel coinages.

A more flexible way to compare the productivity of these three character types is to plot growth curves, which represent how many lexical items (types) in a class are encountered as more of the corpus is sampled (tokens): the steeper the curve, the more productive the process. By exploiting the Zipf-Mandelbrot law (or other frequency models) to account for hapax legomena and all other frequency ranks, we can also extrapolate beyond our actual corpus to predict how steep this growth curve will remain if new characters continued to be encountered indefinitely (Baayen 2001).

Using this approach, as implemented in the 'zipfR' package (Evert and Baroni 2007) in the R statistical software (R Core Team 2018), we get the graph shown in Figure 4.1. This plot includes the growth curves observed empirically in the set of real Chinese characters, as well as those modeled up to the corpus size (14,214,766 character tokens) using a variant of the Zipf-Mandelbrot law that makes the reasonable assumption that actual vocabulary sizes are always finite (Evert 2004), thus dealing, in part, with non-Zipfian aspects of the character frequency distribution (see Section 4.2.1). As can be seen, semantic-phonetic characters, formed through semantic radical affixation, not only have the highest type frequency, but are also associated with the steepest growth curve, even when projected beyond the observed data. By contrast, the growth curves for the other two character types level off quite early on.

We can also conduct a similar analysis on just the 3,353 semantic-phonetic characters with single-edge radicals (8,031,713 tokens) to compare the relative productivity of affixation at the left, right, top, and bottom. The results in Table 4.2 show, unsurprisingly, that the left-edge position is by far the most productive.

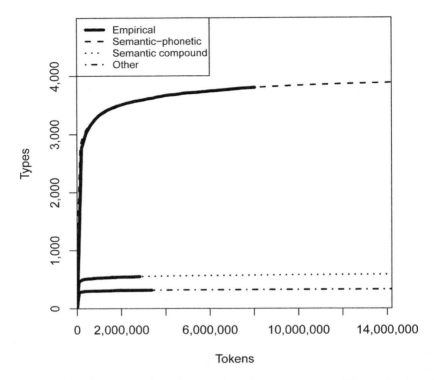

Figure 4.1 Growth curves for three character formation operations, empirical and projected

Table 4.2 Estimated productivity for radical positions in semantic-phonetic characters

Radical position	Productivity	Sample size	Proportion in sample
Left	.70	2,338	.70
Right	.05	221	.07
Top	.12	445	.13
Bottom	.12	349	.10

New is a hint that the productivity for the top and bottom positions may actually be identical, despite there being a slightly greater proportion of characters with top-edge radicals.

The growth curves for these four positions are plotted in Figure 4.2. Again, left-edge radicals are by far the most productive, being the only ones with a rising slope, and again, despite the fact that there are slightly more semantic-phonetic characters with top-edge radicals than with bottom-edge radicals, their flat slopes suggest that both positions are equally unproductive.

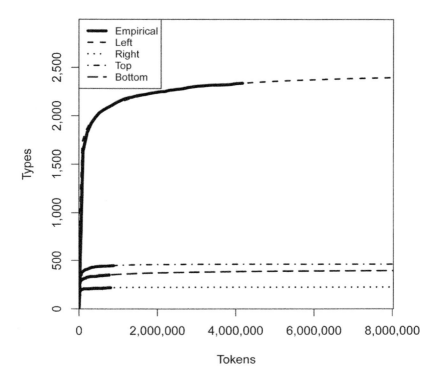

Figure 4.2 Growth curves for single-edge semantic radicals in semantic-phonetic characters

Unfortunately, these sorts of models are not very helpful in testing the productivity of the many other character patterns we have looked at. For example, while the constraints on reduplication shape seem virtually exceptionless, only a hundred or so characters are derived solely via this process. In particular, while there are 58 hapax legomena in the Academia Sinica corpus that contain reduplication, only the two in (3) are derived solely via reduplication. It hardly seems safe to draw any conclusions about reduplication productivity from such paltry evidence.

(3)   幵   㔕

4.2.3. Quantifying exceptions

The productivity of a pattern can be conceived in another way, namely in relation to its exceptions. The simplest way to quantify this would be to count the number of forms (type frequency) that obey the pattern, then divide by the number that the

126   *Corpus-based evidence for character grammar*

pattern should apply to. This idea can be formalized as in (4), where P = productivity, N = number of potential targets, and e = number of exceptions.

(4) $P = \dfrac{N - e}{N}$

Things become more complex when patterns compete with each other (e.g., in the past tense for English verbs ending in -*ing*: *wing* ~ *winged*, *sting* ~ *stung*, *sing* ~ *sang*, *bring* ~ *brought*), leading researchers who adopt this approach to rely on computer modeling (e.g., Albright and Hayes 2003; Kapatsinski 2010). The core idea remains simple, however: the probability that a novel item will undergo a pattern should correlate with the probability that existing lexical items conform to it, an idea dubbed the Law of Frequency Matching (Hayes *et al.* 2009).

For those who think mental grammar should be more decisive than this, Yang (2016) proposes instead that learners use the number of exceptions only to decide whether there are too many of them to bother with a productive rule at all. He proves that, if this rule-vs.-exception model is correct, the maximum number of tolerable exceptions e_{tol} can be estimated using the equation in (5), where N is size of the lexical class and ln N is its natural logarithm (the proof depends on the logarithmic nature of a Zipfian lexicon). If a pattern has fewer exceptions than specified by this equation, it is expected to be learnable, but if it has more, the learner should store all forms in memory as is. Yang tests his Tolerance Principle in wide variety of data sets, including English stress and morphological patterns in English, German, Spanish, Russian, and Polish.

(5) $e_{tol} \approx \dfrac{N}{\ln N}$

Now consider the generalization from Chapters 2 and 3 that semantic radicals favor prosodically weak positions at the left and top. Contrasting these 'regular' positions with the 'exceptional' strong positions along the same axes (right and bottom), we get the class sizes N_{hor} and N_{vert} as in (6) (again counting only semantic-phonetic characters in the Academia Sinica corpus).

(6)   a $N_{hor} = N_{left} + N_{right} = 2{,}338 + 221 = 2{,}559$
       b $N_{vert} = N_{top} + N_{bottom} = 445 + 349 = 794$

These then give us each axis's estimated e_{tol} as shown in (7).

(7)   a $e_{tol}(N_{hor}) = 2{,}559 \,/\, \ln 2{,}559 \approx 326$
       b $e_{tol}(N_{vert}) = 794 \,/\, \ln 794 \approx 119$

As shown in (8), the number of actual exceptions falls below the tolerated number for the horizontal axis, but not for the vertical axis. From this, we predict that the preference for left-edge over right-edge radicals should be learnable, but the slight asymmetry in favor of top-edge radicals over bottom-edge radicals should not be. These predictions are consistent with the corpus-based productivity analyses in Section 4.2.2, and an experiment testing them is reported in Section 5.3.1.

(8)   a $e(N_{hor}) = N_{right} = 221 < 326 = e_{tol}(N_{hor})$
      b $e(N_{vert}) = N_{bottom} = 349 > 119 = e_{tol}(N_{vert})$

The estimates from the gradient frequency matching and categorical rule-vs.-rote models can be computed for all of the patterns described in the previous two chapters. For example, in Section 3.4.6, we saw a curious relationship, first observed by Wang (1983), whereby strokes with leftward hooks tend to make contact on the top. In our sample, the 22 constituents in (9a) obey this generalization, while the ten in (9b) violate it. While the generalization is defined for constituents, in case what might matters to learners is the number of characters containing them, I calculated these as well (using the Chinese Character Decomposition page in the Wikimedia Commons: Wikimedia Commons 2017). This yielded 1,392 characters that obey Wang's generalization and 2,751 that violate it.

(9)   a 了 可 子 手 竹 乎 爭 亦 承 予 丁 京 牙 于 亨
         矛 糸 孑 孓 亍 亇 爭
      b 小 事 才 水 求 寸 事 隶 刂 扌

Since the character counts imply that the pattern should be essentially unproductive according to either of the competing learning models (Frequency Matching and the Tolerance Principle), we will restrict our attention to the constituent counts. For Frequency Matching, the relevant equation simply gives the ratio of regular cases divided by the total; as shown in (10a), we expect that learners will generalize this pattern more often than not. By contrast, as shown in (10b), the number of actual exceptions is higher than that permitted by the Tolerance Principle, so it predicts that the pattern is not learnable at all. These predictions will be tested in other experiments described in Section 5.3.2.

(10) a $22/(22 + 10) = .69$
      b $e_{tol} = (22 + 10)/\ln (22 + 10) = 9.23 < 11$

4.3. Diachronic change

While my primary interest is in the productive character grammar in the minds of contemporary readers and writers, the systematicity of earlier Chinese script systems and the systematic ways in which they differ from the modern system remind us that ancient readers and writers had minds too. I first compare modern traditional characters with the small seal script, the best-studied ancient system (Section 4.3.1), and then I do the same for simplified characters, the most widely used modern system (Section 4.3.2).

128 *Corpus-based evidence for character grammar*

4.3.1. The grammar of small seal script

Small seal script (小篆書 *xiǎozhuànshū*), which arose during the Qin dynasty (221 to 206 BCE), has a special place in character history: it is the system described in Xu Shen's *Shuowen* of the first century CE (see Sections 1.2.1.2 and 1.2.2.1) and remains culturally important (e.g., for personal seals and calligraphy). A practical benefit of this importance is that typefaces for it are readily available. Small seal script also makes an instructively sharp contrast with modern characters; the differences between the oracle bone and small seal scripts, on the one hand, and those between the clerical and modern regular scripts, on the other, are much subtler (as has often been noted; e.g., Jiang 1959; Qiu 2000).

This section sketches the synchronic grammar of this system, an exercise like the morphological and phonological analyses that have been given for the similarly extinct Proto-Austronesian (Blust 2003) and Proto-Indo-European (Byrd 2015), except that the data here have literally been left in writing and do not have to be reconstructed. I first examine the character morphology of small seal script (Section 4.3.1.1) and then its character phonology (Section 4.3.1.2).

4.3.1.1. The morphology of small seal script

Most small seal script characters were decomposable. The examples in (11) illustrate this with a constituent that maintains the same form and interpretation whether used as a free character (11a), as the semantic radical in a semantic-phonetic character (11b), as part of a semantic compound (11c), or as a reduplicated constituent (11d); 'A > B' indicates that B descends historically from A. Keep in mind that my small seal script typeface shows only one variant in a system that was less standardized than modern regular characters (Cheng 1980; Galambos 2006; Ho *et al.* 2010; Qiu 2000).

(11) a 米 > 木 *mù* 'wood'
      b 棍 > 根 *gēn* 'root'
      c 樂 > 樂 *yuè* 'music'
      d 林 > 林 *lín* 'grove'

In some ways, the small seal script was even more morphologically transparent than the modern system. For example, the row of four dots in modern characters (see Section 2.2) neutralizes a distinction in the older system: the quasi-morpheme associated with animals (12a–b) had begun to merge with the constituent for 'fire' (12c) but remained distinct from stroke groups in other animal-related constituents (12d–e). The productivity of this animal constituent has itself waxed and waned over the centuries; Galambos (2014, p. 68) mentions that, in the regular script of the much later Sui and Tang dynasties (581–907 CE), the character in (12f) also sometimes added this row of four dots.

(12) a 魚 > 魚 *yú* 'fish'
      b 燕 > 燕 *yàn* 'swallow'

c 爇 > 熱 *rè* 'hot'
d 馬 > 馬 *mǎ* 'horse'
e 鳥 > 鳥 *niǎo* 'bird'
f 象 *xiàng* 'elephant'

In other ways, morphological structure has become clearer in the modern form. This is illustrated by the semantic compounds in (13), where the constituents for 'moon' and 'water' showed greater formal variation in the small seal script than they do now. As an aside, note also that the constituent on the left in the small seal script character in (13b) was different as well, representing not the sun but a window that the moon is shining through.

(13) a 泉 > 泉 *quán* 'spring (source)'
  水 > 水 *shuǐ* 'water'
 b 明 > 明 *míng* 'bright'
  月 > 月 *yuè* 'moon'

While I have not performed a thorough survey, the examples just cited suggest the intriguing idea that in the small seal script, formal transparency was particularly high for semantic-phonetic characters. This would be consistent with their extremely high productivity even back then, comprising over 86 percent of all small seal script characters (Huang 2003, p. 3; see Section 1.2.2.1). They already showed other affix-like properties as well. Not only did their semantics already tend to be abstract, referring to entire semantic classes, but they also tended to appear in consistent locations, with the left edge already favored over all others (Qiu 2000, pp. 242–243). This generalization may have led Xu Shen and many later scholars to miss the fact, still clear in modern script, that the left-edge constituent in (14) was originally the phonetic component in a semantic-phonetic character, rather than a semantic component in a semantic compound (and likewise for many other such characters; see Section 1.2.2.1).

(14) a 仁 *rén* 'kindness' = 亻(人) *rén* 'person' + 二 *èr* 'two'
 b 仁 = 人 (phonetic) + 二 (semantic)

Nevertheless, semantic radicals were overall less affix-like in the small seal script than in the modern system. Positions were more variable than they are now, and even more so prior to the Qin and Han dynasties (ca. 221 BCE–220 CE) (Qiu 2000, pp. 241–244). Moreover, despite having abstract meanings, small seal script radicals were even less operator-like than modern ones, since they were usually added to an existing character merely to disambiguate it from others. This was done to indicate that a spoken morpheme had split in meaning (15a) (Qiu 2000, p. 332), to adapt a character for a homophonous spoken morpheme (15b) (Qiu 2000, p. 225), or to clarify the original meaning of a character that had been borrowed for its pronunciation (15c) (Qiu 2000, p. 226) (see Qiu 2000, especially

130   *Corpus-based evidence for character grammar*

pp. 225–228, 264–266, and 328–332, for complexities and further character coinage strategies).

(15)   a   輌 > 輛 *liàng* (vehicle classifier)
      = 車 > 車 *chē* 'vehicle' +
      兩 > 兩 *liǎng* 'pair' (for ancient two-wheeled vehicles)
   b   獅 > 獅 *shī* 'lion'
      = 犬 > 犬 *quǎn* 'dog' +
      師 > 師 *shī* 'master' (originally ambiguously 'army' or 'lion')
   c   背 > 背 *bèi* 'back'
      = 肉 > 肉 *ròu* 'flesh' +
      北 > 北 *běi* 'north' (originally 'back')

Semantic radicals still did not reduce either. It is true that Xu Shen had noticed that constituents sometimes seemed to be simplified from how they appear in other characters (using the terms 省聲 *shěng shēng* 'reduced phonetic' and 省形 *shěng xíng* 'reduced semantic'). However, these simplifications applied differently in different characters and typically involved dropping entire constituents, as illustrated in (16) (from Qiu 2000, p. 234 and p. 240, respectively). Moreover, Qiu (2000, p. 239) notes that reduced semantics were relatively rare, and Boltz (1994, p. 117), following Boodberg (1937), even argues that apparently reduced phonetic components may actually indicate polyphony (i.e., that the constituents had multiple pronunciations of their own, rather than inheriting them from the complex forms that they putatively simplify).

(16)   a   潸 > 潸 *shān* 'tearful'
      = 水 > 水 *shuǐ* 'water' (semantic) + 散 > 散 *sǎn* 'scatter' (phonetic)
   b   弒 > 弒 *shì* 'kill one's superior'
      = 殺 > 殺 *shā* 'kill' + 式 > 式 *shì* 'style' (phonetic)

Truly systematic reductions of modern semantic radicals were almost entirely absent in their small seal script ancestors. The regular phonological processes of dotting, diagonalization, and stretching did not yet apply (17a–c), though shrinking did (17d).

(17)   a   木 ~ 根 > 木 ~ 根
   b   土 ~ 地 > 土 ~ 地
   c   走 ~ 起 > 走 ~ 起
   d   竹 ~ 筆 > 竹 ~ 筆

Even the idiosyncratic allomorphy of modern semantic radicals had yet to appear, as illustrated in (18).

(18)   a   心 ~ 悟 > 心 ~ 悟
   b   人 ~ 但 > 人 ~ 但

c 氵~祁 > 水~泥
d 扌~㧺 > 手~打
e 阝~隙 > 阜~院

The inflection-like semantic radical 'agreement' in disyllabic spoken morphemes (see Section 2.3.1.4) also took time to develop, indeed long after the demise of the small seal script. Qiu (2000, p. 28) cites the example in (19), which appeared as (19a) in a dictionary compiled around 230 CE, was reanalyzed as (19b) in a later commentary, and today appears as in (19c).

(19) a 吳公
      b 蜈公
      c 蜈蚣 *wúgōng* 'centipede'

Put together, these observations suggest that in the small seal script, semantic radicals had not traveled as far along the root-affix cline as they have reached in modern characters. This development looks like diachronic grammaticalization, consistent with the evidence given in Section 2.3.1.4.

The historical development of reduplication also involves an increase in formal regularity, even as ever fewer characters were formed via this operation. Reduplication was already attested in oracle bones (Chen 1997; Behr 2006; Liu 2008; Qiu 2000, pp. 197–199), but it was always rare and became proportionally rarer with the growing dominance of semantic-phonetic characters. This is reflected in Figure 4.3 (derived from Table 2.2 in Liu 2008, p. 31), with years representing the onset of the political era associated with each script: oracle bones of the Shang king Wu Ding, bronze inscriptions of the Western Zhou, small seal script of the Qin, and regular script of the Cao Wei (see Chen 1997 and Behr 2006, pp. 96–98, for similar estimates of this quantitative decline).

This drop in productivity was nevertheless accompanied by an increase in formal consistency. In oracle bones, Behr (2006) finds at least nine different reduplication shapes, as opposed to the mere three (horizontal doubling, vertical doubling, upward-pointing triangle) robustly attested in modern characters. He also counts several types of mirror reflections, but even in his sample of 88 oracle bone characters (74 distinct characters, plus variants, not counting one mixed type), only 11 (12.5 percent) are mirrored. Even if mirroring was once a productive process, it is no longer; Tan and Cheng (2017) survey a variety of ancient characters that seem to mirror others, and virtually none continue to be reflections of each other in modern regular script (see Chapters 2 and 3 for other arguments against mirroring being part of modern character grammar). Counts of reduplication shapes in Behr's sample are given in Table 4.3, using his reduplication shape symbols. Interestingly, the three modern shapes already dominated, even when variants are set aside.

The dominance of the three modern reduplicative shapes continued to increase in the small seal script system. Table 4.4 counts the 95 reduplicated characters extracted by Liu (2008, pp. 16–19) from *Shuowen*, including character variants, not including

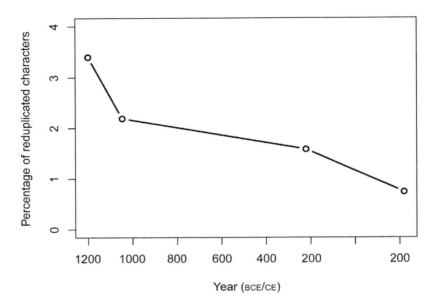

Figure 4.3 The percentage of characters formed via reduplication in oracle bone script (ca. 1200 BCE), bronze inscriptions (1046 BCE), small seal script (221 BCE), and regular script (220 CE)

Source: Derived from Table 2.2 in Liu (2008, p. 31).

mirrored reflections, re-counts of characters containing the same reduplicative form, or apparently non-decomposable constituents. Note the loss of four reduplication categories and the continuing dominance of the three still-dominant shapes.

Based on this brief historical overview, character morphology has been relatively well preserved in the modern system. This stability presumably results from the need to maintain external interpretability, the primary function of orthography, across generations of readers and writers. Nevertheless, small seal script morphology was less systematic than it is today: semantic radicals were less affix-like than they are now, and reduplication, though accounting for an ever-shrinking proportion of characters, has also become more consistent.

4.3.1.2. *The phonology of small seal script*

The historical changes in character phonology, involving externally uninterpreted units and regularities, have been much more dramatic than those in character morphology. Two changes are particularly obvious (see, e.g., Jiang 1959; Qiu 2000): the wholesale replacement of the stroke inventory, from meandering curves to straight lines mostly restricted to just four axes, and the reanalysis of many stroke groups, often via splitting or merging. The linear strokes of regular script may be better suited to rapid ink brush writing than small seal script, but the stroke group

Table 4.3 Reduplication in oracle bone script

Shape	Oracle bone example		Modern	Total (%)	Sole variant (%)
		'sacrificial object'	珏 *jué*	36 (46.8%)	30 (47.6%)
		(name of a person)	炎 *yán*	14 (18.2%)	10 (15.9%)
		'star'	晶 *jīng*	10 (13.0%)	7 (11.1%)
		'multitude of agricultural laborers'	眾 *zhòng*	4 (5.2%)	1 (1.6%)
		'little, young'	少 *shǎo*	3 (3.9%)	1 (1.6%)
		(name of a place)	豩 *bīn*	3 (3.9%)	0 (0.0%)
		(name of a place)	畕 *jiāng*	3 (3.9%)	2 (3.2%)
		(name of a place)	麤 *cū*	2 (2.6%)	1 (1.6%)
		(name of a place)	羴 *shān*	2 (2.6%)	0 (0.0%)

Notes: Classifications, historical glosses, modern characters, and modern pronunciations from Table 3 in Behr (2006, pp. 88–96); first seven oracle bone images from Academia Sinica (2018), and last two based on images in Appendix I of Behr (2006, p. 114).

Table 4.4 Reduplication in small seal script

Shape	Small seal script example	Modern	Count (%)
	'forest'	林 *lín*	54 (56.8%)
	'commodity'	品 *pǐn*	28 (29.5%)
	'more'	多 *duō*	8 (8.4%)
	'multitude of grass'	芔 *mǎng*	4 (4.2%)
	'multitude of agricultural laborers'	眾 *zhòng*	1 (1.1%)

Note: Last two seal script images from Academia Sinica (2018).

134 *Corpus-based evidence for character grammar*

reanalyses, as well as other observations noted later, suggest that the history of character phonology cannot be reduced solely to changes in technology.

Reanalysis in regular script has obscured many small seal script constituents, as seen in the distinct modern reflexes of the 'hand' icon in (20) (the last two highlighted by Qiu 2000, p. 128). This kind of change seems to reflect duality of patterning, with writers sacrificing external interpretability in favor of a new system of strokes and stroke combinations.

(20) a 肅 > 聿 *yù* 'writing brush'
      b 𣪠 > 取 *qŭ* 'take'
      c 彐 > 寸 *cùn* 'Chinese inch'
      d 𠬞 > 弄 *nòng* 'do'
      e 𩙿 > 丞 *chéng* 'assist'

Reanalysis worked the other way as well. The modern stroke group in (21a) neutralizes four distinct seal script constituents, as shown in (21a–d) (see also Section 4.4.1). This may also relate to duality of patterning, but perhaps also to "morphology by itself" (Aronoff 1994b), whereby morphemes are defined structurally rather than via external interpretations.

(21) a 𠂊 > 月 *yuè* 'moon'
      b 𩵋 > 青 *qīng* 'green'
      c 𦘠 > 服 *fú* 'clothing'
      d 𠕄 > 朋 *péng* 'friend'

However, focusing just on differences from modern characters neglects the fact that small seal script had its own synchronic phonological system; its unmistakable visual panache itself represents a sort of duality of patterning. For example, despite their very differently shaped modern descendants, the seal script constituents in (22) all share the same U-shaped stroke. The examples in (22a–f), and perhaps also (22g–h), also show a stroke interaction typical of the system, whereby the U extends 'horns' rather than making endpoint contact.

(22) a 𠂇 > 大
      b 彐 > 又
      c ㅂ > 口
      d 𠂊 > 月
      e 𪅓 > 鳥
      f 𢎨 > 巴
      g 百 > 百
      h 𠀁 > 也

Other seal script regularities are similar to those still found in modern character phonology. This includes the strong tendency for strokes to be parallel, as seen in most of the examples so far; more examples are given in (23a) and exceptions in

Corpus-based evidence for character grammar   135

(23b). Recall that the bias towards parallel strokes (Sections 3.4.2 and 3.6.1) may have a universal perceptual motivation, and in Section 4.4.3, we will see further evidence for this. Thus, its persistence through character history need not result from diachronic transmission.

(23) a 川 > 火   水 > 水   川 > 川
         爪 > 爪   毛 > 毛   飛 > 飛
      b 九 > 九   身 > 身

A less obvious but theoretically more important difference between the phonologies of small seal script and modern regular characters is the virtual lack of prosodic structure in the older system. In Section 4.3.1.1, we saw that the preference for left-edge radicals was already present, but not regular reduction or idiosyncratic allomorphy. None of the other stroke-level consequences of prosody were present either. Stroke size was not even used for lexical contrast, as seen in the lack of size differences in the small seal characters in (24). At the same time, however, absolute distance was occasionally used distinctively, as shown in (25), something never seen in the modern system.

(24) a 日 > 日
      b 曰 > 曰
      c 未 > 未
      d 末 > 末
      e 土 > 土
      f 土 > 士

(25) a 王 > 王
      b 王 > 玉

As illustrated in (26), small seal script did not reliably show bottommost prominence either (see Section 3.4.4 for this pattern).

(26) a 二 > 二
      b 示 > 示
      c 工 > 工
      d 豆 > 豆
      e 車 > 車
      f 羊 > 羊
      g 革 > 革

Small seal script did predictably curve vertical strokes, but symmetrically at both the left and right, not just at the left as in modern characters (see Section 3.4.5). This is true whether curving still appears in the modern forms (27) or not (28). Other modern curved strokes correspond to a different sort of small seal

136   *Corpus-based evidence for character grammar*

curving (29a–b) or to analogy with this (29c), or else had no curved source at all (30). Diachronic transmission seems irrelevant here.

(27) a 爿 > 片
      b 𤔔 > 介
      c 廾 > 井
      d 弗 > 弗
      e 爪 > 爪
      f 月 > 丹
      g 周 > 周
      h 用 > 用

(28) a 冊 > 冊
      b 岡 > 岡
      c 內 > 內
      d 向 > 向
      e 兩 > 兩
      f 角 > 甬
      g 同 > 同

(29) a 巛 > 川
      b 州 > 州
      c 卅 > 卅

(30) a 并 > 并
      b 夕 > 月
      c 角 > 角

It seems equally hopeless to look to the small seal script for explanations of the modern rightward-pointing hook (see Section 3.4.6 for analyses of all modern hook types). As shown in (31), not only are such hooks generally absent in the small seal ancestors of the modern characters that have them, but the crossing-stroke context is generally absent too. At most, we might speculate that the most modern-looking constituents (31f–g) seeded analogical change in the rest.

(31) a 長 > 長
      b 艮 > 艮
      c 衣 > 衣
      d 喪 > 喪
      e 辰 > 辰
      f 氏 > 氏
      g 民 > 民

The history of the leftward-pointing hook is somewhat clearer (see also Wang 1983, pp. 34–37). There were two major diachronic sources: the modern hooks

Corpus-based evidence for character grammar 137

in (32b) are associated with curved strokes in the small seal script forms in (32a), whereas those in (33b) are associated in (33a) with straight strokes that had material to their left. Other leftward hooks had more idiosyncratic sources, like that in (34). These signs of diachronic continuity suggest that modern hooking is not solely due to the mechanical tendency for ink brushes to flick upward at the end of a vertical stroke.

(32) a 卩 可 孚 業 乎 乎 于
　　 b 了 可 子 事 手 乎 于

(33) a 才 水 艸 个 京 牙 寸
　　 b 才 水 竹 丁 京 牙 寸

(34) a 丞
　　 b 丞

However, straight strokes often remained unhooked even when there was material to the left, as in (35), and the reinterpretation of curving as hooking sometimes occurred selectively, as in the minimal pair in (36).

(35) a 木 丬
　　 b 木 丬

(36) a 乎 平
　　 b 乎 平

On the one hand, the synchronic small seal script system suggests that simple stroke parameters and prosody are not obligatory in an orthographic system, even one already as complex as Qin-era Chinese. On the other hand, the fact that regular script has remained far more stable than all earlier Chinese scripts raises the possibility that a sophisticated orthographic phonology does indeed have benefits for efficient reading and writing.

4.3.2. Modern simplified characters

The modern system of simplified characters developed in the People's Republic of China is now the most widely used Chinese character system (Li 1996; Zhao 2005). Roughly speaking, simplification reduced the number of characters, character components, and strokes per character, while maintaining some continuity with traditional characters either by preserving them unchanged or by adapting obsolete, calligraphic, or variant characters and constituents.

The mixed nature of the simplification procedure is illustrated in (37) with the traditional and simplified versions of my Chinese name. Note that I abuse the historical linguist's '<' symbol to mean 'replaced by' rather than 'derived from.' Both of the simplified characters here are old variant forms, but the change in (37a)

138   *Corpus-based evidence for character grammar*

seems merely to involve stroke reduction while that in (37b) involves wholesale character substitution, indeed neutralizing a traditional character contrast; Tsai and Tai (2018) count at least 149 traditional character pairs that are neutralized like this.

(37)   a   麦 < 麥 *mài* 'wheat'
       b   杰 < 傑 *jié* 'hero'

Stroke reduction led to subtler changes too, such as the replacement of the two-stroke ⌐-shaped group at the top of the traditional character in (38) with the single complex stroke ⁊ in the simplified form (the constituent at the bottom also differs, as discussed further in Section 4.4.1).

(38)   骨 < 骨 *gǔ* 'bone'

Handel (2013) argues that character simplification was motivated by a psycholinguistic misunderstanding: strokes per se actually have much less influence on reading and writing than stroke groups and constituents (see Section 5.2.3.2). Nevertheless, simplified characters provide intriguing evidence for the psychological reality and productivity of the grammar we have been analyzing, given that it was developed by scholars who transferred their traditional character intuitions to the new system even while replacing many components in the lexical inventory. I first demonstrate this for simplified character morphology (Section 4.3.2.1), and then I do the same for simplified character phonology (Section 4.3.2.2).

4.3.2.1. Simplified character morphology

While simplification itself lies outside synchronic mental grammar, it has had grammatical consequences. Regarding character morphology specifically, simplification often changed character constituents. Not only have the 214 semantic radicals of the traditional Kangxi system been reduced, in the current government standard (GF 0011–2009: Ministry of Education of the People's Republic of China 2009b), to a mere 201, but many simplified characters contain constituents different from their traditional counterparts. This includes characters that have become monomorphemic (39a) and those with different and (as Handel 2013, p. 44, points out) sometimes inconsistently chosen phonetic components (39b–c).

(39)   a   开 < 開 *kāi* 'open'
       b   灯 < 燈 *dēng* 'lamp'
       c   邓 < 鄧 *dèng* (surname)

More grammatically interesting, however, are changes relevant to character morphology as a system. For example, simplification of a four-dot row into a single stroke is generally permitted only if it is not an independent constituent.

Corpus-based evidence for character grammar   139

This principle helps explain why it is simplified in (40) but not in (41a) (where the row of dots may indicate an animal) and (41b) (where it is the idiosyncratic allomorph of 火 'fire'). As usual, there are exceptions, as shown by the row of dots retained in the apparently single-constituent character in (42).

(40)   a   马 < 馬 *mǎ* 'horse'
       b   鸟 < 鳥 *niǎo* 'bird'
       c   鱼 < 魚 *yú* 'fish'

(41)   a   熊 < 熊 *xióng* 'bear'
       b   热 < 熱 *rè* 'hot'

(42)   燕 < 燕 *yàn* 'swallow'

Simplification has generally increased the grammaticalization trend as well, as suggested by many changed characters that now place the semantic radical at the canonical left edge. While I have not conducted a quantitative survey (which would be complicated by the fact that simplification often ignores character type), the examples in (43) in seem typical, even applying constituent-internally in (43f).

(43)   a   听 < 聽
       b   响 < 響
       c   体 < 體
       d   肤 < 膚
       e   惊 < 驚
       f   热 < 熱

Similarly, the idiosyncratic allomorphy in (44) consistently appears only in the prosodically weak left-edge position, extending the traditional system's alternation to a greater number of semantic radicals (see also Handel 2013, p. 45).

(44)   a   词～警 < 詞～警
       b   铅～鉴 < 鉛～鑒
       c   红～紫 < 紅～紫

These new idiosyncratic allomorphs also help confirm that the split characters in (45) do not involve true horizontal reduplication, given that the central constituent is now overtly reduced, just like the constituent in the leftmost position of the whole character. That is, as argued in Sections 2.3.3.2 and 2.3.3.3, these characters have the structure [X[Y[X]]], with left-edge idiosyncratic allomorphy applying recursively.

(45)   a   狱 < 獄
       b   辩 < 辯
       c   辫 < 辮

140 *Corpus-based evidence for character grammar*

However, character simplification has sometimes reversed the normal course of grammaticalization, with the traditionally bound semantic radicals in (46) now also used as free characters. While such reversals most likely result from the unnaturalness of the system's committee-driven creation, degrammaticalization has also been claimed to occur in spoken language history as well (though see a critical review in Haspelmath 2004).

(46) a 厂 < 廠
      b 广 < 廣
      c 产 < 產

Reduplication also shows grammatically interesting changes in simplified characters, though as usual they are not consistent. Table 4.5 illustrates several simplification strategies.

Though seemingly trivial, the first three strategies (a–c) preserve a key morphological component of reduplication, namely the reduplicated constituent itself. The next strategy (d) is even more grammatically interesting, since it preserves the abstract prosodic template, even while changing the reduplicated constituent. The next three strategies (e–g) preserve, or even create, reduplicative structures in other ways. Only the final two strategies (h–i) fail to preserve any aspect of the traditional reduplicative structure. This is so even though reviving obsolete templates along with the obsolete characters would have served the goal of reducing stroke

Table 4.5 The treatment of reduplication in character simplification

Strategy	*Examples*		
a. Do not change	林 比 兢 朋 弱 窳 替 昌		
	圭 多 炎 哥 品 器 缀 < 綴		
b. Simplify each constituent	骉 < 驫		
c. Do not reduplicate, but preserve constituent	虫 < 蟲	齿 < 齒	奸 < 姦
d. Preserve reduplicative template abstractly	枣 < 棗	双 < 雙	莹 < 瑩
	两 < 兩	办 < 辦	变 < 變
	丧 < 喪	来 < 來	伞 < 傘
	晋 < 晉	聂 < 聶	轰 < 轟
	奔 < 犇		
e. Remove/replace non-reduplicated part	丽 < 麗	从 < 從	丝 < 絲
f. Apply more canonical reduplicative template	众 < 眾		
g. De novo reduplication	宫 < 宮	丛 < 叢	
h. Merge reduplicants into a new constituent	戋 < 戔	继 < 繼	质 < 質
	金 < 僉		
i. Eliminate reduplication entirely	尔 < 爾	吓 < 嚇	选 < 選
	粗 < 麤	刍 < 芻	灵 < 靈
	钥 < 鑰		

Corpus-based evidence for character grammar 141

count just as well. For example, the simplified character in (47) was taken from an old variant that conformed to the triangular template, rather than maintaining the horizontal tripling of 人 seen in small seal script. The standard traditional form in the middle of (47) avoids violating the modern reduplication template in another way, by reanalyzing horizontal tripling as split doubling. The variant character in (48) illustrates yet another strategy: recursive affixation.

(47)   众 < 眾 < 屭

(48)   伙

Finally, reduplication in simplified characters also continues to obey the generalization that it may only undergo regular reduction processes, as illustrated by the presence of dotting but not idiosyncratic allomorphy in (48) (see also Section 3.3.1.2).

(49)   从 < 從

4.3.2.2. Simplified character phonology

The most obvious effect of simplification on character phonology is the increase in duality of patterning. In (50), each row of simplified characters shows new (near) minimal contrasts.

(50)   a 龟 < 龜   电 < 電
       b 发 < 發/髮   龙 < 龍   友 < 友
       c 无 < 無   天 < 天

As with character morphology, however, character phonology in simplified characters remains very similar to that in the traditional system. The traditional stroke inventory is preserved, though sometimes in different roles. For example, the complex stroke in the simplified idiosyncratic allomorph in (51a) was already attested in the regularly diagonalized form in (51b).

(51)   a 语 < 語
       b 九 ~ 鳩

Stroke groups also continue favor the same interactions as in traditional characters. In the simplified constituents in (52a–c), for instance, all non-contacting strokes are parallel to an adjacent stroke (see Section 3.4.2). Note that the oblique stroke in (52d) makes contact, exempting it from axis assimilation just like (52e).

(52)   a 旧 < 舊
       b 鱼 < 魚
       c 马 < 馬

142 *Corpus-based evidence for character grammar*

    d 长 < 長
    e 才 < 才

The treatment of dots in simplified characters also retains traditional patterns. The default direction continues to be the unmarked falling main diagonal (53a–b), and the tendency for dots to favor the top right (see Section 3.4.2) remains too (53c–e).

(53) a 门 < 門
      b 义 < 義
      c 书 < 書
      d 发 < 發/髮
      e 龙 < 龍

Bottommost prominence (see Section 3.4.4) is also retained under simplification (54). Particularly interesting are (54f–g), where simplification has created a new target for it.

(54) a 车 < 車
      b 晋 < 晉
      c 并 < 並
      d 丧 < 喪
      e 专 < 專
      f 来 < 來
      g 金 < 僉

The restriction of prominence to strokes without endpoint contact also generalizes in simplified characters, as illustrated by the loss of topmost prominence in the simplified forms in (55a–b) now that the central stroke in the 'hand' constituent no longer crosses on the right end. The decision in (55c) to simplify the row of four dots into a single dot, rather than the usual horizontal stroke, may have a similar motivation, given the small space available.

(55) a 寻 < 尋
      b 雪 < 雪
      c 为 < 為

In contrast to prominence, curving and hooking are treated somewhat differently in simplified characters; in Chapter 3 we saw that even in traditional characters they have more exceptions. Regarding curving, the simplified system has adopted the non-curved variant of the character in (56a) (see also Section 4.4.1). This may be because the constituent consists of two separate parts, which tends to disfavor curving, as we saw in Section 3.4.5. Alternatively, curving could be blocked by analogy with the similar character in (56b), due to its inapplicability with bottom stroke contact.

Corpus-based evidence for character grammar   143

(56)   a 非 < 非
       b 韭 < 韭

The simplified system also tends to preserve the etymological form of the leftmost stroke despite changes in the conditioning environment. In (57a), for example, simplification frees the bottom of the left-edge stroke, but it remains straight anyway, unlike the contrasting simplified characters in (57b).

(57)   a 贝 < 貝
       b 月   目

Similarly, in (58a), two stroke groups are combined into one, but unlike the contrasting traditional pair in (58b), this change does not trigger left-edge curving.

(58)   a 门 < 門
       b 周   門

Curving also ignores changes in constituent width (see Section 3.4.5): in (59a), simplification has changed a taller-than-wide traditional constituent into a wider-than-tall one, but curving is retained. Compare this with the width-dependent change in curving shown by the idiosyncratic alternation in (59b), retained in the simplified system.

(59)   a 风 < 風
       b 肉 ~ 月

Regarding hooking, the character in (60a) seems to violate what in traditional characters is an exceptionless generalization, whereby a true rightward hook always has crossed strokes to its right (see Section 3.4.6). However, even in traditional characters rightward hooks can also be derived from L-shaped complex strokes, and the simplified system seems to have lexicalized the output of this latter process, as shown by the newly idiosyncratic allomorphs in (60b–c). The hook in (60a) may thus be lexically specified. Alternatively, its upper oblique stroke may suffice as a 'crossing' trigger.

(60)   a 长 < 長
       b 金 ~ 银 < 金 ~ 銀
       c 言 ~ 话 < 言 ~ 話

The link between leftward hooking and asymmetry, already rather weak in traditional characters, is further obscured in the simplified system. In some cases, the creation of, or increase in, asymmetry in the simplified system does not trigger hooking of the central vertical stroke, as in (61).

(61)   a 车 < 車
       b 书 < 書

144 *Corpus-based evidence for character grammar*

In other cases, newly created asymmetry does correlate with a newly added hook, as in (62a–b). Alternatively, this may simply be due to analogy with the character in (62c).

(62) a 东 < 東
      b 拣 < 揀
      c 小

Finally, the simplified and traditional systems are virtually identical in character phonetics, aside from the arbitrary variation in prescriptive stroke orders noted in Section 3.6.2.2. For example, recall that in the traditional system, the semantic radical in (63a) undergoes diagonalization when used as a semantic radical, reversing the stroke order so that the diagonalized stroke can be put last, minimizing the distance to the top of the next constituent. The simplified system retains this reversal, but also shows precisely the same dependence of stroke order (phonetics) on stroke form (phonology) in the semantic radical in (63b). This example thus demonstrates not just the continuing productivity of diagonalization but also its phonological, not phonetic, nature.

(63) a 牛～物 < 牛～物
      b 车～较 < 車～較

Put together, the observations in this and the previous section suggest that the simplified character system was compiled by people for whom traditional character grammar was psychologically real and productive, enough so that it was maintained, to a large extent, even in novel stroke groups and constituent combinations.

4.4. Character variation

In this section, I consider how Chinese character grammar is reflected in the ways writers go beyond canonical character forms. I first look at different calligraphic and typeface styles (Section 4.4.1), then individual writing habits and accidents (Section 4.4.2), and finally the playful or artistic creation of new characters (Section 4.4.3).

4.4.1. Conventional stylistic variation

The grammatical analyses in the previous two chapters are intended to apply to modern traditional characters in general, so when I cited examples in support, I used a form of regular script (楷書 *kǎishū*, literally 'model writing'; for discussion of the term and concept, see Qiu 2000, p. 147).

However, calligraphic styles (Gu 2017; Tseng 1993) and typefaces (Palmer 2015; Wilkinson 2000; Wittern 2017) are systematically different, and even within a system, characters may have variants (Galambos 2006, 2014, 2017), and individual writers may have their own habits (see Section 4.4.2). Such variation cannot be analyzed solely in terms of faithfulness to regular script (contra Goldberg and Cohen-Goldberg, in preparation), since they often show lexical idiosyncrasies and may modify, add, or drop individual regularities or entire constituents. Cross-style differences may thus be lexical, morphological, and/or phonological, not merely phonetic.

Morphological variation includes differences in constituent position, as shown in (64). Note that one variant in each row in (64a–b) puts the semantic radical in the default left-edge position. The variation in (64c) may stem from scribal indecision about the constituents' interpretations as semantic or phonetic components.

(64)　a　裡 裏 *lǐ* 'inside'
　　　　　= 衣(衤) 'clothes' + 里 *lǐ*
　　　b　匯 滙 *huì* 'concourse'
　　　　　= 匚 'container' + 氵(水) 'water' + 隹 *zhuī*
　　　c　夠 够 *gòu* 'enough'
　　　　　= 多 *duō* 'more' + 句 *jù* 'sentence'

Character constituents are also sometimes analyzed differently across different styles. Continuing a discussion from Section 4.3.1.2, in (65a) the lower constituents are kept distinct in the regular script forms, but they are neutralized in the sans serif forms in (65b) (黑體 *hēitǐ*).

(65)　a　胃　　青
　　　b　**胃　青**

Even idiosyncratic allomorphy can vary, on a constituent-by-constituent basis, across typefaces. For example, my regular example typeface shows idiosyncratic variation in the semantic radical in the characters in (66a), but in the sans serif typeface (66b), the radicals (often) retain their canonical form.

(66)　a　木～桌　糸～絲　示～神～禮
　　　b　**木～桌　糸～絲　示～神～禮**

Character styles may also differ in decomposition. Close examination of the Song (宋體 *Sòngtǐ*) characters in (67a) and the regular script characters in (67b) reveals a subtle difference in the length of the second-from-bottom horizontal stroke. The Song typeface preserves the etymological structure, with a long horizontal stroke at the bottom of the upper constituent, while the latter style treats the character as if it had become monomorphemic, the extra prominence lost due to stress clash (see Section 3.4.4).

(67)　a　美＝羊＋大　　姜＝羊＋女
　　　b　美≠羊＋大　　姜≠羊＋女

146 *Corpus-based evidence for character grammar*

Cross-typeface differences in decomposition are also revealed via left-edge curving. In my regular script typeface, character-internal curving only occurs in (68a) when the constituents are completely separate (in the first character), but in the sans serif typeface in (68b), curving also applies to the conjoined stroke groups of the last character (a variant of the more common non-curved character in the center).

(68) a 朋 冊 冊
      b 朋 冊 冊

The variant characters in (69) show another phonological consequence of morphological decomposition. While both show leftmost curving, the dots only show reflective symmetry in the monomorphemic form in (69a). Moreover, in the reduplicated variant in (69b), bottommost prominence now applies twice and the lower stroke on the left undergoes diagonalization.

(69) a 并
      b 并

Reduplication also shows a slight phonological difference across character styles. Recall from Sections 3.3.2 and 3.4.5 that in triangular reduplication, the constituent at the lower left may show reduction. In my scheme, the topmost constituent is also in a prosodically weak position, but its weak status is usually not visually obvious. Thus, in the regular typeface, curving only occurs at the left in (70a). However, the sans serif typeface in (70b) shows curving in both weak positions, at the top as well as the left. The process is lexicalized, however, as shown by a similar curving contrast in the individual constituent in (71), where the sans serif font treats the vertical stroke as intrinsically left-edged, like 尹.

(70) a 艸
      b 艸

(71) a 屮
      b 屮

Variation in curving across typefaces may also provide further evidence for the prosodic analysis given in Section 3.4.5, intended to explain why curving is disfavored in wider constituents. In my usual example typeface, the 月 -shaped stroke group retains its leftmost curving in all of the characters in (72a), but the sans serif typeface in (72b) loses it when the stroke group is 'flattened' by material above.

(72) a 月 有 青
      b 月 有 青

Corpus-based evidence for character grammar 147

The variant characters in (73) demonstrate the productivity of stroke axis assimilation: it occurs only in (73a) because the corresponding stroke in (73b) makes contact and that in (73c) is a dot.

(73) a 尸
      b 戶
      c 户

The blocking of stroke axis assimilation by contact is also illustrated by the cross-typeface variation in (74).

(74) a 糸
      b 系

Given the complexity of dot-related generalizations (see Section 3.4.3), it is not surprising that character styles also show considerable variation in their treatment. For example, while the regular script form of the character (75a) arranges the dots to point away from the center, in the sans serif typeface in (75b) the dots retain their default axis.

(75) a 雨
      b 雨

Some of the stylistic variation in dot axis seems to relate to axis assimilation. In (76a), the sans serif typeface assimilates dot axis, unlike regular script (76b). The simplified and traditional characters in (76c) show a similar contrast.

(76) a 雲 舟
      b 雲 舟
      c 氏 < 氐

The preference to start strokes at stroke contact (see Section 3.4.2) is overtly visible in certain styles, as in the simplified regular typeface in (77), whereas it is hidden in the traditional typeface.

(77) a 月 < 月
      b 日 < 日

Prominence, curving, and rightward hooking work exactly the same way in all modern character styles (aside from the simplified characters discussed in Section 4.3.2.2), but the regular script characters in (78a) systematically receive leftward hooks in the sans serif typeface in (78b). This contrast may possibly be due to analogy with 小 and/or 水. However, the same contrast in (79) suggests another factor as well: perhaps hooking is blocked in (79a) because of (near) contact with another stroke, extending the pattern seen in 月 vs. 目. There are exceptions, as always: the character in (80) retains its nearly contacting hook in both of these

148 *Corpus-based evidence for character grammar*

typefaces, and there is no apparent rhyme or reason for the variation in hooking in the traditional and simplified regular typefaces in (81).

(78) a 示 眾
      b 示 眾

(79) a 少 哥
      b 少 哥

(80) a 丞
      b 丞

(81) a 茶
      b 茶

Due to their different physical implementations, character styles of course also vary considerably in phonetics. Individual strokes in regular script, for example, show predictable variations in width, as spelled out explicitly in Wang (1983, pp. 201–203), conventionalizing the marks left naturally by a brush pen. By contrast, cardinal-axis strokes in Song typefaces are entirely straight and of unvarying width, originally because they were carved as embossed reliefs on wooden blocks. The more rapidly written semi-cursive (行書 *xíngshū*) and cursive (草書 *cǎoshū*) styles have different phonetics yet. They may also require strokes to be written in a different order from regular script, though apparently only as a consequence of changes in stroke group structure, again suggesting that phonetics depends on phonology and not just physics.

4.4.2. Individual variation

Handwritten characters often deviate from any conventionalized style, both intentionally and accidentally, shedding further light on the productive knowledge of character grammar.

For example, Wang (1983, pp. 129–134) observes that some writers write some characters, like those in (82), with the embedded semantic radical 'raised' to the left-edge position of the character as a whole (i.e., affixed 'last'), as in (83).

(82) a 哲
      b 塗

(83) a 哲
      b 塗

As (84) shows, only the standard forms are recursively decompositional, but the alternative forms are nevertheless tempting because they put an idiosyncratically reduced semantic radical into its standard left-edge position. These variants are

Corpus-based evidence for character grammar 149

thus something like the English folk decomposition of *helicopter* as *helicopt-er*, etymologically incorrect but grammatically better formed.

(84) a 哲 *zhé* 'wise' = 折 *zhé* + 口 'mouth'
      b 塗 *tú* 'daub' = 涂 *tú* + 土 'earth'

Similar to slips of the tongue and (signing) hand (Fromkin 1971; Hohenberger, Happ, and Leuninger 2002), spontaneous slips of the pen are also revealing about character morphology and phonology. In a small corpus of such slips in simplified Chinese characters, Moser (1991) describes many that manipulate character constituents. Examples of character blends, where the constituents of one intended character are combined with those of another to create a non-lexical character, are shown in (85a–b) (respectively his Ex. 94, p. 34, and Ex. 85, p. 32). The spontaneous creation of novel characters clearly demonstrates productive knowledge of character grammar. Note also that constituent interpretability does not seem crucial: the error in (85a) involves a semantic radical but the error in (85b) involves constituents (立 and 田) that are not synchronically interpretable here.

(85) a Intended: ... 在比较高的层次
                      ... *zài bǐjiào gāo de céngcì*
                      '... at a <u>relatively high</u> level'
         Error: ... 在比辐的层次
                      ... *zài bǐ X de céngcì*
                      '... at a compared to X level'
      b Intended: 真没意思
                      zhēn méi yìsi
                      'really uninteresting'
         Error: 真没畜
                      zhēn méi X
                      'really not X'

Moser's database also shows that character constituents can be extracted from reduplicated structures: 王 is extracted from 琴 in (86a) and 又 from 嗓 in (86b) (respectively his Ex. 86 and Ex. 87, p. 32).

(86) a Intended: 西方的音乐呢, 有<u>小提琴</u>....
                      Xīfāng de yīnyuè ne, yǒu <u>xiǎotíqín</u>. . . .
                      'As for Western music, there's the <u>violin</u>. . . .'
         Error: 西方的音乐呢, 有<u>小捏</u>....
                      Xīfāng de yīnyuè ne, yǒu <u>xiǎo X</u>. . . .
                      'As for Western music, there's the <u>small X</u>. . . .'
      b Intended: 他不唱, <u>他嗓子</u>....
                      Tā bù chàng, <u>tā sǎngzi</u>. . . .
                      'He didn't sing, <u>his voice</u>. . . .'

150 *Corpus-based evidence for character grammar*

Error:　　　　　他不唱，他又....
　　　　　　　　Tā bù chàng, tā yòu. . . .
　　　　　　　　'He didn't sing, he again. . . .'

Slips in alphabetic orthographies show that writers also have knowledge of reduplicative templates; Moser (1991, p. 24) cites the shift in doubling when <letter> is miswritten as <leeter>, and Caramazza and Miceli (1990) describe a dysgraphic Italian writer who made many such errors. Unfortunately, Moser's only Chinese example, in (87) (Ex. 63, p. 24), seems more likely to show the writer anticipating the meaning ('pair') than the orthographic doubling.

(87)　　Intended:　　你到芝加哥我就给你买一双
　　　　　　　　　　Nǐ dào zhījiāgē wǒ jiù gěi nǐ mǎi yī shuāng
　　　　　　　　　　'When you get to Chicago I'll buy you a pair'
　　　　Error:　　　你到芝加哥我就给你买二双
　　　　　　　　　　Nǐ dào zhījiāgē wǒ jiù gěi nǐ mǎi èr shuāng
　　　　　　　　　　'When you get to Chicago I'll buy you two pairs'

Moser (1991) reports errors relating to character phonology as well. The examples in (88a–b) (respectively Ex. 83 and Ex. 84, p. 31) show character substitutions that seem to be motivated by shared strokes. Nihei (1988) elicited similar errors in an experiment where Japanese writers repeatedly wrote the same kanji, and Liu *et al.* (2013) found natural examples in a corpus of handwritten simplified characters used to train recognition software (though in Section 5.2.2.1, I will discuss an experiment that failed to show stroke-level effects on writing).

(88)　a　Intended:　　...那种防火的纸....
　　　　　　　　　　　... *nà zhǒng fánghuǒ de zhǐ.* . . .
　　　　　　　　　　　'. . . that kind of flame-resistant paper. . . .'
　　　　　Error:　　　...那种防光的纸....
　　　　　　　　　　　... *nà zhǒng fáng guāng de zhǐ.* . . .
　　　　　　　　　　　'. . . that kind of light-resistant paper. . . .'
　　　b　Intended:　　你不会因此而生我的气吧？
　　　　　　　　　　　Nǐ bù huì yīncǐ ér shēng wǒ de qì ba?
　　　　　　　　　　　'You wouldn't get mad at me for this, would you?'
　　　　　Error:　　　你不会因此而生我的生吧？
　　　　　　　　　　　Nǐ bù huì yīncǐ ér shēng wǒ de shēng ba?
　　　　　　　　　　　'You wouldn't get get at me for this, would you?'

Though I interpret Moser's examples in morphological and phonological terms, Moser himself, following the literature on slips of the pen in alphabetic writing systems (e.g., Hotopf 1983) and action slips more generally (e.g., Norman 1981), describes all of his writing errors as motoric in nature, that is, as taking place in character phonetics. However, the gestures in his errors are always defined top-down by constituents and stroke groups, and he himself admits (p. 31) that the tops

Corpus-based evidence for character grammar   151

of 光 and 火 are not even written in the same stroke order, suggesting an amodal level of mental representation.

The difficulty of ascribing the properties of handwriting solely to motor control is also suggested by a common habit, observed by Nakagawa and Matsumoto (2004) in their corpus of spontaneous Japanese kanji writing, wherein the constituent 口 is written as a clockwise circle, as in the character in (89). While this modification clearly simplifies the articulation, it is equally clear that the goal is to preserve the visual target.

(89)   癌

Another piece of evidence that handwriting variation, even at the stroke level, is not merely motoric comes from the examples in (89). The typeset regular character in (88a) shows the canonical form, but the handwritten variant in (90b) is also found; Ch'en *et al.* (1989, p. 73) even offer this form as a prototype for students of Chinese as a second language. In (90a), the row of four dots is treated as a separate constituent, allowing bottommost prominence to apply within the stroke group above it, whereas in (90b) it triggers prominence clash, treating the character as monomorphemic.

(90)   a 黑
        b 黑

4.4.3. Artistic and playful characters

While Chinese calligraphy is an art, it is still intended to communicate actual linguistic content using actual characters (at least traditionally; Gu 2017). Artistic and playful impulses have also led to the creation of entirely new characters, however, further demonstrating the psychological reality and productivity of character grammar. As cautious as dictionary-makers and Unicode developers are about expanding the canon, the urge to create new characters remains unabated.

The central role of grammatical knowledge in character coinage is particularly apparent when this knowledge is entirely absent. Figure 4.4 shows Popeye the Sailor hard at work studying what is supposed to be Chinese, as depicted in a 1930s newspaper comic strip by the American cartoonist E.C. Segar. Obviously, however, Segar had never looked at actual Chinese characters very carefully.

Just as non-natives only seem sensitive to the most superficial phonetic features (the supposed 'gutturals' of German, the 'sing-song' nature of tone languages, the hand waving of sign languages), Segar picks up on the variation in stroke thickness that is a phonetic hallmark of regular script, but nothing else. A similar obsession with stroke width is found in faux Chinese fonts for Roman letters, still often seen on Chinese restaurant menus in the West. The rest is pure fantasy, from the circular and twisted strokes of Segar's character phonology to the total lack of morphological decomposition. His inventions do favor the cardinal directions (horizontal and vertical) and the strokes tend to cross or be parallel rather than being arranged every

152 *Corpus-based evidence for character grammar*

Figure 4.4 Popeye studying 'Chinese'

Source: From the July 7, 1932, strip of *Thimble Theatre*. Reprinted with permission of King Features Syndicate. All rights reserved.

which way, but these similarities with real characters most likely follow from the visual universals of orthographic phonetics (see Section 3.6.1).

By contrast, when native Chinese speakers create new characters for joking or artistic effect, they almost always do so via genuine character morphology, just as speakers (or signers) of a language generally coin new words by recombining existing morphemes. Precisely how they do this depends on their metalinguistic beliefs about how characters are supposed to work, making their coinages impure evidence for 'natural' character grammar. In particular, despite the fact that semantic-phonetic characters have been dominant since small seal script, artistically minded writers seem to have a special affection for semantic compounds (see, e.g., Galambos 2014; Behr 2006, 2010). For example, Behr (2006, p. 77) cites a variant of the character in (91a), coined by Daoists by the 1600s, that was composed of the constituents listed in (91a'), with all but the left-edge radical stacked vertically, as a commentary on the foreignness of a rival religion. The example in (91b), apparently coined in Japan (Mair 2011), is similarly witty. The familiar artistic character in (91c) is also interesting in that it conforms to

Corpus-based evidence for character grammar   153

a grammatical reduplicative template (horizontal doubling). However, all such characters are rare in actual text; even the one in (91c) is meant for decoration.

(91)   a   佛 *fó* 'Buddha'
       a' 亻 *rén* 'person' + 西 *xī* 'west' + 域 *yù* 'region' + 哲 *zhé* 'wisdom'
       b   圕 *túshūguǎn* 'library' (cf. 圖書館 *túshūguǎn* 'library')
       c   囍 *shuāngxǐ* 'double happiness'   (cf. 雙喜 *shuāngxǐ* 'double happiness')

The same point is illustrated by those decorative 'characters' containing entire phrases, like that in (92a), and by signage where idiosyncratic allomorphs are returned to full form or even drawn pictorially, as described in (92b).

(92)   a   招財進寶 *zhāo cái jìn bǎo* (expression of wishes for wealth and success)
       b   煮 *zhǔ* 'cook' (with 火 or ● instead of ⺗ for 'fire' at the bottom)

Other playful character coinages are semantic-phonetic, as when psycholinguists create so-called pseudocharacters for their reading experiments (see Chapter 5), or when the linguist Chao Yuan-Ren (趙元任) 'translated' Lewis Carroll's notorious nonsense poem 'Jabberwocky' with the help of novel semantic-phonetic characters for the made-up English words of the original (Chao 1969). Reflecting the folk-linguistic predilection for semantic compounds, playfully coined semantic-phonetic characters often take the meaning of the phonetic component into consideration, but since the forces of character morphology remain mentally active, the coinages still end up with well-formed affix-plus-stem structures.

An amusing example illustrating these points is shown in (93a), which was created by internet users in the People's Republic of China to poke fun at a nonsense syllable uttered by film star Jackie Chan in a TV commercial (Mair 2015). Of course an essential part of the joke is that the character is constructed from Chan's stage name in (93b), but the coiners still recognized that it looked natural to combine an actual semantic radical (龙 < 龍 'dragon'), in one of its common positions (at the bottom edge), with an actual phonetic component (成 *chéng*) that happens to have the same coda as the target syllable (a close enough match for modern readers all too familiar with the opacity of many phonetic components).

(93)   a   夢 *duāng* (nonce interjection)
       b   成龙   Chéng Lóng

Less amusingly, the nonce characters in (94) come from a recent defamation case in Taiwan where it was ruled that the writer's intent was clear, despite burying the offensive word within two layers of semantic radicals (Yan 2018). Both invented characters are nevertheless perfectly well formed.

(94)   蘐莁 (cf. 妓女 *jìnǚ* 'prostitute')

154 *Corpus-based evidence for character grammar*

In another coinage that blurs the line between semantic-phonetic characters and semantic compounds, Ho (2014) describes the brilliantly designed character in (95a), created by Cantonese speakers to express support for the 2014 Umbrella Movement protest in Hong Kong. It not only shows a hand holding an umbrella, but also places the 'hand' radical in its usual left-edge location and makes the remainder a plausible (if ahistorical) phonetic component, given the similar Cantonese pronunciations for the characters in (95b–c).

(95)   a 撑

      b 撐 *caang¹* 'support'

      c 傘 *saan³* 'umbrella'

A rare case of artistic character creation at the level of character phonology is the work of Chinese artist Xu Bing (徐冰). For his installation *Book from the Sky* (天书 *Tiān Shū*, a Chinese idiom for 'it's Greek to me'), first presented in 1988, he invented hundreds of characters with both attested and invented components arranged in ways that preclude interpretation in either meaning or pronunciation (see discussion in Andreeva 2015 and numerous images online). For example, in his characters, genuine semantic radicals, when used at all, tend not to appear in their usual positions. Yet even his non-lexical components use strokes from the genuine inventory and obey formal generalizations like leftmost stroke curving and bottommost prominence. Before I learned of this work, I made a similar (but much less effective) pastiche of an unreadable ancient Chinese book for the cover of Myers (2012), using some of the test items for the experiments discussed in Section 5.3.

4.5. Summary

In this chapter, I gave a brief survey of corpus-based methods that may be used to study character grammar, starting with quantitative models of component combinations, potential character coinage, and the learnability of character regularities. Quantitative methods could potentially also be applied to any of the qualitative evidence I discussed in the remainder of the chapter, from the shifting proportions of character formation operations (in small seal script and simplified regular characters) to the likelihood of making one sort of slip of the pen rather than another, or certain patterns being preserved in a given calligraphic or typographical style. However, not all of the relevant corpora have been compiled to a sufficient size and level of detail for quantitative analysis, and in some cases, it is not clear how they ever could be, as with characters created for playful or artistic purposes.

There are two key grammatical observations that arise from all of this corpus data. First, though the number of characters that people actually recognize and use in daily life is limited to only a few thousand, characters themselves do not form a fixed inventory. We already saw this with the exponential growth in character inventories in Section 1.2.1.2: the productive power of the character system is enormous. If people can invent new characters that maintain the look of existing

Another way to test psychological reality and productivity, of course, is to study how readers and writers read and write characters in real time, under controlled experimental conditions. This is the topic of the next chapter.

ones, they must have knowledge about how characters are supposed to look, above and beyond their own rote memory. Second, this knowledge has a life of its own, since it can be readily transferred across different systems, whether in the shift from small seal script to modern regular script, in the cobbling together of the modern simplified character system, in the composing of nonsense poems and unreadable books, or even in the influence of Chinese character grammar on other orthographic systems (see Vietnamese character morphology in Section 2.3.2, and the orthographic phonology of Korean Hangul in Sections 3.3.1.2 and 3.4.4).

Another way to test psychological reality and productivity, of course, is to study how readers and writers read and write characters in real time, under controlled experimental conditions. This is the topic of the next chapter.

References

Academia Sinica, 2018, 小學堂文字學資料庫 [Primary school text database]. http://xiaoxue.iis.sinica.edu.tw/, accessed 11/17/2018.

Albright, A. and Hayes, B., 2003, "Rules vs. analogy in English past tenses: A computational/experimental study", *Cognition*, 90(2), pp. 119–161.

Altmann, G. and Schwibbe, M.H., 1989, *Das Menzerathsche Gesetz in informationsverarbeitenden Systemen* [Menzerath's law in information processing systems], Olms, Hildesheim.

Andreeva, P., 2015, "From Xu Bing to Shu Yong: Linguistic phenomena in Chinese installation art", *Sino-Platonic Papers*, 256, pp. 54–72.

Aronoff, M., 1994b, *Morphology by itself: Stems and inflectional classes*, MIT Press, Cambridge, MA.

Baayen, R.H., 2001, *Word frequency distributions*, Kluwer, Dordrecht.

Baayen, R.H. and Renouf, A., 1996, "Chronicling the Times: Productive lexical innovations in an English newspaper", *Language*, 2(1), pp. 69–96.

Barabási, A.L., 2003, *Linked: How everything is connected to everything else and what it means for business, science, and everyday life*, Plume, New York.

Behr, W., 2006, "Homosomatic juxtaposition and the problem of 'syssymantic' (*huìyì*) characters", in F. Bottéro and R. Djamouri, eds., *Écriture chinoise: données, usages et représentations* [Chinese writing: Data, uses and representations], pp. 75–114, École des hautes études en sciences sociales, Centre de recherches linguistiques sur l'Asie orientale [Graduate School of Social Sciences, East Asian Language Research Center], Paris.

Behr, W., 2010, "In the interstices of representation: Ludic writing and the locus of polysemy in the Chinese sign", in A.J. de Voogt and I.L. Finkel, eds., *The idea of writing: Play and complexity*, pp. 281–314, Brill, Leiden.

Blust, R.A., 2003, "Three notes on early Austronesian morphology", *Oceanic Linguistics*, 42(2), pp. 438–478.

Bohn, H., 1998, *Quantitative Untersuchungen der modernen chinesischen Sprache und Schrift* [Quantitative investigations of modern Chinese language and script], Verlag Dr. Kovač, Hamburg.

Boltz, W.G., 1994, *The origin and early development of the Chinese writing system*, American Oriental Society, New Haven, CT.

Boodberg, P.A., 1937, "Some proleptical remarks on the evolution of Archaic Chinese", *Harvard Journal of Asiatic Studies*, 2(3/4), pp. 329–372.

156 *Corpus-based evidence for character grammar*

Byrd, A.M., 2015, *The Indo-European syllable*, Brill, Leiden.

Caramazza, A. and Miceli, G., 1990, "The structure of graphemic representations", *Cognition*, 37(3), pp. 243–297.

Chao, Y.R., 1969, "Dimensions of fidelity in translation with special reference to Chinese", *Harvard Journal of Asiatic Studies*, 29, pp. 109–130.

Chen, K.J., Huang, C.R., Chang, L.P. and Hsu, H.L., 1996, "Sinica corpus: Design methodology for balanced corpora", *Proceedings of the 11th Pacific Asia Conference on Language, Information and Computation (PACLIC 11)*, pp. 167–176.

Ch'en, T.T., Link, P., Tai, Y.J. and Tang, H.T., 1989, *Chinese primer: Character workbook*, Harvard University Press, Cambridge, MA.

Chen, W. [陈伟武], 1997, 同符合体字探微 [A close study of Chinese characters constructed by juxtaposition of the same sign]. 中山大学学报，社会科学版 [Journal of Sun Yat-sen University, Social Sciences Edition], 4, pp. 106–118.

Cheng, H.C. [鄭孝淳], 1980, 中華七體大字典 [Dictionary of Chinese characters in seven styles]. 天工書局 [Tiangong Publishers], Taipei.

Evert, S., 2004, "A simple LNRE model for random character sequences", *Proceedings of JADT 2004*, pp. 411–422.

Evert, S. and Baroni, M., 2007, "zipfR: Word frequency distributions in R", *Proceedings of the 45th Annual Meeting of the Association for Computational Linguistics, Posters and Demonstrations Sessions*, pp. 29–32.

Fromkin, V.A., 1971, "The non-anomalous nature of anomalous utterances", *Language*, 47(1), pp. 27–52.

Fujiwara, Y., Suzuki, Y. and Morioka, T., 2004, "Network of words", *Artificial Life and Robotics*, 7(4), pp. 160–163.

Galambos, I., 2006, *Orthography of early Chinese writing: Evidence from newly excavated manuscripts*, Budapest Monographs in East Asian Studies, Budapest.

Galambos, I., 2014, "Medieval ways of character formation in Chinese manuscript culture", *Scripta*, 6, pp. 49–74.

Galambos, I., 2017, "Variant characters", in R. Sybesma, W. Behr, Y. Gu, Z. Handel, C.T.J. Huang and J. Myers, eds., *Encyclopedia of Chinese language and linguistics*, vol. 4, pp. 483–484, Brill, Leiden.

Goldberg, S.J. and Cohen-Goldberg, A.M., In preparation, "Constraint interaction in the analysis of calligraphic scripts", Tufts University ms, Medford, MA.

Gu, Y., 2017, "Calligraphy", in R. Sybesma, W. Behr, Y. Gu, Z. Handel, C.T.J. Huang and J. Myers, eds., *Encyclopedia of Chinese language and linguistics*, vol. 1, pp. 331–335, Brill, Leiden.

Ha, L.Q., Silicia-Garcia, E.I., Ming, J. and Smith, F.J., 2003, "Extension of Zipf's law to word and character N-grams for English and Chinese", *International Journal of Computational Linguistics and Chinese Language Processing*, 8(1), pp. 77–102.

Handel, Z., 2013, "Can a logographic script be simplified? Lessons from the 20th century Chinese writing reform informed by recent psycholinguistic research", *Scripta*, 5, pp. 21–66.

Handel, Z., Forthcoming, "The cognitive role of semantic classifiers in modern Chinese writing as reflected in neogram creation", in I. Zsolnay, ed., *Seen not heard: Composition, iconicity, and the classifier systems of logosyllabic scripts*, The Oriental Institute of the University of Chicago, Chicago.

Handian [汉典], 2015, 汉典 [Chinese dictionary]. www.zdic.net/, accessed 11/17/2018.

Haspelmath, M., 2004, "On directionality in language change with particular reference to grammaticalization", *Typological Studies in Language*, 59, pp. 17–44.

Hayes, B., Siptár, P., Zuraw, K. and Londe, Z., 2009, "Natural and unnatural constraints in Hungarian vowel harmony", *Language*, 85(4), pp. 822–863.

Ho, J.M. [何建明], Hwang, M.C. [黃銘崇], Yuen, K.W. [袁國華] and Lin, J.W. [林正偉], 2010, 國際電腦漢字及異體字知識庫 [International encoded han character and variants database]. http://chardb.iis.sinica.edu.tw/, accessed 11/17/2018.

Ho, T.L.M., 2014, "Letters from Hong Kong: Characters under the Cantonese umbrella", *Asian review of books*, www.asianreviewofbooks.com/pages/?ID=2053, accessed 11/17/2018.

Hohenberger, A., Happ, D. and Leuninger, H., 2002, "Modality-dependent aspects of sign language production: Evidence from slips of the hands and their repairs in German Sign Language", in R.P. Meier, K. Cormier and D. Quinto-Pozos, eds., *Modality and structure in signed and spoken languages*, pp. 112–142, Cambridge University Press, Cambridge.

Hotopf, W.H.N., 1983, "Lexical slips of the pen and tongue: What they tell us about language production", in B. Butterworth, ed., *Language production*, vol. 2, pp. 147–199, Academic Press, Cambridge, MA.

Huang, D.K. [黃德寬], 2003, 汉字构形方式的动态分析 [Dynamic analysis of the formation of Chinese characters]. 安徽大学学报(哲学社会科学版) [Journal of Anhui University (Philosophy and Social Sciences)], 27(4), pp. 1–8.

Hue, C.W., 2003, "Number of characters a college student knows", *Journal of Chinese Linguistics*, 31(2), pp. 300–339.

Jiang, S. [蔣善国], 1959, 汉字形体学 [The study of Chinese character form]. 文字改革出版社 [Writing Reform Press], Beijing.

Kapatsinski, V., 2010, "Velar palatalization in Russian and artificial grammar: Constraints on models of morphophonology", *Laboratory Phonology*, 1(2), pp. 361–393.

Kordek, N., 2013, *On some quantitative aspects of the componential structure of Chinese characters*, Wydawnictwo Rys, Poznań.

Li, J. and Zhou, J., 2007, "Chinese character structure analysis based on complex networks", *Physica A: Statistical Mechanics and Its Applications*, 380, pp. 629–638.

Li, L. [李乐毅], 1996, 简化字源 [The origins of simplified Chinese characters]. Sinolingua, Beijing.

Liu, C.L., Yin, F., Wang, D.H. and Wang, Q.F., 2013, "Online and offline handwritten Chinese character recognition: Benchmarking on new databases", *Pattern Recognition*, 46(1), pp. 155–162.

Liu, M. [刘曼], 2008, 叠体字的历时考察与认知比较研究 [The diachronic study and cognitive comparison of stacked characters]. Ph.D. thesis, Tsinghua University, Beijing.

Mair, V., 2011, "Polysyllabic characters in Chinese writing", *Language Log*, August 2, http://languagelog.ldc.upenn.edu/nll/?p=3330, accessed 11/17/2018.

Mair, V., 2015, "Duang", *Language Log*, March 1, http://languagelog.ldc.upenn.edu/nll/?p=17913, accessed 11/17/2018.

Mandelbrot, B., 1953, "An informational theory of the statistical structure of language", in W. Jackson, ed., *Communication theory*, pp. 468–502, Butterworths Scientific Publications, London.

Menzerath, P., 1954, *Die Architektonik des deutschen Wortschatzes* [The architectonics of the German lexicon], Dümmler, Bonn.

Ministry of Education of the People's Republic of China, 2009b, 汉字部首表 [The table of indexing Chinese character component]. www.china-language.gov.cn/fw/zwxxhpt/201707/t20170703_5392.html, accessed 11/17/2018.

Moser, D., 1991, "Slips of the tongue and pen in Chinese", *Sino-Platonic Papers*, 22, pp. 1–45.

158 Corpus-based evidence for character grammar

Myers, J. ed., 2012, *In search of grammar: Empirical methods in linguistics*, Language and Linguistics Monograph Series 48, Taipei.

Nakagawa, M. and Matsumoto, K., 2004, "Collection of on-line handwritten Japanese character pattern databases and their analyses", *Document Analysis and Recognition*, 7(1), pp. 69–81.

Nihei, Y., 1988, "Effects of pre-activation of motor memory for kanji and kana on slips of the pen: An experimental verification of the recency hypothesis for slips", *Tohoku Psychologica Folia*, 47(1–4), pp. 1–7.

Norman, D.A., 1981, "Categorization of action slips", *Psychological Review*, 88(1), pp. 1–15.

Palmer, T., 2015, *The practice of Chinese typography*, CreateSpace Independent Publishing Platform, North Charleston, SC.

Prün, C., 1994, "Validity of Menzerath-Altmann's Law: Graphic representation of language, information processing systems and synergetic linguistics", *Journal of Quantitative Linguistics*, 1(2), pp. 148–155.

Qiu, X., 2000, *Chinese writing*, compiled and translated from Chinese by G.L. Mattos and J. Norman, The Society for the Study of Early China and The Institute of East Asian Studies, University of California, Berkeley.

R Core Team, 2018, R: A language and environment for statistical computing, [computer program] R Foundation for Statistical Computing, www.R-project.org/, accessed 11/17/2018.

Schindelin, C., 2017a, "Zipf's law", in R. Sybesma, W. Behr, Y. Gu, Z. Handel, C.T.J. Huang and J. Myers, eds., *Encyclopedia of Chinese language and linguistics*, vol. 4, pp. 723–734, Brill, Leiden.

Schindelin, C., 2017b, "Menzerath's law", in R. Sybesma, W. Behr, Y. Gu, Z. Handel, C.T.J. Huang and J. Myers, eds., *Encyclopedia of Chinese language and linguistics*, vol. 3, pp. 1–3, Brill, Leiden.

Stalph, J., 1989, *Grundlagen einer Grammatik der sinojapanischen Schrift* [Foundations of a grammar of the Sino-Japanese script], Harrasowitz Verlag, Wiesbaden.

Tan, F. [谭飞] and Cheng, B.X. [程邦雄], 2017, 汉字形变构字现象研究 [A study on the morphological variation of Chinese characters]. 语文研究 [Linguistic Research], 1, pp. 55–60.

Tsai, P.Y. [蔡邦佑] and Tai, H.Y. [戴浩一], 2018, 漢字文化圈現行常用漢字字形比較 [A systematic comparison of commonly used Chinese]. 第八屆「漢字與漢字教育」國際研討會論文集 [Proceedings of the 8th International Conference on Han Characters Education and Research], pp. 331–379.

Tseng, Y., 1993, *A history of Chinese calligraphy*, Chinese University Press, Hong Kong.

Uttal, W.R., 2003, *Psychomythics: Sources of artifacts and misconceptions in scientific psychology*, Psychology Press, London.

Wang, J.C.S., 1983, *Toward a generative grammar of Chinese character structure and stroke order*, Ph.D. thesis, University of Wisconsin, Madison.

Wikimedia Commons, 2017, *Chinese character decomposition*, https://commons.wikimedia.org/wiki/Commons:Chinese_characters_decomposition, accessed 11/17/2018.

Wiktionary, 2018, *Wikitionary*, www.wiktionary.org/, accessed 11/17/2018.

Wilkinson, E.P., 2000, "The characters: Evolution and structure", in E.P. Wilkinson, ed., *Chinese history: A manual*, pp. 407–426, Harvard University Asia Center, Cambridge, MA.

Wittern, C., 2017, "Encodings, fonts, and input systems", in R. Sybesma, W. Behr, Y. Gu, Z. Handel, C.T.J. Huang and J. Myers, eds., *Encyclopedia of Chinese language and linguistics*, vol. 2, pp. 169–173, Brill, Leiden.

Xiao, H., 2008, "On the applicability of Zipf's Law in Chinese word frequency distribution", *Journal of Chinese Language and Computing*, 18(1), pp. 33–46.

Yan, H.J. [顏宏駿], 2018, 自創文字罵人「妓女」判拘30天 [Person who invented characters to call somebody a prostitute receives 30-day sentence]. 自由時報 [Liberty Times], March 20, http://news.ltn.com.tw/news/society/paper/1185367, accessed 11/17/2018.

Yang, C., 2013, "Ontogeny and phylogeny of language", *Proceedings of the National Academy of Sciences*, 110(16), pp. 6324–6327.

Yang, C., 2016, *The price of linguistic productivity: How children learn to break the rules of language*, MIT Press, Cambridge, MA.

Zaixian hanyu zidian [在线汉语字典], 2018, 在线汉语字典 [Online Chinese dictionary]. http://xh.5156edu.com/, accessed 11/17/2018.

Zhao, S., 2005, "Chinese character modernisation in the digital era: A historical perspective", *Current Issues in Language Planning*, 6(3), pp. 315–378.

Zipf, G.K., 1935, *The psychobiology of language*, Houghton-Mifflin, Boston.

5 Experimental evidence for character grammar

5.1. Introduction

As rich as Chinese character corpora are, their unconstrained nature makes it hard to draw causal inferences from them about the processing of character knowledge, and as records of character production, they say nothing at all about character comprehension. This chapter thus supplements the previous one with evidence for character grammar from controlled laboratory experiments.

Like corpus data, experiments reflect processing, not grammar directly, yet as explained in the first chapter, language use entails grammatical knowledge: in order to process a language, one needs to know it. In particular, if the way in which experimental participants read or write characters depends in part on productive generalizations and not merely rote memory, then a great deal about character grammar can already be gleaned from the ever growing psycholinguistic literature on characters, even if the researchers themselves did not think of their studies in grammatical terms (Section 5.2).

As we will see, however, the fact that psycholinguists generally focus on processing for its own sake means that they have not yet explored character grammar in much depth. I therefore review some of my own experiments on character reading that incorporate a grammatical focus directly into their design, particularly character phonology, which has been almost entirely neglected in the psycholinguistic literature (Section 5.3).

5.2. Grammar and processing

I start my review of the existing literature on Chinese character reading and writing by looking at experimental studies that address one of the most basic properties of character grammar, namely abstractness (Section 5.2.1). Next I turn to the many studies that have probed character morphology (Section 5.2.2) and finally to the few studies related to character phonology and phonetics (Section 5.2.3).

It is important to note at the outset that the psycholinguistic literature is hopelessly inconsistent in the nomenclature for character structure. For example, many studies use 'radicals' for all character constituents (e.g., Taft and Zhu 1997), while others call the same things 'stroke patterns' (Chen, Allport, and Marshall 1996) or 'logographemes' (e.g., Chen and Cherng 2013). When reviewing the studies

Experimental evidence for character grammar   161

in this section, I continue to use my usual terms: semantic radicals and phonetic components are constituents, which in turn are stroke groups. The one new term that I will adopt from the psycholinguistic literature is the PSEUDOCHARACTER, a non-lexical combination of character constituents in their usual positions, making them, in essence, morphologically grammatical accidental gaps.

5.2.1. *Abstract knowledge*

As outlined in Section 1.3.1.4, a key property of grammar is abstractness. Here, I review character experiments relating to non-iconicity (Section 5.2.1.1), amodality (Section 5.2.1.2), and modularity (Section 5.2.1.3).

5.2.1.1. *Experiments on character iconicity*

A handful of experimental studies have tested the hypothesis that iconicity plays a mentally active role in Chinese characters. The basic logic is always the same: if the meaning of a character can be intuited from its form alone, a reader with no prior knowledge of Chinese should have a better than chance ability to guess what the character means.

All of these studies are problematic, however. Some only tested intuitive 'meaningfulness' (Koriat and Levy 1979; Nelson and Ladan 1976), and even those that elicited guesses about actual meanings (e.g., Luk and Bialystok 2005) tested quite small samples (50 characters, 42 character pairs, and 20 characters, respectively, in these three studies). In the most recent study, Xiao and Treiman (2012) made some methodological improvements. To get an objective estimate of how many single-constituent characters really are iconic, they gave 40 English speakers without Chinese experience 213 simple (and simplified) characters used in elementary school textbooks in the People's Republic of China. To remove biases intrinsically favoring certain meanings over others, in each trial they presented a single meaning in English and had participants guess which of two visually matched characters related to it. They were also quite careful in their statistics, running their analyses character by character to determine which ones were associated with the correct meaning significantly more often than chance, taking into account the fact that the same character was tested repeatedly (as correct or incorrect choice). This resulted in the list of 15 significantly 'iconic' characters in Table 5.1 (after their Table 1, p. 957, using their glosses).

As with the earlier studies, however, the results are not very convincing. To start with, there are questions about the test items: the authors translate 丁 as 'man' even though it is most commonly used as a meaningless surname, and translate 个 as 'individual' even though it is most commonly used as a semantically bleached function morpheme. The paired forced-choice design also artificially inflates the accuracy rate; asking people to link all 213 English meanings to all 213 characters would likely result in virtually no hits at all. In any case, finding only 15 putatively iconic characters out of 213 (7 percent) hardly demonstrates that iconicity is a core property of the character system, especially when one remembers that the vast majority of characters are morphologically complex, unlike these. Even in

162 *Experimental evidence for character grammar*

Table 5.1 The results of Xiao and Treiman (2012)

Character		Percent correct
爪	'claw'	95
凹	'concave'	95
内	'inner'	95
贝	'shell'	90
气	'air'	90
川	'river'	90
个	'individual'	90
丁	'man'	85
小	'small'	85
耳	'ear'	85
田	'field'	85
三	'three'	85
门	'door'	85
雨	'rain'	85
云	'cloud'	85

morphologically simple characters, iconicity is routinely overridden by character phonology, as when bottommost prominence causes unequal 'wheel' sizes in the traditional character in (1) (recall from Section 1.4.1 that phonology beats iconicity in sign languages as well).

(1)   車 *chē* 'vehicle'

5.2.1.2. *Experiments on the amodal processing of characters*

Character grammar is also abstract in that it is amodal, rather than being restricted just to articulation or just to perception. Of course, processing takes place within each of these subsystems as well: it is not impossible to read without being able to write (as Bi, Han, and Zhang 2009 conclude from a case study of a brain-damaged Chinese adult), and in fact, the ubiquity of digital key-in systems has led to an epidemic of 'character amnesia' (Hilburger 2016; Xu 2017), whose sufferers cannot handwrite many characters that they readily recognize.

Nevertheless, consistent with the speculations of Bever (1975) (see Section 1.3.1.4), character grammar seems to emerge through learning to bridge input and output systems. For example, in an experiment that asked 131 Chinese children to read aloud 200 simplified characters taken from schoolbooks in the PRC, Tan *et al.* (2005) found that each child's reading ability was most strongly predicted by his or her ability to correctly copy 60 characters, even when they statistically controlled for other variables. The same children were then tested on their ability to copy pseudocharacters (non-lexical combinations

Experimental evidence for character grammar 163

of real constituents in their standard locations). Factoring out nonverbal IQ and line drawing accuracy, this ability predicted a statistically significant proportion of the variance in the reading ability of beginning readers, though the influence dropped to non-significance in intermediate readers. Tan *et al.* (2013) also found a positive correlation between children's reading ability and the amount of time they spent writing Chinese by hand in daily life. Similarly, Hsieh (2010) taught Taiwanese children rare (but well-formed) traditional characters and found that their comprehension was improved with writing practice, though also with the more visually oriented stroke-counting practice; Xu and Liu (2018) report related results in children learning simplified characters. Writing also helps second-language character learners. For example, Guan *et al.* (2011) found that handwriting practice significantly improved character recognition in adult American students. Other studies on character learning will be discussed in Chapter 6.

The amodal nature of character knowledge is observed in mature readers as well. Flores d'Arcais (1994) found that adult readers of simplified Chinese were significantly faster to name characters when they were preceded by fragments that are written earlier in standard stroke order, as with the strokes on the left in (2a) and on the top right in (2b), despite the characters' overall visual similarity. Misidentifying paired characters as identical in a same-different task was also significantly more common for characters sharing early strokes. No such stroke order effects were found in Dutch participants, showing that the mental linking of articulation with perception emerged through experience using the system.

(2)   a   讯
        b   迅

Stroke order per se only seems to have limited effects on character knowledge, however. Tamaoka and Yamada (2000) tested 91 Japanese-speaking undergraduates on their knowledge of various aspects of kanji and then used a structural path model (a statistical method for drawing causal inferences) to determine which variables affect which other ones. They concluded that stroke order knowledge significantly influenced only semantic radical knowledge, and it was this, not stroke order itself, that influenced knowledge of character pronunciation and meaning. The correlation between stroke order and radical knowledge likely reflects the fact that character constituents are conceived of, and hence written as, wholes. I discuss other stroke order experiments in Section 5.2.3.2.

5.2.1.3. *Experiments on the neural modularity of character processing*

In Section 1.4.3.1, I noted that the brain seems to treat orthographic processing as a specialized task, not reducible to the processing of vision, pronunciation, or meaning, though of course these other processes are involved in reading as well (e.g., Dehaene *et al.* 2015; Perfetti, Liu, and Tan 2005; Tao and Healy 2016). In particular, the so-called Visual Word Form Area (VWFA) becomes activated not just by viewing alphabetic text, but also by viewing Chinese characters. In an early

164 *Experimental evidence for character grammar*

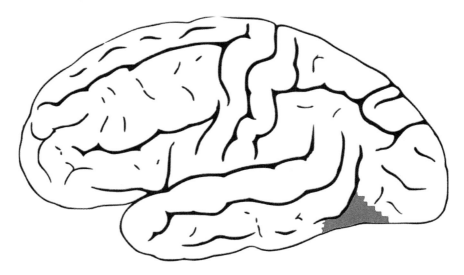

Figure 5.1 The rough location of the Visual Word Form Area (in the fusiform gyrus)

Source: Brain image derived from Gray (1918), via https://commons.wikimedia.org/wiki/File:Gray726.svg.

Chinese study on the VWFA, Liu *et al.* (2008) presented Chinese readers with genuine simplified characters, pseudocharacters, and mere jumbles of Chinese strokes, while their brain activity was scanned via fMRI (functional magnetic resonance imaging, which measures blood oxygen levels as a proxy for neural activity). Pseudocharacters were associated with greater activation, as compared with stroke jumbles, within an area in the left hemisphere called the fusiform gyrus, which lies between the temporal lobe at the side of the cerebral cortex and the occipital lobe at the back, as indicated roughly in Figure 5.1 (this is the left hemisphere, so the back of the head is on the right).

In a later fMRI study, Wang *et al.* (2011) asked simplified Chinese readers to decide if a character was repeated from the previous experimental trial. Again, activation in the VWFA differed for pseudocharacters as compared with two types of ungrammatical characters (stroke jumbles and characters with constituents in illegal positions), though in the opposite direction from the Liu *et al.* (2008) study. The authors speculate that this reversal was due to their use of a task that burdens visual working memory: ungrammatical characters are harder to remember, prompting the VWFA to exert more effort.

The time course of Chinese character recognition was studied in readers of simplified Chinese by Lin *et al.* (2011) using the event-related potentials (ERP) brainwave recording technique. They found that pseudocharacters and real characters elicited the same brainwave component called the N170, which is negative-going

Experimental evidence for character grammar 165

and occurs about 170 milliseconds (ms, or one thousandth of a second) after stimulus onset, while ungrammatical characters with constituents in illegal positions in turn showed a slightly greater N170 than stroke jumbles. This signal was again associated with the VWFA. Lu *et al.* (2011) found similar results using similar techniques.

In other words, the VWFA discriminates among character-like forms in accordance with their degree of well-formedness. Of course, unsurprisingly for a brain area that existed long before writing was invented, the VWFA handles more than just orthographic patterning (recall from Chapter 1 that it is also involved in face recognition). Hsu *et al.* (2009) and Zhao *et al.* (2016) found that this area is also involved in processing character pronunciations, and Chan *et al.* (2009) found that activation in nearby areas is associated with character meanings. Nevertheless, the literature is reasonably consistent in showing that the knowledge of character structure requires a particular kind of neural skill, one that is productively extended to novel characters.

5.2.2. Character morphology

I now turn to experiments on character morphology (for more conventional psycholinguistic reviews of character processing, see Chen and Yeh 2009; Lee 2017; Liu and Wu 2017; Su and Law 2017; Tan *et al.* 2005). I start with studies that provide evidence that characters are decomposed into constituents (Section 5.2.2.1). Then I look at the processing of the two key types of externally interpreted constituents: semantic radicals and phonetic components (Section 5.2.2.2).

5.2.2.1. Decomposition

Characters are not only structurally decompositional, but readers really do decompose them in real time. As has been found for morphological processing in spoken languages (e.g., Roelofs and Baayen 2002), external interpretability (in meaning or pronunciation) is not crucial if there are sufficient formal clues to decomposition, consistent with the notion of "morphology by itself" (Aronoff 1994b).

For example, Hsiao and Cottrell (2009) displayed pairs of traditional characters composed of two vertically stacked constituents, and asked readers from Taiwan and participants without any Chinese experience to decide if just the upper or just the lower constituents in each character pair were the same or different. The stimuli included those shown in Table 5.2 (from their Figure 2, p. 456), which share the

Table 5.2 Sample materials from Hsiao and Cottrell (2009)

		Upper constituents	
		Same	Different
Lower constituents	**Same**	盟 盟	盗 盛
	Different	集 售	架 吾

166 *Experimental evidence for character grammar*

constituent at the top, at the bottom, in both positions, or in neither position. In comparison with the Chinese readers, the non-Chinese readers showed much lower accuracy when characters matched in the irrelevant half of the character (e.g., the upper half when they were asked to focus on the lower half). From this, the authors conclude that Chinese readers have learned to decompose characters into their constituents, whether or not they are also interpreted for pronunciation or meaning.

Using a similar experimental paradigm, Liu *et al.* (2016) found that distraction due to the irrelevant half of the characters was greater for traditional character readers from Hong Kong and Taiwan than for simplified character readers from the Chinese mainland. However, whereas simplified characters were decomposed more readily by simplified character readers, particularly if they were better at writing them (more evidence for amodality), traditional characters were decomposed equally well by both reader groups. The authors therefore conclude that experience with simpler cases may help learners generalize to more complex cases, a principle that happens to apply to grammar acquisition as well (e.g., Elman 1993; Hayes 2004). Regardless of the precise mechanism, the transfer of decomposition skills beyond one's experience clearly suggests productive morphological knowledge and also supports the argument in Section 4.3.2 that traditional and simplified characters have virtually identical grammars.

Decomposition seems to be spontaneous, occurring even when readers are focused on other things. Chen, Allport, and Marshall (1996) presented simplified character readers with pairs of real characters, pseudocharacters (accidental morphological gaps), and non-lexical characters with constituents in illegal positions (systematic morphological gaps). Stimuli were further divided into those with two or three constituents (including uninterpreted ones), as illustrated for some of their real characters in Table 5.3 (based on Figure 2, p. 1032). Participants had to decide if the characters in each pair were the same or different in their entirety. They found that correctly judging identical pairs as identical was slower for characters with three than with two constituents, even when the number of strokes was taken into account. A similar but weaker pattern was observed for pseudocharacters, while no such effect was found with ungrammatical systematic gaps, suggesting that decomposition into constituents is a productive and grammar-guided process.

Further evidence for automatic character decomposition comes from an experiment by Wang and Dong (2013) in which readers had to determine if simplified characters contained a specified stroke group while ERP recordings were made. Not only were responses less accurate when the stroke group was not a full lexical constituent (even when the number of strokes was controlled), but such stimuli also elicited stronger brainwave components associated with the processing of

Table 5.3 Sample materials from Chen *et al.* (1996)

Character type	Different pairs	Same pairs
Two constituents	袭 杂	雪 雪
Three constituents	喝 唱	读 读

Experimental evidence for character grammar   167

Table 5.4 Sample materials from Taft and Zhu (1997), Experiment 3

		Average frequency of two constituents on right	
		High	Low
Frequency of constituent compound on right	**High**	扮	饰
	Low	浇	脖

lexically challenging stimuli, including the N400, a negative-going brainwave component about 400 ms after stimulus onset (and one of the best established of all linguistic ERP components; Kutas and Federmeier 2011).

If readers automatically decompose characters into their constituents, we expect constituent frequency to matter, similar to the way the recognition of morphologically complex words is affected by morpheme frequency (see, e.g., Myers 2006, 2017f for reviews of Mandarin compound words). Taft and Zhu (1997) tested this prediction in simplified characters via the lexical decision task, where participants had to make an immediate judgment of whether or not a test item is a real character. Their non-lexical foil characters were pseudocharacters (accidental morphological gaps).

For example, in their Experiment 3, they presented readers with real characters constructed as in Table 5.4 (from their Table 3, p. 770), in which the average frequency of the two basic constituents stacked on the right (e.g., 八 and 刀 in 扮) was crossed with the frequency of the two-constituent compound that they form (e.g., 分 in 扮). The results showed that characters with more frequent basic constituents were responded to faster, suggesting that even deeply embedded constituents are mentally activated in character reading.

It is also possible to use constituent frequency effects to detect when the mental representations for abstract character constituents first become activated. Wu *et al.* (2012) found in an ERP study on simplified characters that overall constituent frequency affected brain waves about 50 ms later than position-specific frequency (e.g., how often a particular constituent appears on the right), though only the latter continued to affect processing through 400 ms post-stimulus.

Characters sharing the same constituents also activate each other. For example, in a pair of experiments on traditional characters, Tsang and Chen (2009) had participants give a yes/no judgment about whether a target character had been presented in one of the previous two trials. The task is illustrated with two 'no' conditions in Table 5.5 (from their Table 1, p. 953), one in which the target shared each of its two constituents with one of the previously presented pair and one in which it did not. Reaction times were significantly longer and error rates significantly higher when constituents were shared, as if readers had automatically decomposed the earlier characters and activated their constituents.

Writers decompose characters as well. We already saw in Section 4.4.2, from a corpus of slips of the pen, that writers may substitute or shift character

168　*Experimental evidence for character grammar*

Table 5.5 Sample materials from Tsang and Chen (2009)

Condition	Target character	Preceding two characters
Shared constituents	和	秋 吐
No shared constituents	個	妙 振

constituents. Law and Leung (2000) and Han *et al.* (2007) observed similar writing errors in patients with dysgraphia due to brain damage and explicitly argued from their results that the key writing unit in Chinese is the character constituent ('logographeme,' in their terms), whether or not it has any external interpretation.

Chen and Cherng (2013) confirmed this point using an experimental method for probing the mental preparation of word production originally developed by Meyer (1990) for spoken Dutch (see Chen, Chen, and Dell 2002; Myers, Lee, and Tsay 2005, for applications to Mandarin and Taiwan Sign Language, respectively). In this experimental paradigm, participants are first trained on sets of prompts and targets so that in the main part of the experiment they know which target to produce for which prompt. The sets of prompt–target pairs either include formally similar targets (homogeneous sets) or not (heterogeneous sets), which allows one to test which formal features matter to language producers.

In the case of Chen and Cherng (2013), the prompt–target pairs came from two-(traditional) character words (reversed if necessary) and target homogeneity was defined orthographically, with training sets sharing the first-written one or two strokes (Experiments 1 and 2), the first-written semantic radical (Experiments 3 and 4), or the first-written uninterpreted constituent (Experiments 5 and 6). This design is illustrated with the target characters in Table 5.6 (after their Table 1, p. 3).

After the Taiwanese writers had been trained on each set (counterbalancing homogeneity vs. heterogeneity across participants), they were shown a prompt character and had to handwrite its associated target character, with their onset times measured with a touchpad. The results showed that training targets sharing initial strokes had no effect on the mental processing time it took to prepare to write, but training target characters sharing constituents, whether semantic radicals or uninterpreted stroke groups, both sped up writing onset time. Consistent with the corpus-based studies on slips of the pen, writers activate constituents (but not individual strokes) during writing, regardless of external interpretability. The failure to show stroke-level effects needs follow-up, however, given that similar-looking constituents may be substituted for each other in slips of the pen (see Section 4.4.2). Moreover, in an experiment on writing simplified characters, Wang *et al.* forthcoming) found an effect of stroke number on character initiation latencies (see Section 5.2.3.2).

5.2.2.2. *Externally interpreted constituents*

Given the functional logic of character structure, we expect readers to activate not just the forms of semantic radicals and phonetic components, but also their external interpretations in meaning and pronunciation. To help quantify this idea,

Experimental evidence for character grammar 169

Table 5.6 Sample target characters used in Chen and Cherng (2013)

Experiment 1: first stroke	Homogeneous sets (columns)			
	ノ	Ⅰ	一	ヽ
Heterogeneous sets (rows)	狗	野	雄	冰
	信	對	期	歉
	須	頻	划	就
	錄	輝	静	補
Experiment 3: first semantic radical	**Homogeneous sets (columns)**			
	阝	禾	糸	彳
Heterogeneous sets (rows)	院	利	紙	後
	陶	秋	細	行
	陽	私	紅	律
	陳	秘	紀	往
Experiment 5: first uninterpreted constituent	**Homogeneous sets (columns)**			
	立	口	人	士
Heterogeneous sets (rows)	競	跑	錄	聲
	毅	號	領	鼓
	彰	嗣	劍	毅
	龍	鄙	創	款

Feldman and Siok (1997) proposed the now-commonly used measure of COM-
BINABILITY, that is, a constituent's type frequency in a specified role, regardless of
its precise form. For example, the semantic radical combinability for the constituent in (3a) would only count characters in which this constituent is the semantic
radical (as in (3b), but not in (3c), where it is the phonetic component), even if it
appears in its idiosyncratic allomorph as in (3d). This makes combinability related
to variables commonly used in experiments on morphological processing in spoken languages, like morphological family size (Schreuder and Baayen 1997), and
like these variables, it is expected to facilitate character recognition via the spreading of activation from lexical neighbors to the target character.

(3)   a   火 *huǒ* 'fire'
      b   燙 *tàng* 'scalding hot'
      c   伙 *huǒ* 'companion'
      d   熱 *rè* 'hot' (灬)

Feldman and Siok (1997) tested this hypothesis by crossing combinability with
position for both semantic radicals and phonetic components, using materials like
those in Table 5.7 (from their Table 1, p. 778, and Table 3, p. 780). These were
then mixed with non-lexical characters (including pseudocharacters and characters modified by changing strokes) and given to simplified character readers in a
lexical decision task.

170 *Experimental evidence for character grammar*

Table 5.7 Sample materials from Feldman and Siok (1997)

| | | Semantic radicals | |
| | | Position | |
		Left	Right
Combinability	High	诲 *huì* 'instruct'	鸭 *yā* 'duck'
	Low	躺 *tăng* 'lie down'	瓶 *píng* 'bottle'
		Phonetic components	
		Position	
		Left	Right
Combinability	High	郊 *jiāo* 'suburb'	躺 *tăng* 'lie down'
	Low	鸭 *yā* 'duck'	诲 *huì* 'instruct'

The results showed that high combinability characters were consistently responded to more quickly than low combinability characters, confirming that readers take the functional roles of character constituents into account. Semantic radicals and phonetic components were also treated differently. For semantic radicals, there was an interaction between combinability and position: high combinability sped responses to characters with left-edge radicals but not to characters with right-edge radicals. For phonetic components, however, responses were faster with higher combinability, regardless of constituent position. This asymmetry is consistent with the different morphological roles of the two types of constituents: as argued in Section 2.3.1.2, position matters more to the affix-like semantic radicals than it does to the stem-like phonetic components.

In a follow-up study, Feldman and Siok (1999) adopted experimental techniques often used to study morphologically complex words. In a morphological priming lexical decision experiment, each target item is preceded by a word that either shares a morpheme (the prime) or does not (the control). However, since morphologically related words are also related in form and meaning, morpheme-level and word-level variables must be deconfounded. One method is to include semantically opaque words (e.g., *strawberry* is a compound despite not being semantically related to *straw*), and another is to have other items intervene between prime and target, which tends to reduce or eliminate purely form-based and purely semantic priming while preserving morphological priming (Feldman 2003).

Feldman and Siok (1999) applied both techniques in a pair of experiments on simplified characters. The prime-target character pairs shared semantic radical semantics, whole-character semantics, both, or neither. The targets also varied in the combinability of their semantic radical. This yielded the design illustrated in Table 5.8 (after their Figure 1, p. 564).

In their first experiment, where targets were immediately preceded by primes, whole-character semantics had the usual facilitative effect, speeding up responses

Experimental evidence for character grammar   171

Table 5.8 Sample materials from Feldman and Siok (1999)

High combinability

Target: 论 *lùn* 'discuss'		Semantic radical primes	
		Same	Different
Character meaning primes	**Related**	评 *píng* 'appraise'	述 *shù* 'narrate'
	Unrelated	诸 *zhū* 'various'	竿 *gān* 'pole'

Low combinability

Target: 翅 *chì* 'wing'		Semantic radical primes	
		Same	Different
Character meaning primes	**Related**	翼 *yì* 'wing'	膀 *bǎng* 'upper arm'
	Unrelated	翠 *cuì* 'emerald'	缘 *yuán* 'margin'

to the target. Semantic radical combinability also sped up responses, showing yet again that the characters were decomposed into constituents. For semantically related prime-target pairs, it did not matter if the primes and targets also shared the same semantic radical, but crucially, when the prime was semantically unrelated to the target, sharing the radical slowed responses, as if the radical had been giving misleading information. This shows that the semantic radical was not only mentally activated, but actually interpreted in terms of its meaning.

In their second experiment, the prime and target were separated by 7 to 13 other items. Similar to what has been found in morphological priming experiments on spoken languages, the sharing of semantic radicals still sped responses, though only when the primes and targets also shared whole-character semantics. This study thus makes a strong case for considering semantic radicals as true morphemes, in precisely the same sense as in spoken or signed languages. A replication and extension of this study by Yang and Wu (2014) on traditional characters suggests that semantic radical activation may merely be optional, but this is also like morpheme processing.

These conclusions are further backed up by a variety of additional evidence. In a brain-imaging study on traditional characters using magnetoencephalography (MEG, similar to ERP but with better spatial resolution), Hsu, Lee, and Marantz (2011) found that function influenced the order in which constituents became mentally active: around 100 ms after stimulus onset, phonetic component combinability had a significant effect on the M100 component (as did visual complexity, quantified via number of strokes) but semantic radical combinability did not, whereas 70 ms later semantic radical combinability significantly affected M170 while phonetic component combinability did not. These brainwave components were observed in the right hemisphere, though, and thus not in the VWFA.

The role of semantics in semantic radical processing was also demonstrated when Chen and Weekes (2004) asked readers of simplified characters to classify characters for meaning and found that the consistency of radical semantics

172 *Experimental evidence for character grammar*

mattered, particularly when the radical had high combinability (see also Chen *et al.* 2006). In a similar experiment on traditional characters, Hsiao, Shillcock, and Lavidor (2007) found that a cue to focus on the left side (where the semantic radical always appeared in the test items) benefited semantic judgments for characters containing radicals with low combinability more than a right-side cue, again showing that the affix-like positional preferences and semantic classificatory functions of semantic radicals have genuine processing effects.

Another way in which semantic radicals are affix-like is that they are closed class (Section 2.3.1.1), while phonetic components are not. Mattingly and Hsiao (1999) tested the processing implications of this with non-lexical simplified characters that combined real semantic radicals either with constituents often used as phonetic components, like that in (4a), or with constituents never used this way, like that in (4b). These were then mixed with real characters for lexical decisions. While the second type of non-lexical character was rejected slightly more easily, the effect was small and non-significant, leading the authors to conclude that readers have few expectations about what can or cannot be a phonetic component, treating it essentially as an open class.

(4) a 革 'leather' + 昆 *kūn*
     b 革 'leather' + 书 *shū*

Phonetic components are also interpreted, however. In one of the experiments in Chua (1999), simplified character readers were presented with a series of definitions, each of which was immediately followed by a character; the participants' task was to decide if the character matched the definition. Responses were significantly less accurate both for characters sharing pronunciation with an appropriate answer character and for those sharing just the phonetic component. The results suggest that phonetic components are indeed associated with pronunciations, so automatically in fact that they are even activated during a semantic judgment task.

To test if readers productively infer pronunciations from phonetic components, Lee *et al.* (2006) created pseudocharacters from real left-edge semantic radicals and real right-edge phonetic components with highly consistent pronunciations. For example, one of their pseudocharacters was constructed of the semantic radical in (5a) on the left and, on the right, the phonetic component shared by the characters in (5b), all of which are pronounced *yáo* (from their Figure 1, p. 624).

(5) a 月 (肉)
     b 搖 遙 謠 徭 傜 瑤

They then presented these pseudocharacters to traditional character readers, along with an audio recording of a syllable that either matched the expected pronunciation (*yáo*) or did not (e.g., *chèn*). A second later, participants saw an orthographically unrelated real character that either did or did not match the recorded pronunciation, like the matching character in (6), and they had to decide if the pronunciations were homophonous. When the pronunciation assigned to the

Experimental evidence for character grammar   173

pseudocharacter differed from the expectation set up by the phonetic component, participants were slower to correctly identify 'non-homophonous' pairs, as if the expected pronunciation was difficult to suppress. Concomitant ERP measurements further backed up this conclusion.

(6)   姚 *yáo*

In addition to the just-illustrated gradient variable of CONSISTENCY, or the proportion of characters in which the phonetic component is pronounced as in the target character, there is also the categorical variable of REGULARITY, which reflects whether or not the phonetic component is pronounced identically with the target character as a whole. The two variables seem to tap into different aspects of processing: Liu, Chen, and Sue (2003) found that consistency affects character naming speed while regularity affects character naming accuracy, and Lee *et al.* (2005) found that consistency has a particularly influential effect on naming irregular characters. In essence, readers behave as if they hope that the pronunciation of a character is identical to that of its phonetic component (using regularity), but if this is not the case, they estimate pronunciation probabilistically (using consistency). The latter process thus depends on generalizing beyond rote memory, a hallmark of productive grammatical knowledge.

A rather different way of testing the external interpretation of character constituents was used by Williams and Bever (2010) in a series of experiments using simplified semantic-phonetic characters in which either the semantic radical or the phonetic component was blurred. Unsurprisingly, they found that responses in a semantic categorization task were affected more when the semantic radical was blurred, whereas responses in a homophone detection task were affected more when the phonetic component was blurred. Blurring of the semantic radical also had a greater effect in a lexical decision task, perhaps for morphological reasons (radical affixation being dominant in character formation) but prosodic or even visual explanations are also possible (41 of their 48 test items had left-edge radicals).

Since studies on character constituent interpretation have always focused on semantic-phonetic characters, there are no experiments, as far as I am aware, explicitly testing if the constituents in semantic compounds are also interpreted in real time. An indirect hint that they are not comes from the writing study of Wang *et al.* (forthcoming) (see also Sections 5.2.2.1 and 5.2.3.2), which found no effect of etymologically defined semantic-phonetic status on writing latencies or durations, after regularity was taken into account. This suggests that semantic-phonetic characters with opaque pronunciations are not processed differently from semantic compounds. Studies explicitly testing the idea are needed, however, given the structural differences between the two character types (see Chapter 2), as well as the strong tendency for artistic and playful characters to be coined with constituent semantics in mind (see Section 4.4.3).

Put together, such studies leave no doubt that semantic radicals and phonetic components are mentally activated and interpreted during reading, similar to morphemes in spoken and signed languages. Semantic radicals, similar to affixes,

174 *Experimental evidence for character grammar*

are also processed in a more position-sensitive and closed-class way than phonetic components.

5.2.3. *Character phonology and phonetics*

In comparison with character morphology, experimental research on character phonology and character phonetics is rather sparse. This is already suggested by the kinds of non-lexical characters used in the experiments reviewed earlier: there is a huge and largely unexplored gap between well-formed pseudocharacters and hopelessly scrambled strokes. This research lacuna means that I have to be rather generous in order to have anything from the existing literature to review here at all. I start with studies that have looked at the effects of overall character structure, akin to character prosody (Section 5.2.3.1), then turn to studies on the perception and production of strokes, aspects of character phonetics (Section 5.2.3.2).

5.2.3.1. *Character structure*

Character prosody is essentially character structure for its own sake, with character morphology factored out. In the studies most relevant to this topic, Yeh and colleagues (Yeh, Li, and Chen 1997; Yeh, Li, and Chen 1999; Yeh and Li 2002) asked traditional character readers to sort characters, written on individual cards, into separate piles based on whether they looked similar. Yeh and Li (2002) supplemented this with a task in which participants saw a single target character on a computer screen and had to judge whether it appeared in a following display of up to 24 characters. In both experimental paradigms, the experimenters' goal was to quantify the underlying parameters of perceived similarity via statistical methods like cluster analysis and multidimensional scaling.

Their central finding was that characters are perceived as similar not only when they share constituents, but also when they share overall structure. In particular, characters that arrange their constituents horizontally are perceived as different from characters with vertically arranged constituents, and characters that place their constituents into separable areas are perceived as different from characters in which one constituent surrounds another. Yeh and Li (2002) call these the horizontal-vertical and the open-bounded dimensions, respectively, as illustrated in Table 5.9 (from their Figure 1 on p. 937, based on results from a sorting task).

Note the interaction between the two dimensions: horizontally oriented characters tend to be perceived as intermediate between open and bound, whereas vertically oriented characters run along the full range of the open-bound dimension. This does not quite jibe with the observations in Chapters 2 and 3 regarding the greater splittability of horizontally oriented reduplication, nor with the universal perceptual and cognitive constraints favoring the horizontal axis, discussed in Section 6.2.2; further research seems warranted to account for the discrepancy. Easier to interpret is the finding that characters with a left/bottom radical (e.g., 遍) clustered with the horizontally arranged characters, unlike characters with top/left radicals (e.g., 曆): recall that the regular stretching process, which creates left/

Experimental evidence for character grammar　175

Table 5.9 Sample materials and schematic results from Yeh and Li (2002)

	Horizontal	↔	Vertical
Open			售　姿　菲
↕	排　師　褊		重　事
Bound	遍		曆　圍　幾

Table 5.10 Sample materials from Sun and Yan (2006)

Target	Correct	Homophone	Shared constituent	'Symmetrical'
朋 *péng*	狐朋狗友 Full identity	狐彭狗友 *péng*	狐服狗友 月	狐✗✗狗友 [XX]

bottom structures, targets what are otherwise left-edge constituents (see Chapters 2 and 3).

Another study with possible implications for character prosody is that of Sun and Yan (2006), which is unusual in that it seems to have tested reduplicated structures (see also Section 5.3.2). Unfortunately, the authors tested only eight simplified characters, do not list any besides 朋, and confusingly call them 'structurally symmetrical characters' (结构对称汉字 *jiégòu duìchèn hànzì*) rather than using more standard terms (like 叠体字 *diétǐzì* 'stacked-body characters'), so it is not clear if all of their test items truly involved reduplication. In any case, their experimental task involved presenting a target character and asking readers to decide if it was contained in a four-character string. As illustrated in Table 5.10 (based on their text description on p. 40), these strings either contained the target character, a homophonous character that did not contain any of the target character's constituents, a non-homophonous character that contained one of the target character's constituents, or a non-lexical character that was likewise 'symmetrical' (though they are not clear if this was more Chinese-looking than the abstract symbols they use to illustrate it). Their key finding was that participants were slower and less accurate in rejecting the two visually similar foils (sharing a constituent or the 'symmetrical' structure) than the homophonous foil. Assuming that all of their 'symmetrical' characters did indeed involve reduplication, these results seem to support the notion that readers activate not just character constituents or overall character shapes, but also abstract reduplicative templates.

5.2.3.2. *The perception and production of strokes and stroke order*

In this section, I briefly review some experiments on the perception and production of strokes, an aspect of character phonetics. Curiously, one stroke-related

176 *Experimental evidence for character grammar*

factor has proven to have only weak effects at best: visual complexity (a fact that Handel 2013 cites in criticizing the motivations behind character simplification). For example, Chang *et al.* (2016) found no effect of the number of strokes in naming times for traditional characters, Chen *et al.* (1996) found none in a same-different task on simplified characters (see Section 5.2.2.1), and Chen and Cherng (2013) found no stroke-level priming in a writing task (also reviewed in Section 5.2.2.1). Sze, Liow, and Yap (2014) claim that stroke number did affect their lexical decision times for simplified characters (in a replication of Leong, Cheng, and Mulcahy 1987), but the only examples they cite reveal a confound with the number of stroke groups (from their Table 3, p. 270): the few-stroke characters in (7a) generally also have fewer stroke groups (mostly just two) than the many-stroke characters (three or more) in (7b).

(7)　　a　和　没　扒　吠　呐
　　　　b　就　解　慷　塌　寥

In a recent and admirably large writing experiment (203 participants producing 1,600 simplified characters, 200 per participant), Wang *et al.* (forthcoming) attempted to deal with this confound by including both stroke number and constituent number together in statistical analyses of character initiation and completion times. While they did find that stroke number affected both measures, its high correlation with constituent number led to the latter having no statistically significant effects, a result they admit is inconsistent with the literature (see Section 5.2.2). It may be that simplified character constituents have too few strokes for this kind of statistical analysis to work properly, especially if writing latency depends heavily on the first constituent (as implied by the results of Chen and Cherng 2013), or perhaps conventional stroke counts do not accurately reflect how readers and writers actually decompose stroke groups (see Section 3.4.1).

Despite the surprisingly weak influence of visual complexity, there is ample experimental evidence that character recognition goes through a perceptual stage similar to that of phonetics. For example, we saw in Section 5.2.2.2 that Hsu *et al.* (2011) found that the number of strokes affects an early brainwave component in reading, and in Section 5.2.2.1, we saw that experience with simplified characters makes readers more skilled in character decomposition; interestingly, this skill that turns out to be associated with visual discrimination more generally (Peng, Minett, and Wang 2010; McBride-Chang *et al.* 2005). Moreover, in arguing for the amodality of character grammar in Section 5.2.1.2, I discussed how familiarity with conventional stroke order affects the perception of statically presented Chinese characters, so it is no surprise that it also does so for animations of characters being written (e.g., Tse and Cavanagh 2000). Particularly interesting is an fMRI study in which Yu *et al.* (2011) presented simplified character readers with animations that either followed the standard stroke order or else shifted the order of one or two strokes: the greater the number of stroke order violations, the greater the activity in the VWFA. This combines two of the arguments for the abstractness of character grammar: the amodal linking of perception with production and its dependence on a specialized brain area.

Just as spoken and signed phonetics reflects higher-level phonological representations, stroke order also depends on constituent structure (see Section 3.6.2.1). Experimental evidence for this comes from another brain-imaging study on the perception of stroke order in simplified characters, this time using ERP. When Qiu and Zhou (2010) presented animations of two-constituent characters, they found that stroke order reversals yielded significantly greater brain activity when they crossed constituents than when they were constituent-internal.

Similar conclusions follow from experiments on the physiology of writing. Kao *et al.* (1986) had participants write the character 永, commonly used in calligraphic training because it contains all of the traditionally recognized stroke types. In separate conditions, participants were asked to write just the first stroke, just the first two, and so on. Mean stroke pressure (measured via a pressure-sensitive plate) was at its greatest when only one stroke had to be written and dropped continually with each additional stroke, though for the full character the mean pressure slightly increased again (recall the discussion of constituent-final emphasis in Section 3.6.1). The effort of writing a constituent thus seems to be distributed across the strokes that make it up, again suggesting that articulation serves higher linguistic goals.

In a related experiment on writing time rather than pressure, Chau *et al.* (1986) asked participants to write horizontally oriented two-constituent traditional characters. In the 'writing separately' conditions, participants had to write just the left-edge constituent or just the right-edge constituent, and in 'displacement' conditions, they had to write the left-edge or right-edge constituent 10 cm to the left of the other. In both types of conditions, writing times were slower when writing a single constituent on its own as compared with writing it as part of a whole character (cf. Menzerath's law in Section 4.2.1). The difference in writing times between the 'writing separately' and the 'displacement' conditions was also much larger for left-edge constituents than for right-edge constituents, suggesting that the latter was mentally prepared ahead of time. This too is consistent with what we know about the sequential nature of word form preparation prior to actual articulation, as demonstrated, for example, by implicit priming experiments (see also Section 5.2.2.1).

5.3. Experiments on character phonology using acceptability judgments

Many gaps have yet to be filled in the experimental study of character grammar, particularly in character phonology. In this section, I review a handful of studies that I have conducted myself. All of these were run on traditional character readers in Taiwan and used the acceptability judgment task (also known as the wordlikeness judgment task when applied to lexical grammar), where participants are shown non-lexical forms (here, non-lexical characters) and asked to judge whether, or to what degree, they resemble genuine lexical items. This task is

178 *Experimental evidence for character grammar*

occasionally used in psycholinguistics (e.g., Bailey and Hahn 2001), but because of the light it sheds on grammatical knowledge, it is far more common in theoretical linguistics (see review in Myers 2017c).

The acceptability judgment task is arguably less natural than the more common psycholinguistic tasks of naming and lexical decision, since it takes participants one step further away from natural language use. Nevertheless, it has a number of advantages for the study of grammar, most obviously by using non-lexical items so that participants must generalize beyond rote memory. While the lexical decision task also requires non-lexical items as foils, they are generally designed to be as word-like as possible to force lexical access, precisely what we want to avoid in the study of productivity. Moreover, the focus of the acceptability judgment task on permanent grammatical knowledge makes reaction times less important than the judgments themselves, leaving researchers free to increase judgment sensitivity by providing participants with many points along a continuum from 'acceptable' to 'unacceptable.' Of course, as with any psycholinguistic experiment, the results reflect not just knowledge but also real-time processing; acceptability is not identical with the grammar that partly underlies it (see Section 1.3.2), and reaction times can in fact help clarify their relation, as we will see.

The first set of my character acceptability judgment experiments looked at semantic radical position (Section 5.3.1), the second looked at reduplication (Section 5.3.2), and the third looked at generalizations relating to stroke features (Section 5.3.3).

5.3.1. Semantic radical position and form

The experiment described here, designed and run in collaboration with Tsung-Ying Chen, was intended to address the hypothesized prosodic motivation for semantic radical position. Namely, do readers prefer horizontally arranged characters where the left-edge constituent is thinner than the right, and vertically arranged characters with flat top-edge constituents, even when reduction processes like diagonalization and dotting are taken into account?

For our experiment, we created non-lexical characters composed of two constituents, one narrower than the other, that were arranged either horizontally or vertically. We then crossed this axis factor with two others: the hypothesized grammaticality of the constituent positions (left-thin vs. right-thin, and top-flat vs. bottom-flat) and the lexical status of the 'semantic radical,' which was either taken from the actual inventory of 214 traditional lexicographic radicals or was another genuine character constituent never used as a semantic radical. This $2 \times 2 \times 2$ design resulted in quartets of non-lexical characters sharing an axis, 'phonetic component,' and 'radicals,' like those in Table 5.11 (a Song typeface was used because it is the most commonly encountered in print). There were a total of 32 such sets, yielding a total of 128 test items (32×4). Note that 'thinness' and 'flatness' were defined solely by the spatial dimensions of the constituents, not by the metric of stroke-crossing used in the analyses in Chapters 2 and 3. Note also that the resolution of these stimuli, though low for print, was sufficient for the

Experimental evidence for character grammar 179

Table 5.11 Two sets of test items in the semantic radical judgment experiment

	Grammatical		Ungrammatical	
Axis	Semantic radical	Not semantic radical	Semantic radical	Not semantic radical
Horizontal	稞	䃜	槷	槷
Vertical	䡥	蓺	熱	墊

Table 5.12 Sample filler items in the judgment experiment

Filler type	Pseudocharacter	Added/removed stroke	Flipped constituent
Expected acceptability	High	Medium	Low
Examples	豞 霝 居	旙 畜 曆	頋 尭 庖

computer displays in which the images were actually presented (likewise for the other acceptability judgment experiments reviewed later).

The items were then divided into four lists, one per participant group, counterbalancing the sets so that each participant judged 32 items (= 128/4) with an equal number of each of the four types (grammatical/radical, grammatical/non-radical, ungrammatical/radical, ungrammatical/non-radical) but only one item per set (e.g., the grammatical/radical item of set 1, the grammatical/non-radical item of set 2, and so on), in what is known as a Latin square design.

These items were combined with a large number of non-lexical filler items, both to hide the patterns that we were particularly interested in and to define a range of well-formedness. The 64 fillers were presented to all participants, so that each participant saw twice as many fillers as test items. They represented three levels of well-formedness, as illustrated in Table 5.12: 20 were pseudocharacters (non-lexical combinations of real semantic radicals and phonetic components in their standard positions), 20 started as pseudocharacters but then had one stroke added or removed, and 20 started as pseudocharacters but then had one constituent flipped. No grammatical hypotheses were tested with them, so I do not discuss their analysis in this section, but they did indeed elicit the expected three levels of acceptability.

All items were preceded by abstract visual primes to highlight character structure (an earlier experiment without these primes yielded similar results). As

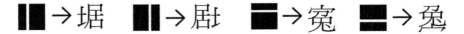

Figure 5.2 Sample prime/target pairs in the second semantic radical judgment experiment

illustrated in Figure 5.2, these consisted of arrangements of thin/wide or flat/tall black rectangles that corresponded to the relative dimensions of the constituents in the target items that followed them.

A fourth experimental factor is also relevant to some of the analyses that follow. Namely, of the 64 horizontal-axis characters, 38 (about half) contained a constituent with regular reduction, as with the first and third items in the first row in Table 5.12 (dotting) and the first two items in Figure 5.2 (diagonalization).

The experiment was run using the Web-based experimental control program Worldlikeness (Chen and Myers 2017), which can be used either online or in a lab; here we did the latter. Participants were 98 traditional character readers (college students) in Taiwan, divided into four Latin square groups of up to 25 each; participants were paid a nominal fee. They were told that none of the items in the experiment would be genuine Chinese characters (實驗中所出現的字皆不是中文字) and instructed to judge if each item was similar to a Chinese character (是否像中文字) by pressing one of two labeled keys, the 'S' key for 'no' (不像中文字) and the 'L' key for 'yes' (像中文字) (at the left and right ends of the keyboard, respectively). Within each trial, the abstract visual prime was displayed for 500 ms and then replaced with the large target item, which remained until a response was given. One of the test items (without reduction) was miscoded and had to be dropped. Also dropped was one impossibly fast response (less than 100 ms), possibly due to preparing to press the key before the trial had even started.

Judgment choices were analyzed with mixed-effects logistic regression, which models the probability (strictly speaking, the log odds) of choosing 'yes' vs. 'no' in terms of fixed variables (those of theoretical interest) while also taking into account the random variables (participants and items). We analyzed reaction times (RT) in milliseconds for 'yes' and 'no' responses together (transformed via the logarithm function to make them more normally distributed), using mixed-effects linear regression, computing the p values using the so-called Kenward-Roger approximation (Judd *et al.* 2012) as implemented in the 'afex' package (Singmann 2018) in the R statistical software (R Core Team 2018). The algorithm fitting mixed-effects models is notoriously crash-prone (Matuschek *et al.* 2017), so our models were as simple as possible, only including random intercepts (random variation in overall response levels across participants and items) but not random slopes (random variation in the strengths and directions of the fixed effects).

We modeled both judgment choices and log RT in terms of character axis (horizontally vs. vertical arranged constituents), hypothesized grammaticality (thin/flat constituent at left/top vs. at right/bottom), and constituent type (whether the thin constituent is or is not a true semantic radical), as well as all possible interactions

Experimental evidence for character grammar 181

among these factors. I also included the average of both constituents' positional frequencies (derived from the Academia Sinica corpus: Chen *et al.* 1996) as a nuisance 'rote memory' variable (more precisely, the standardized mean log positional frequency, which puts the variable on a standard scale and gives it a more normal bell shape). Each of the binary factors used effect coding so that the interactions could be interpreted just as they would be in an analysis of variance (ANOVA).

Figure 5.3 shows the mean acceptance rates (adjusted to fit a log scale) in the upper plot and the mean log RT in the lower plot. These are so-called effects plots (created in R using the 'effects' package of Fox and Hong 2009), based on the model fits rather than the raw data; the vertical bars represent 95 percent confidence intervals derived from the model.

For response choices, there was a main effect of grammaticality ($B = 0.89$, $SE = 0.11$, $z = 7.78$, $p < .0001$) (see Section 1.2.1.2 for how to interpret statistical reports like these) and no main effect of constituent type ($p > .1$), but these two factors interacted ($B = -0.36$, $SE = 0.1$, $z = -3.52$, $p < .001$): grammaticality effects were stronger for genuine semantic radicals (compare line slopes within each row of plots). As reviewed in Section 5.2.2, one sign of the affix-like nature of semantic radicals, as opposed to other types of constituents, is that readers have stronger positional preferences for them, and this seems to be confirmed here. Grammaticality also interacted with axis ($B = 0.4$, $SE = 0.1$, $z = 4.56$, $p < .0001$): grammaticality effects were stronger for horizontally arranged characters (compare lines slopes within each column). That is, while narrow 'radicals' looked better at the left than at the right, flat 'radicals' were judged roughly the same at either the top or bottom. Finally, there was a significant effect of standardized mean log constituent positional frequency ($B = 0.4$, $SE = 0.13$, $z = 3.17$, $p = .002$): items with more common constituents in their usual positions were judged as better. Because the analysis factored this out separately, however, the other effects just described cannot merely be due to rote memory of constituent position. No other effects or interactions were significant.

For reaction times, there was no main effect of grammaticality ($p > .4$), but there were main effects of axis and constituent type: faster judgments were made for horizontally arranged characters ($B = -0.03$, $SE = 0.01$, $t = -4.95$, $p < .05$) and characters with genuine semantic radicals ($B = 0.02$, $SE = 0.006$, $t = 3.8$, $p < .001$). The greater difficulty participants had in judging vertical-axis characters was reflected in an interaction between grammaticality and axis ($B = -0.02$, $SE = 0.006$, $t = -3.62$, $p < .05$): grammatical characters were faster to judge for horizontal-axis characters but not for vertical-axis characters. No other effects or interactions were significant. Again, all of these results factor out the possibly confounding influence of constituent positional frequency (non-significant for RT).

While readers did not seem to care about radical dimensions along the vertical axis (i.e., top vs. bottom edges), for horizontally arranged characters, they generalized the grammaticality pattern beyond genuine semantic radicals (i.e., preferring any sort of thin constituent to appear at the left rather than right edge). Figure 5.4 shows the effects plots for horizontal axis non-semantic-radical characters, not

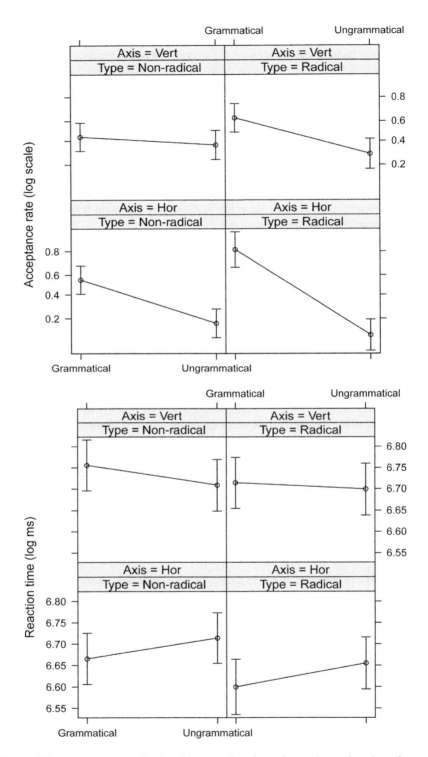

Figure 5.3 Acceptance rates (top) and log reaction times (bottom) as a function of grammaticality, constituent type, and character axis

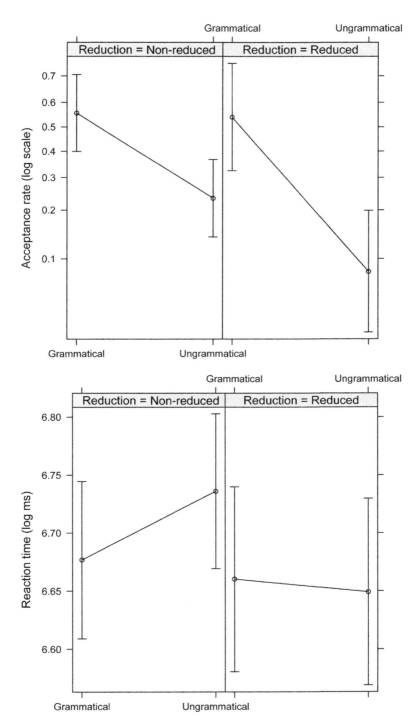

Figure 5.4 Acceptance rates (top) and log reaction times (bottom) for items with a horizontal axis and non-radical constituents as a function of grammaticality and constituent reduction

184 *Experimental evidence for character grammar*

only after factoring out constituent positional frequency, but also after taking into account constituent reduction and possible interactions with it. The grammaticality effect for response choice remained highly significant ($B = 1$, $SE = 0.21$, $z = 4.87$, $p < .0001$), and there were also independent but marginal positive effects of constituent frequency ($B = 0.36$, $SE = 0.18$, $z = 1.96$, $p = .05$) and reduction ($B = 0.32$, $SE = 0.19$, $z = 1.7$, $p = .09$). Characters with reduction were also judged significantly more quickly ($B = 0.03$, $SE = 0.01$, $t = 2.20$, $p = .03$). The tendency for reduction to improve acceptability and judgment speed is itself interesting, suggesting that knowledge of this regular process is also mentally active, though to be sure of its generalizability it would have to be tested in novel constituents, not the real ones that we used. Nevertheless, reduction did not interact with grammaticality either in response choices or reaction times ($ps > .1$); readers seemed to feel that thin constituents always look better on the left, whether or not they also reduce. There were no other significant main effects or interactions.

This experiment suggests that Chinese readers not only know where genuine semantic radicals tend to appear (lexical knowledge), but also that the constituent on the left edge of a character should be thinner than the one on the right and that only the left-edge constituent can undergo reduction processes like dotting or diagonalization (prosodic knowledge). Because of the dependence of reader judgments on constituent dimensions (boosted via the visual primes) rather than semantic radical status or positional frequency, they must have abstracted the left-edge radical generalization beyond any particular set of exemplars; in other words, this looks like grammar, not ad hoc analogy.

Nevertheless, readers did not seem to have any prosodic expectations about the vertical axis: flat constituents were judged as equally good (or bad) whether they appeared at the top or the bottom. This asymmetry may result from universal perceptual and cognitive constraints favoring the horizontal axis (see Section 6.2.2), but it may also emerge from experience with the Chinese character system itself. Recall from Section 4.2.3 that Yang (2016) argued that a pattern is only learnable if the number of exceptions falls below a threshold determined by the total number of items. In particular, we saw in that chapter that the number of characters with right-edge radicals does fall below this threshold, making the left-better-than-right generalization learnable, but the top-better-than-bottom generalization has too many exceptions (bottom-edge radicals) than is tolerable according to Yang's principle.

5.3.2. Reduplication

In terms of character coinage, reduplication has not been productive for centuries, but the patterns are nevertheless extremely regular: horizontal tripling is vanishingly rare, and vertical tripling and upside-down triangles are not found at all. We thus expect readers to be able to generalize the reduplicative template to novel characters, and exactly this was demonstrated experimentally by Myers (2016). In this section, I reanalyze the original data from that study, first reconstructing the key findings and then pulling out a few more interesting implications (none of the images or analyses in this section appeared in the original paper).

Experimental evidence for character grammar 185

Table 5.13 Sample materials used in the reduplication judgment experiment

Shape	Grammatical		Ungrammatical	
	Lexical	*Non-lexical*	*Lexical*	*Non-lexical*
Horizontal	補	㣲	衈	辮
Vertical	瑷	瑂	瑷	瑂
Triangular	惢	筀	惢	籆

The test items consisted of 48 quartets of non-lexical characters, each containing a lexicographic radical and a reduplicated constituent, that crossed grammaticality (doubling vs. tripling along the horizontal or vertical axis, or upward- vs. downward-pointing triangles) with lexicality of the reduplicated structure (i.e., whether the base element actually reduplicates this way in the traditional character inventory), with 16 quartets for each of the three reduplication shapes (horizontal, vertical, and triangular). Examples are shown in Table 5.13 (see Myers 2016 for others). As in the radical position experiment (Section 5.3.1), the items were shown in a Song typeface and distributed in a Latin square design across four lists, for counterbalanced presentation to participants in four groups, so that each participant only saw 48 of these items, with equal numbers of each of the four character types but with only one item taken from any given set. All participants were also shown 120 non-lexical filler characters of the same three types as in the radical position experiment.

Items were presented in random order to 20 traditional character readers in Taiwan, divided into four groups of five participants each, using the PsychoPy experimental control software (Peirce 2007, 2009). Participants were asked to press labeled keys indicating whether an item did or did not seem like a Chinese character. Each trial started with the symbol '+' for 500 ms (to make sure they were looking the right way), continued with a blank screen for 500 ms, and ended with the test item, which stayed on the screen for 3,000 ms (three seconds) or until a response was given. Participants were paid a nominal fee. No responses were given in 17 trials, including two reduplication trials, so these were dropped from the data set.

For the reanalysis reported here, I created a mixed-effects logistic regression model (with random intercepts but not random slopes for both participants and items) predicting response choices from grammaticality, lexicality, shape, all of their possible interactions, and three numerical variables: log stroke count (ungrammatical tripling also increases the number of strokes, so I wanted to factor out this potential confound), log frequency of the reduplicative structure (e.g., 朋), and log frequency of the reduplicative structure's base element (e.g., 月). I also created a mixed-effects linear regression model with the same structure that

186 *Experimental evidence for character grammar*

predicted log reaction times (log RT) for all responses (see Myers 2016 for separate RT analyses for 'yes' and 'no' responses). The effects plots associated with the three categorical factors (with all other factors controlled for) are shown in Figure 5.5. For the RT analysis, statistical significance (via p values) was computed the same way as for the radical position experiment (see Section 5.3.1).

As reflected in the plot for response choices, grammatical forms were significantly more acceptable than ungrammatical ones ($B = 0.75$, $SE = 0.11$, $z = 6.69$, $p < .0001$), and characters with lexical reduplicative structures were also significantly more acceptable ($B = 0.34$, $SE = 0.15$, $z = 2.26$, $p = .02$). Interestingly, these two factors showed no sign of interacting ($p > .8$): the grammaticality effect was just as strong for novel reduplicative structures as for those that the participants had seen before. The grammaticality effect was also independent of the frequency of the reduplicative structures, even though this also had its own positive effect on acceptability ($B = 0.33$, $SE = 0.13$, $z = 2.52$, $p = .01$). Base element frequency did not have a significant effect ($p > .1$). Forms with reduplication along the horizontal axis tended to be judged as most acceptable ($B = 0.46$, $SE = 0.16$, $z = 2.95$, $p = .003$), though shape also interacted with lexicality ($B = 0.35$, $SE = 0.15$, $z = 2.29$, $p = .02$), such that the constraint against upside down triangles generalized to novel reduplicative structures more readily than the constraints against horizontal or vertical tripling. No other effects or interactions reached significance (including the number of strokes; see Section 5.2.3.2).

The RT analysis did not show any main effects, but there were significant interactions of grammaticality with lexicality ($B = -0.03$, $SE = 0.01$, $t = -3.36$, $p < .05$) and with reduplication shape ($B = 0.04$, $SE = 0.01$, $t = 2.71$, $p < .05$). As shown by the height of the lines in the left side of the RT plot, it took longer to judge grammatical but non-lexical reduplicative structures, indicating that extending grammatical generalizations to novel forms took extra effort. The interaction with shape (see dip in the line at the upper right of the RT plot) again shows the special treatment of triangular reduplication: for them, it took longer to respond to grammatical cases than ungrammatical ones, regardless of lexical status, whereas responses to the other two shapes were more consistent. No other main effects or interactions were significant.

To get another perspective on the time course of acceptability judgments, I went beyond Myers (2016) by adopting a statistical method called dynamic survival analysis (Martinussen and Scheike 2006). As the name suggests, this was originally developed for biomedical researchers wanting to know what factors predict how long an animal will live. This method also turns out to be appropriate for modeling decision making in a psychology experiment, where a trial ends once a decision has been confirmed with a button press (Schmidtke *et al.* 2017).

Specifically, I ran a competing risks regression (using the 'timereg' package in R; Scheike and Zhang 2011) to map out the temporally shifting effects of grammaticality, lexicality, and their interaction on the decision to respond 'yes' rather than 'no' (I left out the stroke and frequency variables, since the analyses discussed earlier showed that they had little to no effect). To allow the underlying algorithm to converge properly for all three reduplication shapes, I capped the

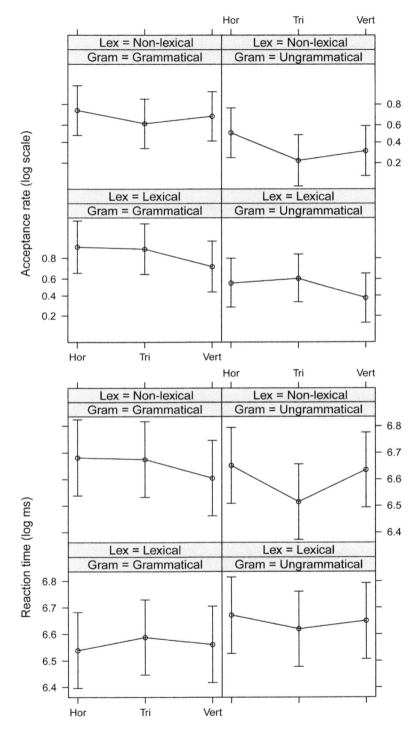

Figure 5.5 Acceptance rates (top) and log reaction times (bottom) for non-lexical characters with reduplication as a function of grammaticality, lexical status of reduplicative structure, and reduplication shape

188 *Experimental evidence for character grammar*

responses at 2,500 ms (dropping the five slowest responses). After building the model, I used an R function written by Harald Baayen (Baayen and Blanche 2017) to plot the temporally varying regression coefficients, which represent the cumulative risk of giving a 'yes' response, and its associated 95 percent confidence band, for grammaticality, lexicality, and their interaction. The results are shown in Figure 5.6. The vertical dotted line marks the time, in milliseconds, where the confidence band first rises above the baseline coefficient value, showing that this is when the factor first has a statistically significant effect ($p < .05$).

As can be seen from the plots, grammaticality began to affect responses around the same time as lexicality (their interaction only has a brief effect a few hundred milliseconds later). This analysis thus confirms that the decisions did not depend on prior lexical access of familiar reduplicated structures, but instead represent productive grammatical knowledge.

Demonstrating productivity with reduplication is particularly important because of the abstract nature of the reduplicative templates; characters like 林 and 朋 have nothing in common except their [XX] structure. Like experimental studies on reduplication in spoken languages (Stemberger and Lewis 1986) and signed languages (Berent *et al.* 2014; Berent and Dupuis 2018), Myers (2016) concludes that the knowledge of Chinese character structure must therefore go beyond not just rote memory, but also beyond superficial analogy with specific characters and character constituents.

5.3.3. *Stroke size and shape*

My final pair of acceptability judgment experiments tested reader knowledge of constraints on stroke size and shape (see corpus-based evidence in Chapters 3 and 4). Both experiments were designed and run in collaboration with Tsung-Ying Chen and conducted in the lab with the Worldlikeness Web app. While the experiments overlap somewhat in the patterns they address, the first (Section 5.3.3.1) focused particularly on prominence and curving while the second (Section 5.3.3.2) focused particularly on leftward hooking.

5.3.3.1. *Prominence and curving*

Because stroke shape generalizations apply within rather than across constituents, we tested them in novel stroke groups. Our first experiment crossed the six parameters in Table 5.14 to create 320 ($= 2 \times 2 \times 5 \times 2 \times 2 \times 4$) stroke groups consisting of four parallel strokes and one stroke that crossed them perpendicularly. This time we used a handwriting-like regular typeface to make it easier for participants to tolerate their gradient variability.

Completely crossing all of these parameters created some extremely bizarre forms, like those with contacting hooks, hooked horizontal strokes, and curved horizontal strokes, as illustrated in Figure 5.7.

This bizarreness meant that we could not simply ask participants to give quick binary yes/no judgments of their Chinese-likeness. Instead we told them that all

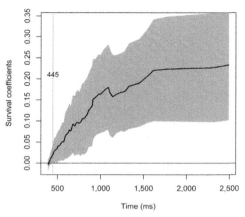
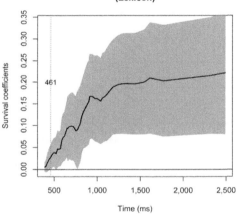
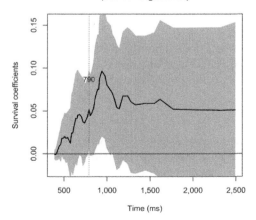

Figure 5.6 Competing risks regression for the reduplication experiment

190 *Experimental evidence for character grammar*

Table 5.14 Sample materials from the first stroke-based acceptability judgment experiment

Axis of strokes in quartet	Vertical	Horizontal		
Examples  				
Position of crossing stroke	Nonhead (left/top)	Head (right/ bottom)		
Examples  				
Crosser contact	Gap at start	Contact at start	Crossing all strokes	Contact at end	Gap at end
Examples     				
Crosser hooking	Hooked	Non-hooked		
Examples  				
Feature of special stroke in quartet	Curved	Long		
Examples 				
Position of special stroke in quartet	First	Second	Third	Fourth
Examples				

Figure 5.7 Examples of bizarre experimental stroke groups

of the figures would look something like the characters in (8), and their task was to rate the degree to which they gave a Chinese character 'feeling' (有中文字的感覺) on a scale from 1 (no feeling) to 7 (strong feeling).

(8)   卅   冊   丰   手

Items were divided into four lists by the position of the crossed stroke. A total of 80 traditional character readers participated, divided roughly evenly into each of the four groups, so that each participant was only tested on 80 (= 320/4) items in a Latin square design. After receiving the instructions and eight practice items

Experimental evidence for character grammar 191

(which either had four identical strokes or a central crossing stroke), the experiment proper began. Each trial began with the symbol '+' for 1,000 ms, immediately followed by the test item, which remained on the screen for 3,000 ms or until a response was given. Because participants had to choose among seven values on a multi-point scale, we did not analyze their reaction times. No responses were given for 137 trials (2 percent).

The responses were rescaled to the range 0–1 and then transformed using the arcsine square root function to make them more normally distributed (following Bailey and Hahn 2001). We then conducted separate analyses for each of the stroke types of interest: curved strokes, lengthened strokes, and hooked strokes. For the first analysis, we looked at the subset of items in which one of four vertical strokes was curved; its position was classified as leftmost vs. non-leftmost. The resulting mixed-effects linear regression analysis (with random intercepts for participants and items) yielded the effects plot in Figure 5.8, showing a significant increase in acceptability when the curved stroke was in the leftmost position ($B = -0.06$, $SE = 0.03$, $t = -2.07$, $p < .05$). Readers seem to know that curving is only licensed at the left edge of a constituent.

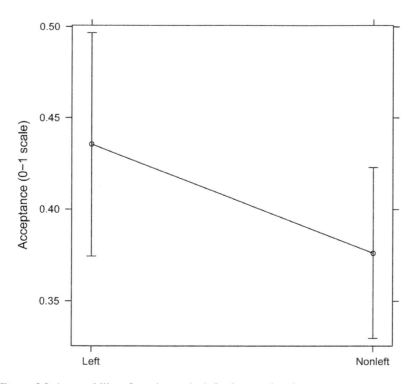

Figure 5.8 Acceptability of curving at the left edge vs. elsewhere

For the analysis of stroke lengthening, we crossed position (head vs. nonhead position according to the prosodic analysis) with axis (horizontal vs. vertical). The results, as reflected in the effects plot in Figure 5.9, showed a significant benefit of head position ($B = 0.04$, $SE = 0.01$, $t = 3.13$, $p < .01$), but there was no effect of axis nor any interaction ($ps > .1$). In other words, readers are aware that strokes are lengthened only in prosodically strong positions, whether at the right or at the bottom.

Finally, we tested if readers prefer leftward hooking on vertical strokes to appear at the right, especially when another stroke appears over the initial point at the top (as in the prototypical hooked complex stroke ⅂). Extracting just the items with a vertical crossing hooked stroke, we classified them by edge (nonhead = left or head = right) and topping (crossing upper stroke vs. not). Hooking was significantly better on the right than the left ($B = 0.03$, $SE = 0.01$, $t = 2.19$, $p < .05$), but there was no main effect of or interaction with the presence of a topping stroke ($ps > .3$); see the effects plot in Figure 5.10.

While this experiment supported the psychological reality of generalizations relating to stroke curving and length, the less than fully successful results for hooking may have resulted from the fact that many items had contacting hooks, which are disallowed regardless of other constituent features. Hence, we decided to run a simpler follow-up experiment.

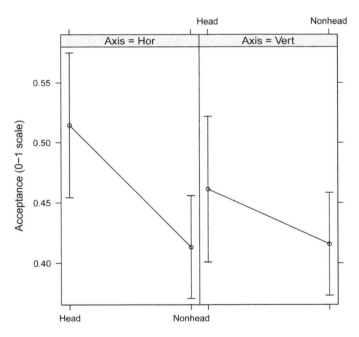

Figure 5.9 Acceptability of stroke prominence in prosodic head (right or bottom) vs. elsewhere

Experimental evidence for character grammar 193

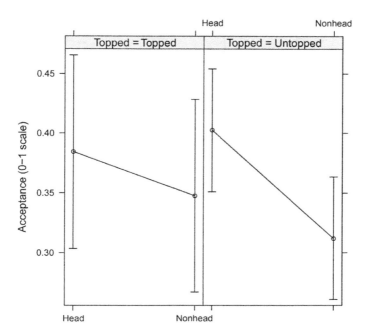

Figure 5.10 Acceptability of leftward hooking on a vertical stroke as the function of prosodic position (head = right vs. nonhead = left) and the presence of strokes at its top

5.3.3.2. Hooking

This time we created a mere 24 items that consisted of two horizontal strokes that were crossed at either the left or right by a straight, curved, or hooked stroke, the topmost point of which either contacted the lower of the two horizontal strokes, contacted the upper of the two, was located in between both strokes, or was located above both strokes (24 = 2 × 3 × 4). All of the stimuli are shown in Figure 5.11.

A total of 77 traditional character readers were presented with all 24 stimuli. The experiment had the same procedure as the previous one, except that there were no practice trials. We then ran two mixed-effects linear regressions on the rescaled acceptability scores (again using the arcsine square root transformation and random intercepts for participants and items).

In the first analysis, we removed all items with the straight vertical stroke and predicted judgments from position and stroke shape (curving vs. hooking). As reflected in the effects plot in Figure 5.12, the right side was favored over the left for both stroke types ($B = -0.07$, $SE = 0.02$, $t = -4.4$, $p < .001$), hooked strokes were favored over curved strokes ($B = -0.05$, $SE = 0.02$, $t = -3.25$, $p < .01$), and there was a marginal interaction such that hooked strokes showed a stronger

Figure 5.11 All materials in the second stroke-based acceptability judgment experiment

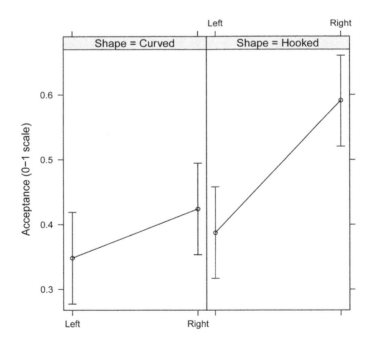

Figure 5.12 Acceptability of curving and leftward hooking as a function of stroke position

right-edge preference than curved strokes ($B = 0.03$, $SE = 0.016$, $t = 2.02$, $p = .07$). The results for the hooked stroke were as expected: readers know that it tends to appear on the right. The unexpected tendency also to prefer curved strokes on the right may have resulted from our mistaken decision to make these strokes more sharply curved than they are in genuine characters (cf. the subtler curve in 尹), which may have led to our 'curved' stroke being perceived as a nonstandard way of writing a hooked stroke. The lesson here is that even when testing phonology, one has to be careful about using stimuli with natural phonetics!

We then looked just at the eight test items with genuine hooks, predicting judgments from position (left vs. right), topping (with other stroke contacting or above the initial point of hooked stroke vs. not), and their interaction. As reflected in the effects plot in Figure 5.13, hooks continued to be more acceptable on the right ($B = -0.09$, $SE = 0.01$, $t = -9.21$, $p < .0001$), but their acceptability was also higher when topped with other strokes ($B = 0.06$, $SE = 0.01$, $t = 6.62$, $p < .0001$). These two factors also enhanced each other in a significant interaction ($B = -0.03$, $SE = 0.01$, $t = -2.77$, $p < .01$), so that the best items were the two where the hooked stroke was both at the right edge and topped. The hooking generalizations of Wang (1983) (see Section 3.4.6) thus seem to be learnable after all (see the competing predictions of alternative learning models in Section 4.2.3). However, because this also made the stroke group look like the lexically attested complex stroke 乛, it is impossible to know from this experiment alone whether these judgments were really due to productive grammar rather than to ad hoc analogy.

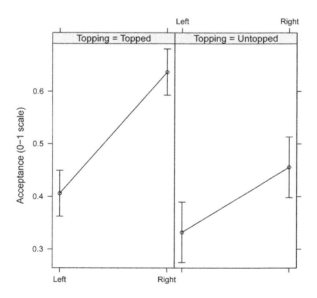

Figure 5.13 Acceptability of leftward hooking on vertical strokes as a function of its position and the presence of strokes on top of it

5.4. Summary

Though most of the experiments reviewed in this chapter were not designed to study character grammar, they still provide considerable evidence for it. Most fundamentally, they show that character knowledge is abstract: iconicity plays almost no role, modality is transcended by linking handwriting experience with print recognition, and a neurologically distinct module is necessary for processing orthographic patterns, their interpretation (e.g., character pronunciation), and their production (e.g., stroke order).

Experiments also show that characters are decomposed into their constituents on the fly, by writers as well as readers (again suggesting amodal knowledge). This even occurs with constituents that are not interpreted, similar to 'morphology by itself' in spoken languages, but when interpretable constituents are mentally activated, so are their interpretations: semantic radicals activate meanings and phonetic components activate pronunciations. These two types of constituents are also processed differently: readers are more sensitive to position for semantic radicals than for phonetic components, and while they seem willing to treat any constituent as a potential phonetic component, they treat semantic radicals as a closed class. Together, these experimental results support my analysis of simple character constituents as morpheme-like, semantic radicals as affix-like, and phonetic components as stem-like.

There is also some experimental support for the productivity of character phonology. Readers are aware of character prosody, classifying characters not just by the constituents they contain but also by their arrangement, and recognizing reduplicative templates and the restrictions on their shapes. Readers also know that constituents tend to be thinner on the left edge than on the right (though they do not seem to pick up on a similar asymmetry along the vertical axis), and that regular reduction processes only apply on the left and not on the right. Moreover, regularities associated with bottommost and rightmost stroke prominence, left-edge curving, and leftward hooking are all generalized by readers to novel stroke groups.

Admittedly, some of these results may reflect superficial analogy rather than grammatical knowledge. I mentioned reasons to doubt this alternative analysis in the case of reduplication and semantic radical position, but the current evidence is not sufficient to rule it out for regular reduction, prominence, curving, or hooking. Moreover, while I argued in Chapter 3 that radical position and reduplication constraints derive from the same prosodic template, other experiments in my lab (not reported here) have so far failed to show that judging one type of pattern affects how readers judge the other. Nevertheless, I hope that more Chinese psycholinguists will go beyond their traditional focus on processing for its own sake and consider studying the productive knowledge of character structure as well.

Whether this knowledge really should be described as 'grammar' at all and whether the study of it has any practical applications are empirical questions that also need to be addressed. This I do in the final chapter.

References

Aronoff, M., 1994b, *Morphology by itself: Stems and inflectional classes*, MIT Press, Cambridge, MA.

Baayen, H. and Blanche, P., 2017, "Dynamic survival analysis", *Talk presented at the Workshop on New Methods in Statistics*, Tübingen, Germany, January 19–20.

Bailey, T.M. and Hahn, U., 2001, "Determinants of wordlikeness: Phonotactics or lexical neighborhoods?", *Journal of Memory and Language*, 44(4), pp. 568–591.

Berent, I. and Dupuis, A., 2018, "The unbounded productivity of (sign) language", *The Mental Lexicon*, 12(3), pp. 309–341.

Berent, I., Dupuis, A. and Brentari, D., 2014, "Phonological reduplication in sign language: Rules rule", *Frontiers in Psychology*, 5, Article 560.

Bever, T.G., 1975, "Psychologically real grammar emerges because of its role in language acquisition", in D.P. Dato, ed., *Developmental psycholinguistics: Theory and application*, pp. 63–75, Georgetown University Press, Washington, DC.

Bi, Y., Han, Z. and Zhang, Y., 2009, "Reading does not depend on writing, even in Chinese", *Neuropsychologia*, 47(4), pp. 1193–1199.

Chan, S.T., Tang, S.W., Tang, K.W., Lee, W.K., Lo, S.S. and Kwong, K.K., 2009, "Hierarchical coding of characters in the ventral and dorsal visual streams of Chinese language processing", *NeuroImage*, 48(2), pp. 423–435.

Chang, Y.N., Hsu, C.H., Tsai, J.L., Chen, C.L. and Lee, C.Y., 2016, "A psycholinguistic database for traditional Chinese character naming", *Behavior Research Methods*, 48(1), pp. 112–122.

Chau, A.W., Kao, H.S. and Shek, D.T., 1986, "Writing time of double-character Chinese words: Effects of interrupting writing responses", in H.S.R. Kao, G.P. van Galen and R. Hoosain, eds., *Graphonomics: Contemporary research in handwriting*, pp. 273–288, North-Holland, Amsterdam.

Chen, J.Y., Chen, T.M. and Dell, G.S., 2002, "Word-form encoding in Mandarin Chinese as assessed by the implicit priming task", *Journal of Memory and Language*, 46(4), pp. 751–781.

Chen, J.Y. and Cherng, R.J., 2013, "The proximate unit in Chinese handwritten character production", *Frontiers in Psychology*, 4, Article 517.

Chen, K.J., Huang, C.R., Chang, L.P. and Hsu, H.L., 1996, "Sinica corpus: Design methodology for balanced corpora", *Proceedings of the 11th Pacific Asia Conference on Language, Information and Computation (PACLIC 11)*, pp. 167–176.

Chen, M.J. and Weekes, B.S., 2004, "Effects of semantic radicals on Chinese character categorization and character decision", *Chinese Journal of Psychology*, 46(2–3), pp. 181–196.

Chen, M.J., Weekes, B.S., Peng, D. and Lei, Q., 2006, "Effects of semantic radical consistency and combinability on Chinese character processing", in P. Li, L.H. Tan, E. Bates and O.J.L. Tzeng, eds., *The handbook of East Asian psycholinguistics, volume 1: Chinese*, pp. 175–186, Cambridge University Press, Cambridge.

Chen, T.Y. and Myers, J., 2017, "Worldlikeness: A web-based tool for typological psycholinguistic research", *University of Pennsylvania Working Papers in Linguistics*, 23(1), Article 4, pp. 20–30.

Chen, Y.C. [陳奕全] and Yeh, S.L. [葉素玲], 2009, 漢字辨識理論模型中的部件表徵 [Radical representation in models of Chinese character recognition]. 應用心理研究 [Research in Applied Psychology], 43, pp. 177–205.

Chen, Y.P., Allport, D.A. and Marshall, J.C., 1996, "What are the functional orthographic units in Chinese word recognition: The stroke or the stroke pattern?", *The Quarterly Journal of Experimental Psychology*, 49(4), pp. 1024–1043.

198 *Experimental evidence for character grammar*

Chua, F.K., 1999, "Phonological recoding in Chinese logograph recognition", *Journal of Experimental Psychology: Learning, Memory, and Cognition*, 25(4), pp. 876–891.

Dehaene, S., Cohen, L., Morais, J. and Kolinsky, R., 2015, "Illiterate to literate: Behavioural and cerebral changes induced by reading acquisition", *Nature Reviews Neuroscience*, 16(4), pp. 234–244.

Elman, J.L., 1993, "Learning and development in neural networks: The importance of starting small", *Cognition*, 48(1), pp. 71–99.

Feldman, L.B., 2003, "What the repetition priming methodology reveals about morphological aspects of word recognition", in J.S. Bowers and C.J. Marsolek, eds., *Rethinking implicit memory*, pp. 124–138, Oxford University Press, Oxford.

Feldman, L.B. and Siok, W.W., 1997, "The role of component function in visual recognition of Chinese characters", *Journal of Experimental Psychology: Learning, Memory, and Cognition*, 23(3), pp. 776–781.

Feldman, L.B. and Siok, W.W., 1999, "Semantic radicals contribute to the visual identification of Chinese characters", *Journal of Memory and Language*, 40(4), pp. 559–576.

Flores d'Arcais, G.B., 1994, "Order of strokes writing as a cue for retrieval in reading Chinese characters", *European Journal of Cognitive Psychology*, 6(4), pp. 337–355.

Fox, J. and Hong, J., 2009, "Effect displays in R for multinomial and proportional-odds logit models: Extensions to the effects package", *Journal of Statistical Software*, 32(1), pp. 1–24.

Gray, H., 1918, *Anatomy of the human body*, 20th ed., Lea and Febringer, New York.

Guan, C.Q., Liu, Y., Chan, D.H.L., Ye, F. and Perfetti, C.A., 2011, "Writing strengthens orthography and alphabetic-coding strengthens phonology in learning to read Chinese", *Journal of Educational Psychology*, 103(3), pp. 509–522.

Han, Z., Zhang, Y., Shu, H. and Bi, Y., 2007, "The orthographic buffer in writing Chinese characters: Evidence from a dysgraphic patient", *Cognitive Neuropsychology*, 24(4), pp. 431–450.

Handel, Z., 2013, "Can a logographic script be simplified? Lessons from the 20th century Chinese writing reform informed by recent psycholinguistic research", *Scripta*, 5, pp. 21–66.

Hayes, B., 2004, "Phonological acquisition in Optimality Theory: The early stages", in R. Kager, J. Pater and W. Zonneveld, eds., *Constraints in phonological acquisition*, pp. 158–203, Cambridge University Press, Cambridge.

Hilburger, C., 2016, "Character amnesia: An overview", *Sino-Platonic Papers*, 264, pp. 51–70.

Hsiao, J.H.W. and Cottrell, G.W., 2009, "Not all visual expertise is holistic, but it may be leftist: The case of Chinese character recognition", *Psychological Science*, 20(4), pp. 455–463.

Hsiao, J.H.W., Shillcock, R. and Lavidor, M., 2007, "An examination of semantic radical combinability effects with lateralized cues in Chinese character recognition", *Perception & Psychophysics*, 69(3), pp. 338–344.

Hsieh, Y.R. [謝侑儒], 2010, 書寫能力對中文閱讀的影響－以弱讀與正常兒童為例 [Learning to read Chinese depends on writing in normal and poor readers], MA thesis, National Chung Cheng University.

Hsu, C.H., Lee, C.Y. and Marantz, A., 2011, "Effects of visual complexity and sublexical information in the occipitotemporal cortex in the reading of Chinese phonograms: A single-trial analysis with MEG", *Brain and Language*, 117(1), pp. 1–11.

Hsu, C.H., Tsai, J.L., Lee, C.Y. and Tzeng, O.J.L., 2009, "Orthographic combinability and phonological consistency effects in reading Chinese phonograms: An event-related potential study", *Brain and Language*, 108(1), pp. 56–66.

Judd, C.M., Westfall, J. and Kenny, D.A., 2012, "Treating stimuli as a random factor in social psychology: A new and comprehensive solution to a pervasive but largely ignored problem", *Journal of Personality and Social Psychology*, 103(1), pp. 54–69.

Kao, H.S., Hong, M.P. and Wah, L.P., 1986, "Handwriting pressure: Effects of task complexity, control mode and orthographic difference", in H.S.R. Kao, G.P. van Galen and R. Hoosain, eds., *Graphonomics: Contemporary research in handwriting*, pp. 47–66, North-Holland, Amsterdam.

Koriat, A. and Levy, I., 1979, "Figural symbolism in Chinese ideographs", *Journal of Psycholinguistic Research*, 8(4), pp. 353–365.

Kutas, M. and Federmeier, K.D., 2011, "Thirty years and counting: Finding meaning in the N400 component of the event-related brain potential", *Annual Review of Psychology*, 62, pp. 621–647.

Law, S.P. and Leung, M.T., 2000, "Structural representations of characters in Chinese writing: Evidence from a case of acquired dysgraphia", *Psychologia*, 43, pp. 67–83.

Lee, C.Y., 2017, "Sublexical processes for reading Chinese characters, neurolinguistic studies", in R. Sybesma, W. Behr, Y. Gu, Z. Handel, C.T.J. Huang and J. Myers, eds., *Encyclopedia of Chinese language and linguistics*, vol. 4, pp. 214–218, Brill, Leiden.

Lee, C.Y., Tsai, J.L., Chiu, Y.C., Tzeng, O.J.L. and Hung, D.L., 2006, "The early extraction of sublexical phonology in reading Chinese pseudocharacters: An event-related potentials study", *Language and Linguistics*, 7(3), pp. 619–636.

Lee, C.Y., Tsai, J.L., Su, E.C.I., Tzeng, O.J.L. and Hung, D.L., 2005, "Consistency, regularity, and frequency effects in naming Chinese characters", *Language and Linguistics*, 6(1), pp. 75–107.

Leong, C.K., Cheng, P.W. and Mulcahy, R., 1987, "Automatic processing of morphemic orthography by mature readers", *Language and Speech*, 30(2), pp. 181–196.

Lin, S.E., Chen, H.C., Zhao, J., Li, S., He, S. and Weng, X.C., 2011, "Left-lateralized N170 response to unpronounceable pseudo but not false Chinese characters: The key role of orthography", *Neuroscience*, 190, pp. 200–206.

Liu, C., Zhang, W.T., Tang, Y.Y., Mai, X.Q., Chen, H.C., Tardif, T. and Luo, Y.J., 2008, "The visual word form area: Evidence from an fMRI study of implicit processing of Chinese characters", *Neuroimage*, 40(3), pp. 1350–1361.

Liu, I.M., Chen, S.C. and Sue, I.R., 2003, "Regularity and consistency effects in Chinese character naming", *Chinese Journal of Psychology*, 45(1), pp. 29–46.

Liu, I.M. and Wu, J.T., 2017, "Reading characters and words, behavioral studies", in R. Sybesma, W. Behr, Y. Gu, Z. Handel, C.T.J. Huang and J. Myers, eds., *Encyclopedia of Chinese language and linguistics*, vol. 3, pp. 532–536, Brill, Leiden.

Liu, T., Chuk, T.Y., Yeh, S.L. and Hsiao, J.H., 2016, "Transfer of perceptual expertise: The case of simplified and traditional Chinese character recognition", *Cognitive Science*, 40(8), pp. 1941–1968.

Lu, Q., Tang, Y.Y., Zhou, L. and Yu, Q., 2011, "The different time courses of reading different levels of Chinese characters: An ERP study", *Neuroscience Letters*, 498(3), pp. 194–198.

Luk, G. and Bialystok, E., 2005, "How iconic are Chinese characters?", *Bilingualism: Language and Cognition*, 8(1), pp. 79–83.

Martinussen, T. and Scheike, T.H., 2006, *Dynamic regression models for survival data*, Springer, Berlin.

Mattingly, I.G. and Hsiao, P.L., 1999, "Are phonetic elements in Chinese characters drawn from a syllabary?", *Psychologia*, 42(4), pp. 281–289.

Matuschek, H., Kliegl, R., Vasishth, S., Baayen, H. and Bates, D., 2017, "Balancing type I error and power in linear mixed models", *Journal of Memory and Language*, 94, pp. 305–315.

McBride-Chang, C., Chow, B.W., Zhong, Y., Burgess, S. and Hayward, W.G., 2005, "Chinese character acquisition and visual skills in two Chinese scripts", *Reading and Writing*, 18(2), pp. 99–128.

200 *Experimental evidence for character grammar*

Meyer, A.S., 1990, "The time course of phonological encoding in language production: The encoding of successive syllables of a word", *Journal of Memory and Language*, 29, pp. 524–545.

Myers, J., 2006, "Processing Chinese compounds: A survey of the literature", in G. Libben and G. Jarema, eds., *The representation and processing of compound words*, pp. 169–196, Oxford University Press, Oxford.

Myers, J., 2016, "Knowing Chinese character grammar", *Cognition*, 147, pp. 127–132.

Myers, J., 2017c, "Acceptability judgments", in M. Aronoff, ed., *Oxford research encyclopedia of linguistics*, Oxford University Press, Oxford, http://linguistics.oxfordre.com/, accessed 11/17/2018.

Myers, J., 2017f, "Morphological processing of compounds, behavioral studies", in R. Sybesma, W. Behr, Y. Gu, Z. Handel, C.T.J. Huang and J. Myers, eds., *Encyclopedia of Chinese language and linguistics*, vol. 3, pp. 94–100, Brill, Leiden.

Myers, J., Lee, H.H. and Tsay, J., 2005, "Phonological production in Taiwan Sign Language", *Language and Linguistics*, 6(2), pp. 319–359.

Nelson, T.M. and Ladan, C.J., 1976, "Judgment of meaningfulness of Chinese characters by English-speaking observers", *Visible Language*, 10(2), pp. 129–143.

Peirce, J.W., 2007, "PsychoPy: Psychophysics software in Python", *Journal of Neuroscience Methods*, 162(1–2), pp. 8–13.

Peirce, J.W., 2009, "Generating stimuli for neuroscience using PsychoPy", *Frontiers in Neuroinformatics*, 2, Article 10.

Peng, G., Minett, J.W. and Wang, W.S.Y., 2010, "Cultural background influences the liminal perception of Chinese characters: An ERP study", *Journal of Neurolinguistics*, 23(4), pp. 416–426.

Perfetti, C.A., Liu, Y. and Tan, L.H., 2005, "The lexical constituency model: Some implications of research on Chinese for general theories of reading", *Psychological Review*, 112(1), pp. 43–59.

Qiu, Y. and Zhou, X., 2010, "Perceiving the writing sequence of Chinese characters: An ERP investigation", *NeuroImage*, 50(2), pp. 782–795.

R Core Team, 2018, *R: A language and environment for statistical computing*. [Computer program] R Foundation for Statistical Computing, www.R-project.org/, accessed 11/17/2018.

Roelofs, A. and Baayen, H., 2002, "Morphology by itself in planning the production of spoken words", *Psychonomic Bulletin & Review*, 9(1), pp. 132–138.

Scheike, T.H. and Zhang, M.J., 2011, "Analyzing competing risk data using the R timereg package", *Journal of Statistical Software*, 38(2), pp. 1–15.

Schmidtke, D., Matsuki, K. and Kuperman, V., 2017, "Surviving blind decomposition: A distributional analysis of the time-course of complex word recognition", *Journal of Experimental Psychology: Learning, Memory, and Cognition*, 43(11), pp. 1793–1820.

Schreuder, R. and Baayen, R.H., 1997, "How complex simplex words can be", *Journal of Memory and Language*, 37(1), pp. 118–139.

Singmann, H., Bolker, B., Westfall, J. and Aust, F., 2018, "Afex: Analysis of factorial experiments", *R package version 0.21–2*, [Computer program], https://CRAN.R-project.org/package=afex, accessed 11/17/2018.

Stemberger, J.P. and Lewis, M., 1986, "Reduplication in Ewe: Morphological accommodation to phonological errors", in C. Ewen and J. Anderson, eds., *Phonology yearbook 3*, pp. 151–160, Cambridge University Press, Cambridge.

Su, I.F. and Law, S.P., 2017, "Character recognition and phonological access, neurolinguistic studies", in R. Sybesma, W. Behr, Y. Gu, Z. Handel, C.T.J. Huang and J. Myers, eds., *Encyclopedia of Chinese language and linguistics*, vol. 1, pp. 362–364, Brill, Leiden.

Sun, S. [孙善麟] and Yan, J. [严建雯], 2006, 结构对称汉字提取特点的研究 [Upon the retrieval of structurally symmetrical Chinese characters]. 宁波大学学报(教育科学版) [Journal of Ningbo University (Educational Science)], 28(2), pp. 39–42.

Sze, W.P., Liow, S.J.R. and Yap, M.J., 2014, "The Chinese Lexicon Project: A repository of lexical decision behavioral responses for 2,500 Chinese characters", *Behavior Research Methods*, 46(1), pp. 263–273.

Taft, M. and Zhu, X., 1997, "Submorphemic processing in reading Chinese", *Journal of Experimental Psychology: Learning, Memory, and Cognition*, 23(3), pp. 761–775.

Tamaoka, K. and Yamada, H., 2000, "The effects of stroke order and radicals on the knowledge of Japanese kanji orthography, phonology and semantics", *Psychologia*, 43(3), pp. 199–210.

Tan, L.H., Laird, A.R., Li, K. and Fox, P.T., 2005, "Neuroanatomical correlates of phonological processing of Chinese characters and alphabetic words: A meta-analysis", *Human Brain Mapping*, 25(1), pp. 83–91.

Tan, L.H., Spinks, J.A., Eden, G.F., Perfetti, C.A. and Siok, W.T., 2005, "Reading depends on writing, in Chinese", *Proceedings of the National Academy of Sciences*, 102(24), pp. 8781–8785.

Tan, L.H., Xu, M., Chang, C.Q. and Siok, W.T., 2013, "China's language input system in the digital age affects children's reading development", *Proceedings of the National Academy of Sciences*, 110(3), pp. 1119–1123.

Tao, L. and Healy, A.F., 2016, "Psycholinguistics: Reading Chinese", in S.W. Chan, ed., *The Routledge encyclopedia of the Chinese language*, pp. 685–705, Routledge, Abingdon.

Tsang, Y.K. and Chen, H.C., 2009, "Do position-general radicals have a role to play in processing Chinese characters?", *Language and Cognitive Processes*, 24(7–8), pp. 947–966.

Tse, P.U. and Cavanagh, P., 2000, "Chinese and Americans see opposite apparent motions in a Chinese character", *Cognition*, 74(3), pp. B27–B32.

Wang, J.C.S., 1983, *Toward a generative grammar of Chinese character structure and stroke order*, Ph.D. thesis, University of Wisconsin, Madison.

Wang, Q. and Dong, Y., 2013, "The N2-and N400-like effects of radicals on complex Chinese characters", *Neuroscience Letters*, 548, pp. 301–305.

Wang, R., Huang, S., Zhou, Y. and Cai, Z.G., Forthcoming, "Chinese character handwriting: A large-scale behavioral study and a database", *Behavior Research Methods*.

Wang, X., Yang, J., Shu, H. and Zevin, J.D., 2011, "Left fusiform BOLD responses are inversely related to word-likeness in a one-back task", *Neuroimage*, 55(3), pp. 1346–1356.

Williams, C. and Bever, T., 2010, "Chinese character decoding: A semantic bias?", *Reading and Writing*, 23(5), pp. 589–605.

Wu, Y., Mo, D., Tsang, Y.K. and Chen, H.C., 2012, "ERPs reveal sub-lexical processing in Chinese character recognition", *Neuroscience Letters*, 514(2), pp. 164–168.

Xiao, W. and Treiman, R., 2012, "Iconicity of simple Chinese characters", *Behavior Research Methods*, 44(4), pp. 954–960.

Xu, M., 2017, "Character amnesia", in R. Sybesma, W. Behr, Y. Gu, Z. Handel, C.T.J. Huang and J. Myers, eds., *Encyclopedia of Chinese language and linguistics*, vol. 1, pp. 356–358, Brill, Leiden.

Xu, Z.A. and Liu, D.P., 2018, "The influence of sensory-motor components of handwriting on Chinese character recognition in second- and fourth-grade Chinese children", *Talk presented at The 17th International Conference on the Processing of East Asian Languages and the 9th Conference on Language, Discourse, and Cognition*, Taipei.

Yang, C., 2016, *The price of linguistic productivity: How children learn to break the rules of language*, MIT Press, Cambridge, MA.

Yang, F.L. [楊馥菱] and Wu, J.T. [吳瑞屯], 2014, 漢字辨識作業中部首相同促發字的形似抑制效果 [Orthographic inhibition between characters with identical semantic radicals in primed character decision tasks]. 中華心理學刊 [Chinese Journal of Psychology], 56(1), pp. 49–63.

Yeh, S.L. and Li, J.L., 2002, "Role of structure and component in judgments of visual similarity of Chinese characters", *Journal of Experimental Psychology: Human Perception and Performance*, 28(4), pp. 933–947.

Yeh, S.L. [葉素玲], Li, J.L. [李金鈴] and Chen, I.P. [陳一平], 1997, 中文的字形分類系統 [The perceptual dimensions underlying the classification of the shapes of Chinese characters]. 中華心理學刊 [Chinese Journal of Psychology], 39(1), pp. 47–74.

Yeh, S.L., Li, J.L. and Chen, K.M., 1999, "Classification of the shapes of Chinese characters: Verification by different predesignated categories and varied sample sizes", *Chinese Journal of Psychology*, 41(1), pp. 65–85.

Yu, H., Gong, L., Qiu, Y. and Zhou, X., 2011, "Seeing Chinese characters in action: An fMRI study of the perception of writing sequences", *Brain and Language*, 119(2), pp. 60–67.

Zhao, L., Chen, C., Shao, L., Wang, Y., Xiao, X., Chen, C., Yang, J., Zevin, J. and Xue, G., 2016, "Orthographic and phonological representations in the fusiform cortex", *Cerebral Cortex*, 27(11), pp. 5197–5210.

6 Implications and applications

6.1. Introduction

So what does it all mean? Why do Chinese characters seem to have a lexical grammar of the same sort seen in spoken and signed languages, and what can we do with this information? In this final chapter, I first discuss the implications for the nature of human language (Section 6.2) and then consider the potential applications for language teaching, clinical linguistics, and computational linguistics (Section 6.3).

6.2. Explaining Chinese character grammar

Even if we grant that the parallels drawn in this book between character structure and the morphology, phonology, and phonetics of spoken and signed languages are not superficial coincidences or terminological sleight-of-hand, we still have to explain where these parallels come from. Do functional pressures in particular cultural contexts cause some orthographic systems to evolve certain grammar-like properties (Section 6.2.1)? Are the parallels with grammar the result of orthography sharing articulatory, perceptual, and cognitive constraints with speech and signing (Section 6.2.2)? Do humans have a biological faculty for grammar that is flexible enough to handle any sophisticated form of communication (Section 6.2.3)? Or does grammar-like structure emerge spontaneously in all sufficiently complex systems (Section 6.2.4)? Let us consider each of these (not mutually exclusive) possibilities in turn.

6.2.1. Cultural context for the evolution of logographic systems

Because of their much more transparent relationship to pronunciation, the structures of syllabic and alphabetic writing systems are almost entirely derived from speech, limiting the value of a grammatical approach to them (though see the discussion of Roman letters and English spelling in Section 1.4.3.2). It therefore seems plausible to speculate that a 'pure' orthographic grammar would arise more readily in a logographic system like that of Chinese, where the formal patterns within each orthographic symbol cannot simply be copied from spoken phonology

204 *Implications and applications*

or morphology. Moreover, mapping to spoken morphemes means that a large number of orthographic symbols need to be learned and processed efficiently, difficulties that an orthographic grammar may ease through devices like decompositionality and duality of patterning.

We do not have a very large sample of logographic systems to speculate about, however. On the one hand, logographic systems have been invented more than once (Sumerian cuneiform, Egyptian hieroglyphs, Chinese characters, Mayan glyphs): logographic systems seem natural. On the other hand, all but Chinese have gone extinct: logographic systems seem unstable.

Before we overgeneralize from this one logographic case, then, we should acknowledge its unique linguistic and cultural context. Sinitic phonology restricts the number of possible morpheme forms, and Sinitic morphology favors compounding over more asymmetrical word structures, making it particularly feasible to write morphemes with separate but equal symbols. These linguistic features are neither sufficient to trigger the adoption of a logographic orthography (the typologically similar Thai, Vietnamese, and Korean are written with letter-like graphs) nor are they necessary (spoken Sumerian, ancient Egyptian, and Mayan had un-Chinese-like phonology and morphology, as we will see). However, Chinese characters also developed in a culture shared by speakers of closely related but mutually unintelligible languages (in the Sinitic family). This situation not only made a logographic system a tool of political unification, but unification itself helped the culture resist pressure to make the transliteration of foreign borrowings more transparent.

In ancient Mesopotamia, by contrast, Sumerian was agglutinative, so its words were multisyllabic and its lexicon large, and there was also considerable multicultural and multi-lingual contact (in fact, the writing system was later adopted for Akkadian, an unrelated and typologically distinct language). Both factors led to the reuse of word symbols as syllable symbols in order to write productively generated words and foreign borrowings (Cooper 1996; Rude 1986). The Mayan language was also agglutinative, so glyph-internal symbols were also often used for their syllabic value (Chiang 2006; Macri 1996). Ancient Egypt was a remarkably stable political power (hieroglyphs were used for four millennia), but its writers and readers spoke a Semitic language in which vocalic prosodic templates were imposed on consonantal root morphemes, as in modern Arabic or Hebrew, so even early Egyptian scribes had to repurpose word symbols to indicate consonants and consonant groups (Ritner 1996).

Despite these contextual differences, logographic systems also share certain structural properties. One prominent trend is that the use of word symbols for pronunciation often causes semantic markers to take on a subordinate, and thus somewhat affix-like, role. We saw this in the history of Chinese in Section 4.3.1.1; in Egyptian hieroglyphs and Mesopotamian cuneiform, writers added so-called semantic determinatives to clarify written word forms that otherwise indicated pronunciation (Cooper 1996; Ritner 1996). A similar process is also occasionally seen in Mayan glyphs, though more often the reverse happened, with syllable

Implications and applications 205

symbols added to a logographic symbol, or even just combined with each other without any semantic marker (Chiang 2006).

According to Rude (1986) (see also Goldwasser 2006), determinatives in Egyptian and cuneiform acted like semantic classifiers, similar to the function that Wiebusch (1995) ascribes to semantic radicals in Chinese characters (see Section 2.3.1.1). In Egyptian hieroglyphs, for example, Rude (1986, p. 134) cites a pair of symbols representing the consonants /x/ and /r/ as being used both for the word meaning 'fire' and for the word meaning 'property' (though in speech they may also have differed in their vowels, which were not written). They would then be distinguished by the addition of a determinative relating to heat or temperature for 'fire,' and one relating to abstractions for 'property.'

Semantic markers in logographic systems also share another affix-like feature: favoring edge positions. Similar to the way semantic radicals in Chinese characters appear most often at the left edge, Ritner (1996) notes that the favored place for semantic determinatives in ancient Egyptian was at the end of the string of symbols making up a word (whether the string was written from right to left, left to right, or top to bottom). In cuneiform, determinatives could appear either before or after a word (Cooper 1996, p. 43), but still always at a word edge.

Even though the components of Mayan glyphs often represent syllables rather than meanings, they shared a different sort of formal property with Chinese semantic radicals: their positions were determined in part by shape, with tall and thin ones tending to appear at the right or left edge and squat and wide ones at the top or bottom. This shape-based restriction follows from another formal property that Mayan glyphs shared with Chinese characters: regardless of how many components it contained, a Mayan glyph maintained an overall square shape (Macri 1996; Chiang 2006).

Another formal property of logographic systems is shared with other types of orthography: the sacrificing of iconicity for simplicity. Simplification was particularly dramatic in the history of Egyptian writing, where the so-called hieratic system was developed early on for handwritten documents, as opposed to the more familiar monumental hieroglyphic style (Ritner 1996). Hegenbarth-Reichardt and Altmann (2008) found that hieratic reduced overall complexity roughly in half, and the most complex hieroglyphs were simplified even more than that. Phoenician letters, ultimately derived from Egyptian writing, were simpler still (Simons 2011). Simplification seems to have had physical as well as cognitive motivations. Mesopotamian cuneiform came into being when scribes realized that it was easier to press a reed end into wet clay, leaving abstract patterns of triangles, than to drag it along the clay to make line drawings (Cooper 1996). A possible exception to this diachronic simplification trend is Mayan glyphs, which tended to retain their ornateness to the bitter end, but even here iconicity was subservient to style; glyphs and glyph components generally are bordered in rounded ridges, for example.

Based on the few examples we have, then, logographic systems all display something like morphology (systematic combinations of interpreted symbols,

206 *Implications and applications*

some formally and functionally affix-like) and something like phonology (formal regularities not directly related to interpretation).

6.2.2. Articulatory, perceptual, and general cognitive influences

Simplification is just one of the many properties of Chinese characters that seem to result from domain-general articulatory, perceptual, and cognitive constraints. In Section 3.6.1, I showed how character phonology is clearly motivated by the physiology of the hand (without, however, being reducible to it), and the same is presumably true for all writing systems (see, e.g., Watt 2015). Writing is also constrained by the physics of the writing instruments, as with the reeds and clay of cuneiform (see Section 6.2.1) and the brush pens and paper of regular Chinese script.

Visual constraints also lead to orthographic universals, as reviewed in Section 3.6.1, such as the preference for strokes along the cardinal horizontal and vertical axes and the avoidance of contrasts that depend on differences in the left and right halves, due to the high salience of left-right symmetry (Changizi *et al.* 2006; Morin 2018). The latter bias seems to underlie several Chinese character patterns, including the strong preference for semantic radicals to appear at the left edge rather than at the top, and the greater productivity and splittability of horizontal reduplication relative to vertical reduplication (see Chapters 2 and 3). Yet as an orthographic universal, its effects are ubiquitous: as we saw in Section 1.4.3.2, vertically asymmetrical Roman capital letters all tend to 'face' the same way (Jameson 1994), and Egyptian hieroglyphs also tended to face the same way in a horizontal line of text, literally so for the hieroglyphs containing faces (Ritner 1996). In the boustrophedon writing of ancient Greek, letters were even mirror-reversed as each horizontal line of text ran in the opposite direction from the previous one (Coulmas 2003). Sign languages also avoid lexical contrasts that depend solely on using the left vs. right hand (Battison 1978). Orthographic learning studies confirm that these generalizations result from innate biases. Preschool Chinese children recall (Kwok and Chan 2008) and produce (Yin and Treiman 2013) characters with left-right symmetry more accurately than asymmetrical ones, replicating the results of Treiman and Kessler (2011) for English-speaking children learning to write letters.

Not all of character grammar interfaces directly with psychophysics: the external interpretation and semantic bleaching of semantic radicals, decompositionality, duality of patterning, and character prosody all seem to require higher-level mental representations and processes. It may be argued, however, that even these processes derive from general cognition, not modules specialized just for language. For example, decompositionality can also be seen in children's drawings (Karmiloff-Smith 1990), and something like the duality of patterning appears outside language as well. While the categorical perception of physically gradient stimuli is a hallmark of phonemic processing in both spoken (e.g., Zhang 2017) and signed (e.g., Morford *et al.* 2008) languages, it may also occur with nonlinguistic stimuli. For example, Goldstone (1994) created sets of visual stimuli varying in features like brightness and size, and trained people to

Implications and applications 207

Figure 6.1 Coarse-grained and fine-grained views of Chinese character reduplication

classify particular subsets of them. When they were then asked to discriminate among a larger set of gradiently varying stimuli, they were more accurate for stimulus pairs that crossed the trained category boundaries than for those that lay within the categories.

Character prosody may also have a basis in general cognition, since it seems related to the ability to perceive the same stimulus in either fine-grained or coarse-grained ways. The main cues for prosody in spoken languages are coarse-grained features like pitch, amplitude, and duration, so even if all but the lowest acoustic frequencies are filtered out, the prosodic structure can still be perceived (e.g., Jusczyk, Cutler, and Redanz 1993). In a similar way, if we blur reduplicative Chinese characters, as in the top row of Figure 6.1, those sharing the same reduplicative template look more similar, whereas if we see the character clearly, as in the bottom row, the internal constituents become more salient. The brain seems to perform similar sorts of manipulations, with different neural pathways handling fine-grained and coarse-grained information in visual images (e.g., Yamaguchi, Yamagata, and Kobayashi 2000).

However, nonlinguistic parallels for decomposition, duality of patterning, and the rest pose a challenge not just to Chinese character grammar, but to the notion of modular grammar in spoken and signed languages as well. In fact, parallels between linguistic and nonlinguistic cognition are sometimes seen as providing clues about how the human language capacity may have evolved out of existing cognitive structures. For example, what I have called the amodal links between articulation and perception are seen not just in language, where a single person is both the producer and recipient of linguistic forms. Even vision, as argued by Bever and Poeppel (2010), depends on linking perceptual input with the implicit production of mental models of three-dimensional space.

208 *Implications and applications*

6.2.3. A flexible human language faculty

I have argued that character grammar is abstract in being non-iconic, amodal, and modular. But according to linguists of a more formal bent, the most important way in which human grammar is more abstract than all other animal communication systems is that it operates via a sort of recursive algebra (what Pinker 1994, p. 84, calls a discrete combinatorial system). If Chinese characters do so too, does this mean that they depend on a species-specific capacity for grammar, a capacity flexible enough to be invoked not just in spoken and signed languages (already physically quite different from each other) but in orthography as well?

The term 'recursion' is used in several different senses (see, e.g., Fitch 2010), but linguists typically use it to describe an operation that can apply to its own output. Recursion is distinct from iteration in at least two ways. First, it is not merely that the same operation is carried out more than once, but that each time the result is something of the 'same kind.' Second, recursion gives rise to embedding, with one thing inside another and so on, all of the 'same kind.' Both properties are clearly seen in the most productive Chinese character formation process: semantic radical affixation.

Recursion is neither necessary nor sufficient for language. It is found in syntax, but not in all types of morphology (template-constrained reduplication is not recursive), nor in all types of phonology: phrasal prosody follows the recursive structure of syntax, but phonemes cannot contain phonemes, nor syllables contain syllables (though see van der Hulst 2010 for a fully recursive model of prosody). Recursion is also found outside of language; for example, we may open the door of the apartment building in order to open the door of the apartment in order to open the door of the bedroom in order to open the door of the closet. Animals can apply recursive algorithms like this when foraging a large area for food, and Hauser, Chomsky, and Fitch (2002) suggest that the neurocognitive underpinnings of such behavior may be part of the evolutionary basis for recursion in human language (though it is not clear exactly what sense of 'recursion' they have in mind here; see critique in Coolidge, Overmann, and Wynn 2011). Some songbirds even seem to structure their calls in accordance with regular grammars (Berwick *et al.* 2011), the same class used in human phonology and morphology (Heinz and Idsardi 2011) and, according to Sproat (2000), in orthography as well.

The similarities between human phonology and some animal communication systems, as well as its tight connection with peripheral processing systems, has led some linguists to argue that phonological cognition does not require specialized processing (e.g., Samuels 2009). However, human phonology does have species-specific properties (Berent 2013; Pinker and Jackendoff 2005), the most important of which is the second part of the formulation I gave at the start of this section: human phonology, like human grammar generally, is algebraic.

Algebra is the math of variables, that is, empty symbols that can take on any valid value assigned to them. For example, as Berent (2013) points out, syllables in human language, unlike the note groupings in birdsong, are formed algebraically, since they are constructed of slots for classes, like consonants and vowels,

Implications and applications 209

that may be filled in by any member of the appropriate class. In Chinese characters, the clearest evidence for variables comes from reduplication, where I have argued that constituents fill in empty templatic slots. Pinker and Prince (1988) were among the first to emphasize that reduplication requires abstract variables, as shown by the failure of computer models to handle this operation without them. Berent, Dupuis, and Brentari (2014) and Berent and Dupuis (2018) make a similar point in experiments on the productive knowledge of sign language reduplication, and Myers (2016), reviewed in Chapter 5, does the same for Chinese character reduplication.

Other aspects of character grammar can also be seen as algebraic. For example, as a class, semantic radicals generally refer to meaning and appear on the left edge, and all character constituents that have the right features can undergo regular processes like bottommost prominence, diagonalization, and curving. The experiments reviewed in Chapter 5 confirm that these patterns are also productively known by readers, and the coinage patterns reviewed in Chapter 4 suggest that writers know them as well.

I end this section with one other argument supporting a human capacity for grammar that is flexible enough to handle Chinese characters, and two arguments against it. The supportive argument is also formal. In the literature on artificial grammar learning (Pothos 2007), adults or children are presented with items obeying certain patterns, and are then asked to judge or otherwise process new items that do or do not obey these patterns. Many of these studies use stimuli written in letters, both genuine (e.g., Chang and Knowlton 2004) and invented (Byrne and Carroll 1989; Taylor *et al.* 2011), and some studies even use two-dimensional visual layouts (Fiser and Aslin 2001; Pothos and Bailey 2000; Saffran *et al.* 2007). All of these studies confirm that visual grammars (even without the temporal sequencing of sign languages) can be learned and productively generalized. Admittedly, this ability is not entirely restricted to humans: birds can also learn artificial visual grammars (Stobbe *et al.* 2012) and even patterns in English spelling (Scarf 2016). However, neither bird species tested by Stobbe *et al.* (2012) was able to learn anything more complex than a regular grammar, unlike their human participants.

My first critical argument against ascribing Chinese character patterns to a flexible grammar capacity goes back to phonology. Though prosodic templates seem to involve algebraic variables, we have already seen in Section 6.2.2 that they may also relate to low-level perceptual processes. It is not surprising, then, that prosody is not uniquely human: all animals make rhythmic movements, and some are sensitive to, and even synchronize with, the rhythmic communicative signals of others (Samuels 2009). One implication of this is that the binary nature of metrical systems in spoken languages (Gordon 2002b) may derive from the intrinsic alternation between the two extremes in a cyclic movement (e.g., [sw][sw][sw]). The binarity of the reduplicative templates in Chinese characters may ultimately have a similar basis, since writing them also involves repeating motoric subroutines.

My second critical argument is that the VWFA is far closer to the visual cortex at the back of the head than to Broca's area towards the front of the head, and the

210 *Implications and applications*

latter area has long been known to be essential to grammatical processing for both spoken (Sahin *et al.* 2009) and signed (Campbell, MacSweeney, and Waters 2008) languages. Broca's area also processes 'grammatical' structure beyond speech and sign, but only when it is temporal, as in musical cognition (Novembre and Keller 2011) or in artificial grammars involving sequentially presented units (Bahlmann, Schubotz, and Friederici 2008). By contrast, what the VWFA does seems more like an elaboration of visual processing than a variety of grammatical processing.

6.2.4. *The spontaneous emergence of structure in complex systems*

Just as grammar is governed in part by biology and in part by experience, biology and experience are themselves governed in part by something even more general: mathematics (or as Chomsky 2005 calls it, the 'third factor'). As we saw in Section 4.2.1, mathematical laws like Zipf's do not apply just to human language. Similarly, since binarity represents the simplest possible contrast, it appears not only in language (including Chinese character reduplication and basic stroke distinctions), but also in biology (e.g., the sexes) and physics (e.g., matter and antimatter). Even discrete combinatoriality is not unique to language; it is also a hallmark of chemistry and genetics, leading Abler (1989) to argue that in such "self-diversifying systems," structure spontaneously emerges as a mathematical necessity. Abler (2005) explicitly cites Chinese characters as providing another example, and Zhang (2006) independently makes a similar point.

We have encountered emergent structure a few times in this book already, including the young natural sign language studied by Sandler *et al.* (2011) (see Section 1.4.1) and the diachronic streamlining of Chinese characters (see Section 4.3.1); Lindblom (2000) and Mielke, Baker, and Archangeli (2016) are two of several studies advocating the idea that phonological structure is intrinsically emergent. Christiansen and Chater (2008) and Chater and Christiansen (2010) argue that grammar more generally emerges in order to coordinate information exchange with other members of a community within preexisting neural constraints. Grammar emergence has been modeled both computationally (e.g., Kirby 2000) and in learning experiments in which each 'generation' of participants shapes an artificial language into an ever more coherent system (e.g., Cornish, Tamariz, and Kirby 2009).

Even if particular brain areas have evolved different specialties in different species, they may do so under similar functional pressures; birdsong may share similarities with the independently evolved human language capacity because certain kinds of communication systems necessarily require certain kinds of structures. Regarding Chinese character grammar in particular, the VWFA and Broca's area may still be solving mathematically homologous problems, despite being innately equipped to handle physically distinct kinds of data (see Section 6.2.3).

How satisfying one finds purely mathematical explanations in science, as opposed to causal explanations, depends in part on one's personality (Myers 2012). However, given that human-like grammar is clearly not inevitable in nature, it seems reasonable to expect that the full explanation for why Chinese characters seem to have one

Implications and applications 211

will probably involve a variety of messy facts from biology, psychology, culture, and history, rather than a single elegant formula.

6.3. Applications

Is grammar useful to anybody but grammarians? Basic grammatical theory may help second-language students become more conscious of the patterns they need to learn, but the basics may be enough; De Bot (2015) dismisses generative linguistics in particular as too arcane and controversial for use as an actual classroom tool. Consciously knowing is also not the same as fluently doing and in fact can get in the way (Kahneman 2011); repetitious practice is essential not just to language teaching, but to clinical linguistics as well. Automated learning algorithms may capture language data better than handwritten grammars, leading one computational linguist to declare: "Whenever I fire a linguist our system performance improves" (though as Jelinek 2005 later explained, his notorious remark was made in a particular historical context). The tension between theory and practice is not limited to linguistics, of course: engineers do not wait for a full scientific explanation if they hit upon a method that works.

With these caveats in mind, in this final section of the book I review how character grammar already plays a role in applied linguistics and make suggestions along the way about how a more overt exploitation of the concept may provide even more benefits. I first discuss language teaching (Section 6.3.1), then clinical linguistics (Section 6.3.2), and finally computational linguistics (Section 6.3.3).

6.3.1. Teaching Chinese characters

If Chinese characters have a grammar, learning characters goes beyond learning a random set of symbols and visual/motor skills, whether the learners are Chinese-speaking children (Section 6.3.1.1) or non-Chinese-speaking adults (Section 6.3.1.2).

6.3.1.1. Teaching characters to Chinese-speaking children

Children are naturally talented at acquiring languages, and this talent extends to orthography. Figure 6.2 shows that Taiwanese children acquire over 3,500 traditional Chinese characters between the ages of 7 and 15, with the most rapid learning early on.

Like natural language acquisition, character knowledge in child learners depends on building amodal representations linking production and perception, as we have discussed before (see Section 5.2.1.2). The knowledge they build is structural and does not relate solely to the mechanics of handwriting, despite traditional pedagogical focus on the latter. For example, Law *et al.* (1998) found an overall accuracy rate of only 27 percent in the writing of ten traditional characters by children in the first year of primary school in Hong Kong (mean age: six years, four months), but as their study title reflects ("Children's stroke sequence errors

212 *Implications and applications*

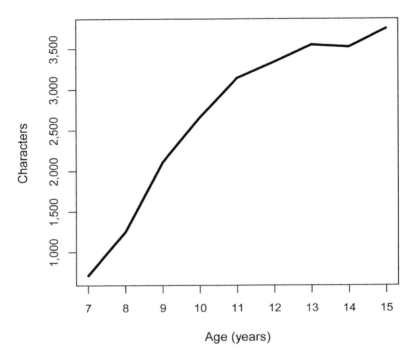

Figure 6.2 The learning of traditional Chinese characters by Taiwanese school children
Source: Data taken from Wang *et al.* (2008, Table 4, p. 560).

in writing Chinese characters"), the researchers thought that the main culprit was inadequate stroke order knowledge, and indeed, about 90 percent of the students said that they thought that correct stroke order was very important. However, most of the students could give no reason other than that their teachers had said so. Even more tellingly, virtually all of the errors reported by the authors relate not to stroke order per se, but to decomposition, for example, misidentifying the top of the character in (1a) as (1b), or stroke analysis, such as writing the constituent in (1c) with the top, right, and bottom lines joined into one clockwise stroke. That is, the errors were in character morphology and character phonology, not character phonetics.

(1) a 畢
    b 田
    c 口

Character learning also depends on learning to parse, just as in the acquisition of words and morphology in spoken and signed languages (e.g., Mintz 2013). The child's first step is to segment characters out of character strings. As Yin and Treiman (2013) found in a study on simplified character learners, even three-year-olds

Implications and applications 213

produce proto-writing clear enough for adults to distinguish attempts at writing single characters from attempts at writing multicharacter names. Next comes learning to analyze individual characters. Yeh *et al.* (2003) found that kindergartners (four to six-and-a-half years old) treated traditional characters in a classification task the same way as non-Chinese speaking foreigners and illiterate Chinese-speaking adults, solely in terms of strokes and stroke groups, whereas literate adults also took overall character configuration into account (see Section 5.2.3.1 for related studies by Yeh and colleagues).

After a bit more experience, children start to treat characters as composed of constituents, as Anderson *et al.* (2013) showed in tasks that asked seven-year-olds to detect a given constituent in a set of simplified characters. Chan and Nunes (1998) found that already by the age of five, children learning traditional characters showed awareness of the positional restrictions of particular constituents, based on their ability to correctly judge the acceptability of non-lexical characters that obeyed or violated these restrictions and to create new characters from a given set of components. Tsai and Nunes (2003) emphasize that the learning of character structure is implicit, with the patterns mostly discovered by the children themselves, further evidence that orthographic acquisition can be as 'natural' as that of spoken and signed languages (see Section 1.4.3.1).

In fact, Liu *et al.* (2010) found that ten-year-olds decomposed traditional characters so readily that in a lexical decision task, they often misclassified pseudocharacters (character-morphological accidental gaps) as real, a rather adult-like behavior (see Chapter 5 for much more on the processing of pseudocharacters). This development is reflected neurologically as well, with Tzeng *et al.* (2017) finding in an event-related potentials (ERP) study on Taiwanese children that the N400 (a negative-going brainwave component that appears about 400 ms after a lexically challenging stimulus) was similar for real characters and non-lexical pseudocharacters, regardless of reading ability. Less advanced readers also showed a stronger N400 for ungrammatical non-lexical characters, as if their less mature character grammars failed to filter them out efficiently. Like adults, children can also parse out character constituents even if they do not indicate meaning or pronunciation (Anderson *et al.* 2013; Shu and Anderson 1999; for adults, see Section 5.2.2.1).

The well-formedness of the individual constituents themselves also matters. Liu (2013) found that five- to six-year-old Taiwanese children rejected a non-lexical complex character more readily the more one of its constituents deviated from its lexical form (by adding ever more parallel strokes), suggesting that learning characters may also depend on learning character phonology (stroke group well-formedness).

The functional design of characters also affects how children learn to interpret them in terms of the spoken language. Phonemic awareness (the ability to recognize or manipulate individual phonemes in non-reading tasks) is vital for children learning to read alphabetic orthographies (e.g., Muter *et al.* 2004), but not for Chinese-speaking children learning characters. Rather, it is much more helpful for them to be aware of syllables and morphemes, which is what characters represent as wholes (McBride-Chang *et al.* 2003; McBride-Chang *et al.* 2008),

214 *Implications and applications*

with the former particularly important early on: Chinese children's reading and writing errors shift from pronunciation-based to meaning-based as they master the system (Tong and McBride-Chang 2010). These findings are particularly remarkable given that they were made in Hong Kong, where children are taught to link characters directly with speech, rather than first teaching them a phonetic notation system as is done in the rest of the People's Republic of China and in Taiwan (McBride-Chang *et al.* 2005).

Character-level mappings with pronunciation and meaning then help children infer the external interpretations for character-internal constituents (i.e., character morphology). Tsai and Nunes (2003) found that novel semantic-phonetic characters were learned more easily by seven- to ten-year-olds if they conformed to what they called this character type's 'schema,' that is, if they had a semantic radical associated with meaning and a phonetic component associated with pronunciation. Reading ability also benefits from an awareness of the semantic classes marked by semantic radicals (Hung *et al.* 2010; Lin 2011; Liu, Li, and Wong 2017) and of the clues that phonetic components provide about pronunciation (Chan and Nunes 1998). Learning how phonetic components work also seems to be a more effective way of mastering character pronunciations than learning via phonetic notation systems, as suggested by a study on eight-year-olds learning traditional characters in Taiwan (Li *et al.* 2018).

Given how quickly children learn characters, via amodal representations that are parsed at ever-deeper levels and then linked to external interpretations, character grammar seems to be acquired as naturally as the lexical grammars of spoken or signed languages. Of course, writing and reading are restricted to social and communicative contexts in which children are unlikely to find themselves without the extra effort of teachers (and parents with sufficient free time). Yet as Chan, Cheng, and Chan (2008) show in a case study of a single child, Chinese literacy can indeed emerge successfully in an environment rich with print and encouragement for the child's own orthographic explorations.

6.3.1.2. Teaching characters to non-Chinese-speaking adults

Aside from having less flexible brains and no prior Chinese experience, the main challenge faced by non-native-speaking adults learning characters is that they know too much. Similar to grammar transfer from a first language, adult learners of a new orthography come biased by their first, and the relative similarity of the two systems makes a difference (Bassetti 2013). In a review of ERP and fMRI studies of bilingual reading, Perfetti *et al.* (2007) highlight an asymmetry in adult Chinese-speaking learners of English and in adult English-speaking learners of Chinese: the former are able to incorporate English letters into the same brain network that they already use for Chinese characters, whereas the latter have to recruit new areas. Kim *et al.* (2016) report related fMRI results for adult native speakers of Korean who had learned both Chinese and English: their brain activation patterns became Chinese-like when reading Chinese but remained Korean-like when reading English, as if they were transferring experience from their own

Implications and applications 215

alphabetic Hangul system. Ehrich and Meuter (2009) even observed an advantage for adult Chinese readers when learning an artificial logographic system based on cuneiform, as compared to English and French readers.

At the same time, however, some of the prior knowledge possessed by adult learners of Chinese characters is useful. Human languages are more or less inter-translatable, so even non-Chinese-speaking adults come equipped with guesses about plausible character meanings. Conventional Chinese phonetic notation is also usually taught early on, providing adult learners with representations for character pronunciations as well. Similarly, Deaf adult signers of Taiwan Sign Language (TSL), even though they naturally have trouble activating character pronunciations (Chiu *et al.* 2016), are still able to piggyback on TSL: Chiu and Wu (2016) found that Deaf adult TSL signers looked longer at a character in a sentence if it was previewed by a character (i.e., replaced in the animated display before their eyes reached it) that had a phonologically similar TSL translation (e.g., sharing handshapes). The benefit of having something to map to orthography may be part of the reason why Hrastinski and Wilbur (2016) found a strong positive correlation between proficiency in American Sign Language and English literacy in American Deaf children (see Lee 2016 for a review of related studies).

Adult learners of Chinese characters also develop the amodal representations essential to the knowledge of formal character grammar. Guan *et al.* (2011) found that handwriting practice improved character recognition in foreign learners, and Ke (1996) found that, by the end of their first semester, American college students studying Chinese showed a strong correlation between how well they recognized characters and how well they wrote them, though eventually their reading ability outstripped their handwriting.

As with children, the benefits of stroke order training is not clear. Despite acknowledging this, Zhang (2014) argues that stroke order is still worth the classroom time because errors in stroke order are associated with the more important errors in stroke configuration and decomposition (recall the child writing study by Law *et al.* 1998, reviewed in Section 6.3.1.1), and because experiments have shown that mature Chinese readers are sensitive to stroke order even when viewing static characters (see Section 5.2.3.2). Neither argument is conclusive, however, for the reasons given in Section 3.6.2.1, and even Zhang admits that stroke order errors are usually invisible to the teacher in the final written form. In fact, overemphasizing stroke order may actually impede literacy: Chang *et al.* (2015) found that when characters were taught to English-speaking learners via animations showing correct stroke order, they were less sensitive to character meanings (as reflected in ERP measurements) than when characters were taught via static displays, presumably, as the authors speculate, due to the unnecessary distraction.

Zhang (2014) also complains that there are more studies on stroke errors in adult learners (e.g., Guo 2008) than on stroke order errors, but this is just as it should be; character knowledge is expected to depend less on character phonetics than on character phonology. Even at the level of phonetics, the fact that adult learners are often confused by visually similar characters (Jiang and Liu 2004; Xiao 2002) suggests that handwriting practice should be supplemented with

216 *Implications and applications*

exercises to strengthen perceptual discrimination (see Section 5.2.3.2 for studies on native Chinese).

Arguably the most important thing students need to learn about Chinese characters is character decomposition (character morphology). This point was emphasized by Tamaoka and Yamada (2000) for kanji writing by native Japanese speakers (see Section 5.2.1.2), and An and Shan (2007) draw similar conclusions for non-Chinese-speaking adult learners of Chinese characters. Non-native adults also learn to interpret semantic radicals for meaning and phonetic components for pronunciation, though the former much more reliably than the latter (Williams 2013), similar to the delayed use of phonetic components by native Chinese children (Shu and Anderson 1999). In both cases, the relative ease of learning semantic radicals may be due, in part, to there being far fewer of them to commit to memory, as compared with the open class of phonetic components.

While children may have a greater ability to absorb language without overt guidance, adults have greater analytical skills, allowing for the use of teaching methods that exploit metalinguistic awareness. Adults also have much wider reading and writing interests than children, and teaching materials should not only reflect this fact, but exploit it. As Shu *et al.* (2003) observe, by introducing the most common and simplest characters first, children's textbooks end up with a preponderance of characters atypical for the lexicon as a whole, non-decomposable or irregular in their phonetic components. By contrast, for adult learners, Tollini (1994) advocates teaching characters (in his case, Japanese kanji) that highlight the overall logic of character form, even if the characters themselves are rarer or more complex.

The adult powers of metalinguistic awareness can also be sharpened through drills and games that explicitly highlight character structure, as has been demonstrated many times (Chang *et al.* 2014; Chen *et al.* 2013; Hong *et al.* 2016; Jin 2003; Shen 2005; Taft and Chung 1999; Zhao and Jiang 2002). In a paper arguing for the relevance of grammatical theory to Chinese language teaching more generally, Li (2015) suggests giving adult learners practice in doing overt linguistic analysis, supplemented with teacher guidance only after the students have tried for themselves. Applying her advice to character grammar, students could be given sets of characters, like those shown in Chapters 2 and 3, and be asked to find the patterns.

Finally, there is no limit to what adult learners may be curious about in the language they are learning. Chinese teachers should therefore be prepared for a wide range of 'why' questions, even about aspects of character form not addressed in their textbooks. For example, I have heard from my Chinese teaching colleagues about students asking why certain characters have hooked strokes while others do not. Needless to say, this very book would provide an excellent resource for answering such questions!

6.3.2. Clinical linguistics

If grammar provides the abstract framework for language processing, we expect character grammar to be relevant to the diagnosis and treatment of reading deficits

Implications and applications 217

(dyslexia). This general point should hold whether we are looking at developmental dyslexia in children (and the adults they grow into) or dyslexia acquired through brain damage.

This is why the model of children's reading ability reviewed in Perfetti (2007) emphasizes the crucial role of mental representations (lexical quality) in reading ability, not merely processing efficiency. That orthographic knowledge structures orthographic processing is also shown by cross-orthography differences in both developmental dyslexia (Miles 2000) and acquired dyslexia (Weekes 2012). Dyslexic universals (see Snowling 2013 and Weekes 2012 for developmental and acquired dyslexia, respectively) also suggest a role for grammar: dyslexia is associated with focal brain anomalies (though not necessarily in the same areas in each case; Hadzibeganovic *et al.* 2010) and is usually accompanied by dysgraphia (writing deficits), showing that the problems reside at a level more abstract than visual processing or motor control alone.

Since Chinese characters represent spoken morphemes, problems in morphemic awareness predict dyslexia in Chinese reading children (Chung and Ho 2010) and, to a lesser degree, so do problems with syllable awareness, visual skills, and productive orthographic knowledge (McBride-Chang *et al.* 2011). Regarding orthographic knowledge, in one common task, children are given a mixture of real characters, well-formed pseudocharacters, and ungrammatical non-lexical characters with constituents in illegal positions. Difficulties in distinguishing the ungrammatical characters from the others predicts Chinese reading and writing difficulties more generally (Chung and Ho 2010; Ho *et al.* 2004); dyslexic children also show less distinct brain responses to well-formed vs. ungrammatical non-lexical characters than normally developing children (Tzeng *et al.* 2018). Problems with interpreting semantic radicals for meaning are similarly predictive (Leung and Ho 2009). In an intriguing case study, Luo *et al.* (2018) found that a hyperlexical Cantonese-speaking child, identified as such by scoring very high in reading aloud but very low in comprehension, did indeed rely atypically heavily on a lexical (rather than grammar-based) route for character recognition, given that the child's ability to select or distinguish word-like characters applied only to genuine characters.

Anomalies in character decomposition are found in acquired dyslexia as well, though in the reverse direction: brain-damaged adults tend to decompose characters too readily. Yin *et al.* (2005) reviews studies showing that some patients have particular trouble reading characters with irregular phonetic components, suggesting that they depend more on them than do unimpaired readers. Han *et al.* (2007) report on a dysgraphic patient who made numerous errors at the level of character constituents, most often by replacing the intended constituent with one similar to it; as we saw in Section 4.4.2, the same types of errors are also made by unimpaired writers, just more rarely. It is as if developmental dyslexia hinders character reading though the delayed learning of character grammar, whereas acquired dyslexia hinders it by damaging pathways for rote character access while leaving character grammar intact. This would make the latter quite different in nature from Broca's aphasia, where grammatical processing itself is a primary casualty (Grodzinsky and Santi 2008).

218 *Implications and applications*

Given these findings, at-risk children benefit from exercises that encourage them to become more aware of the components of their spoken language that are encoded by their orthographic system (Snowling 2013) as well as the internal structure of the orthographic system itself; this also holds of Chinese (Chung and Ho 2010). Such interventions essentially target orthographic morphology. Acquired dysgraphia, as a subtype of acquired apraxia (motor control deficits), also benefits from training in compensatory strategies (e.g., Cicerone *et al.* 2005), thereby targeting an aspect of orthographic phonetics. Exploration of the full richness of character grammar may allow Chinese clinicians to experiment with other regimens as well.

6.3.3. Computational linguistics

Automatic character recognition algorithms often implement aspects of character phonology, such as identification of stroke types (e.g., Fujisawa and Liu 2003; Liu *et al.* 2001; Su 2013), and character databases generally take character morphology into account via character decompositions (see Section 1.2.2.3). Some models also include something like phonology, with frameworks for encoding allomorphy (Haralambous 2013), changes in constituent dimensions (Liu, Duan, and Pi 2009), and stroke-level variation (Bishop and Cook 2007).

Nevertheless, in the past few decades, the general trend among computational linguists has been away from grammar and towards data-driven statistical approaches (Pereira 2000), and the same is true for how they deal with Chinese characters (Dai *et al.* 2007). Natural language grammars are extremely complex and interact with lexical information in even more complex ways, making even the thickest grammar books incapable of capturing all of a language's nuances. Theoretical linguists themselves now agree that the best grammars are those that grow naturally when human learners are exposed to copious amounts of actual language data, leading some to develop computational learning models of their own (e.g., Heinz 2011; Yang 2011). Most computational linguists, however, do not want to model actual human learners, just build a useful product, and if automatic text readers, writers, and translators can make do without any grammar at all, so much the better (though if Neeleman and van de Koot 2010 are right, grammar will emerge as a top-level description anyway; see Section 1.3.1.2).

The grammar-free approach that is particularly prominent in the most recent computational literature involves so-called deep learning (Schmidhuber 2015). This incorporates artificial neural networks in which vast numbers of connections are arranged in many layers, so as each layer recodes input from the previous one, ever more abstract information can be extracted. These models have roots going back to the 1950s (Medler 1998), but only recently have computers become powerful enough to handle the enormous data sets and networks needed to fulfill their potential. For example, in order to model just 1,000 distinct Chinese characters, Cireşan *et al.* (2012) built a network with almost 400,000 nodes, arranged into ten layers, each with its own internal architecture designed to perform a particular type of processing (encoding visual details, generalizing patterns, and

Implications and applications   219

finally identifying characters), and trained it on almost 250,000 character tokens for 14 hours. Among the many other deep-learning character recognition models are those of Wang *et al.* (2017) (which also recognizes constituents within novel characters) and Zhang *et al.* (2018) (which also models character handwriting).

Like all human artifacts, all of these learning models require some manual tweaking to make them suit their human-oriented purposes. Hand-coding is increasingly performed by us, the public, via crowdsourcing tools like Google's reCAPTCHA (von Ahn *et al.* 2008), but model improvement depends on more sophisticated human intervention as well. In the Cireşan *et al.* (2012) study, for example, better results were achieved when the model was initially trained on just ten of the 1,000 character targets, and only after it had reached peak performance on these were just the top five most abstract network layers trained on all 1,000 targets. While this mimics the 'starting small' strategy claimed to hold of natural language acquisition (Elman 1993), it does so (just as in Elman's own network model) only by withholding information in a way that does not occur in natural language acquisition. Investing in traditional scientific research into how characters are actually structured and how this structure is learned by actual humans may ultimately raise character engineering projects above their current ad hoc state.

Even if some computational linguists seem to have lost interest in what grammarians have to say, there is much that grammarians can learn from computational linguists. The theoretical language learning models reviewed in Heinz (2011) and Yang (2011) often make use of methods first developed for engineering purposes, and studies like Silfverberg and Hulden's (2018) continue this tradition by applying deep learning to theoretical linguistic questions. The engineering literature can inspire the scientific study of nature because engineers and nature often stumble across similar solutions to similar problems (see Section 6.2.4). For example, after training only on Chinese characters, the model of Cireşan *et al.* (2012) turned out to recognize uppercase Latin letters as well, inadvertently replicating the finding of Perfetti *et al.* (2007) that Chinese readers co-opt the same brain areas for reading English (see Section 6.3.1.2). Similarly, a grammarian could try training a deep-learning model on psycholinguistic reading data, like reaction times in character lexical decisions, and then examining the intermediate layers to see what sorts of abstract representations might be used by actual readers. Perhaps some layers will encode character morphology, while others encode character phonology (see also Section 4.2.1 for related corpus-based studies).

6.4. Summary

This final chapter started by asking where character grammar might come from: the Chinese social and linguistic context, general physiological and cognitive constraints, a species-specific predilection for grammar, mathematical constraints, or some combination of these. I then turned to possible ways in which the study of character grammar, like theoretical linguistics more generally, might actually be useful to language teachers, clinical linguists, and computational linguists.

220 *Implications and applications*

All of this assumes that Chinese characters do indeed have a grammar that is actually implemented, in some way, in the mind and brain. I have done my best throughout this book to make a case for this very claim and hope that at least some of my readers will take up the pen themselves, proposing improved or alternative analyses, exploring corpora with new techniques, running new experiments, and exploring the implications and applications of character grammar in their own way.

References

Abler, W.L., 1989, "On the particulate principle of self-diversifying systems", *Journal of Social and Biological Structures*, 12(1), pp. 1–13.

Abler, W.L., 2005, *Structure of matter, structure of mind*, Pensoft, Sofia.

An, R. [安然] and Shan, Y. [单韵鸣], 2007, 非汉字圈学生的笔顺问题 – 从书写汉字的个案分析谈起 [The sequence of Chinese characters writing: A case study of foreign students learning Chinese]. 语言文字应用 [Applied Linguistics], 2007(3), pp. 54–61.

Anderson, R.C., Ku, Y.M., Li, W., Chen, X., Wu, X. and Shu, H., 2013, "Learning to see the patterns in Chinese characters", *Scientific Studies of Reading*, 17(1), pp. 41–56.

Bahlmann, J., Schubotz, R.I. and Friederici, A.D., 2008, "Hierarchical artificial grammar processing engages Broca's area", *Neuroimage*, 42(2), pp. 525–534.

Bassetti, B., 2013, "Bilingualism and writing systems", in T.K. Bhatia and W.C. Ritchie, eds., *The handbook of bilingualism and multilingualism*, 2nd ed., pp. 649–670, Wiley-Blackwell, Hoboken, NJ.

Battison, R., 1978, *Lexical borrowing in American Sign Language*, Linstok Press, Silver Spring, MD.

Berent, I., 2013, "The phonological mind", *Trends in Cognitive Sciences*, 17(7), pp. 319–327.

Berent, I. and Dupuis, A., 2018, "The unbounded productivity of (sign) language", *The Mental Lexicon*, 12(3), pp. 309–341.

Berent, I., Dupuis, A. and Brentari, D., 2014, "Phonological reduplication in sign language: Rules rule", *Frontiers in Psychology*, 5, Article 560.

Berwick, R.C., Okanoya, K., Beckers, G.J. and Bolhuis, J.J., 2011, "Songs to syntax: The linguistics of birdsong", *Trends in Cognitive Sciences*, 15(3), pp. 113–121.

Bever, T.G. and Poeppel, D., 2010, "Analysis by synthesis: A (re-) emerging program of research for language and vision", *Biolinguistics*, 4(2–3), pp. 174–200.

Bishop, T. and Cook, R., 2007, "A character description language for CJK", *Multilingual*, 18(7), pp. 62–68.

Byrne, B. and Carroll, M., 1989, "Learning artificial orthographies: Further evidence of a nonanalytic acquisition procedure", *Memory & Cognition*, 17(3), pp. 311–317.

Campbell, R., MacSweeney, M. and Waters, D., 2008, "Sign language and the brain: A review", *The Journal of Deaf Studies and Deaf Education*, 13(1), pp. 3–20.

Chan, L., Cheng, Z.J. and Chan, L.F., 2008, "Chinese preschool children's literacy development: From emergent to conventional writing", *Early Years*, 28(2), pp. 135–148.

Chan, L. and Nunes, T., 1998, "Children's understanding of the formal and functional characteristics of written Chinese", *Applied Psycholinguistics*, 19(1), pp. 115–131.

Chang, G.Y. and Knowlton, B.J., 2004, "Visual feature learning in artificial grammar classification", *Journal of Experimental Psychology: Learning, Memory, and Cognition*, 30(3), pp. 714–722.

Chang, L.Y., Stafura, J.Z., Rickles, B., Chen, H.C. and Perfetti, C.A., 2015, "Incremental learning of Chinese orthography: ERP indicators of animated and static stroke displays on character form and meaning acquisition", *Journal of Neurolinguistics*, 33, pp. 78–95.

Implications and applications 221

Chang, L.Y., Xu, Y., Perfetti, C.A., Zhang, J. and Chen, H.C., 2014, "Supporting orthographic learning at the beginning stage of learning to read Chinese as a second language", *International Journal of Disability, Development and Education*, 61(3), pp. 288–305.

Changizi, M.A., Zhang, Q., Ye, H. and Shimojo, S., 2006, "The structures of letters and symbols throughout human history are selected to match those found in objects in natural scenes", *The American Naturalist*, 167(5), pp. E117–E139.

Chater, N. and Christiansen, M.H., 2010, "Language acquisition meets language evolution", *Cognitive Science*, 34(7), pp. 1131–1157.

Chen, H.C., Hsu, C.C., Chang, L.Y., Lin, Y.C., Chang, K.E. and Sung, Y.T., 2013, "Using a radical-derived character e-learning platform to increase learner knowledge of Chinese characters", *Language Learning & Technology*, 17(1), pp. 89–106.

Chiang, W., 2006, "A comparison of Maya and oracle bone scripts", *Visible Language*, 40(3), pp. 310–333.

Chiu, Y.S., Kuo, W.J., Lee, C.Y. and Tzeng, O.J.L., 2016, "The explicit and implicit phonological processing of Chinese characters and words in Taiwanese Deaf signers", *Language and Linguistics*, 17(1), pp. 63–87.

Chiu, Y.S. and Wu, M.D., 2016, "Use of phonological representations of Taiwan Sign Language in Chinese reading: Evidence from Deaf signers", *Bulletin of Special Education*, 41(1), pp. 91–109.

Chomsky, N., 2005, "Three factors in language design", *Linguistic Inquiry*, 36(1), pp. 1–22.

Christiansen, M.H. and Chater, N., 2008, "Language as shaped by the brain", *Behavioral and Brain Sciences*, 31(5), pp. 489–509.

Chung, K.K. and Ho, C.S.H., 2010, "Dyslexia in Chinese language: An overview of research and practice", *Australian Journal of Learning Difficulties*, 15(2), pp. 213–224.

Cicerone, K.D., Dahlberg, C., Malec, J.F., Langenbahn, D.M., Felicetti, T., Kneipp, S., Ellmo, W., Kalmar, K., Giacino, J.T., Harley, J.P., Laatsch, L., Morse, P.A. and Catanese, J., 2005, "Evidence-based cognitive rehabilitation: Updated review of the literature from 1998 through 2002", *Archives of Physical Medicine and Rehabilitation*, 86(8), pp. 1681–1692.

Cireşan, D.C., Meier, U. and Schmidhuber, J., 2012, "Transfer learning for Latin and Chinese characters with deep neural networks", *The 2012 International Joint Conference on Neural Networks(IJCNN)*, IEEE, pp. 1–6.

Coolidge, F.L., Overmann, K.A. and Wynn, T., 2011, "Recursion: What is it, who has it, and how did it evolve?", *Wiley Interdisciplinary Reviews: Cognitive Science*, 2(5), pp. 547–554.

Cooper, J.S., 1996, "Sumerian and Akkadian", in P.T. Daniels and W. Bright, eds., *The world's writing systems*, pp. 37–57, Oxford University Press, Oxford.

Cornish, H., Tamariz, M. and Kirby, S., 2009, "Complex adaptive systems and the origins of adaptive structure: What experiments can tell us", *Language Learning*, 59(s1), pp. 187–205.

Coulmas, F., 2003, *Writing systems: An introduction to their linguistic analysis*, Cambridge University Press, Cambridge.

Dai, R., Liu, C. and Xiao, B., 2007, "Chinese character recognition: History, status and prospects", *Frontiers of Computer Science in China*, 1(2), pp. 126–136.

De Bot, K., 2015, "Moving where? A reaction to Slabakova *et al.* (2014)", *Applied Linguistics*, 36(2), pp. 261–264.

Ehrich, J.F. and Meuter, R.F., 2009, "Acquiring an artificial logographic orthography: The beneficial effects of a logographic L1 background and bilinguality", *Journal of Cross-Cultural Psychology*, 40(5), pp. 711–745.

Elman, J.L., 1993, "Learning and development in neural networks: The importance of starting small", *Cognition*, 48(1), pp. 71–99.

222 Implications and applications

Fiser, J. and Aslin, R.N., 2001, "Unsupervised statistical learning of higher-order spatial structures from visual scenes", *Psychological Science*, 12(6), pp. 499–504.

Fitch, W.T., 2010, "Three meanings of 'recursion': Key distinctions for biolinguistics", in R.K. Larson, V. Deprez and H. Yamakido, eds., *The evolution of human language: Biolinguistic perspectives*, pp. 73–90, Cambridge University Press, Cambridge.

Fujisawa, H. and Liu, C.L., 2003, "Directional pattern matching for character recognition revisited", *Proceedings of the Seventh International Conference on Document Analysis and Recognition*, IEEE, pp. 794–798.

Goldstone, R.L., 1994, "Influences of categorization on perceptual discrimination", *Journal of Experimental Psychology: General*, 123(2), pp. 178–200.

Goldwasser, O., 2006, "On the new definition of classifier languages and scripts", *Lingua Aegyptia*, 14, pp. 473–484.

Gordon, M., 2002b, "A factorial typology of quantity-insensitive stress", *Natural Language & Linguistic Theory*, 20(3), pp. 491–552.

Grodzinsky, Y. and Santi, A., 2008, "The battle for Broca's region", *Trends in Cognitive Sciences*, 12(12), pp. 474–480.

Guan, C.Q., Liu, Y., Chan, D.H.L., Ye, F. and Perfetti, C.A., 2011, "Writing strengthens orthography and alphabetic-coding strengthens phonology in learning to read Chinese", *Journal of Educational Psychology*, 103(3), pp. 509–522.

Guo, S.L. [郭圣林], 2008, 汉字的笔画特点与外国学生汉字笔画偏误 [The features of Chinese character stroke and foreign learners' errors of Chinese character stroke]. 暨南大学华文学院学报 [Journal of College of Chinese Language and Culture of Jinan University], 2008(4), pp. 63–69.

Hadzibeganovic, T., van den Noort, M., Bosch, P., Perc, M., van Kralingen, R., Mondt, K. and Coltheart, M., 2010, "Cross-linguistic neuroimaging and dyslexia: A critical view", *Cortex*, 46(10), pp. 1312–1316.

Han, Z., Zhang, Y., Shu, H. and Bi, Y., 2007, "The orthographic buffer in writing Chinese characters: Evidence from a dysgraphic patient", *Cognitive Neuropsychology*, 24(4), pp. 431–450.

Haralambous, Y., 2013, "New perspectives in Sinographic language processing through the use of character structure", in A. Gelbukh, ed., *Computational linguistics and intelligent text processing (CICLing 2013)*, pp. 201–217, Springer, Berlin.

Hauser, M.D., Chomsky, N. and Fitch, W.T., 2002, "The faculty of language: What is it, who has it, and how did it evolve?", *Science*, 298(5598), pp. 1569–1579.

Hegenbarth-Reichardt, I. and Altmann, G., 2008, "On the decrease of complexity from hieroglyphs to hieratic symbols", in G. Altmann and F. Fan, eds., *Analyses of script: Properties of characters and writing systems*, pp. 105–114, Mouton de Gruyter, Berlin.

Heinz, J., 2011, "Computational phonology, Part II: Grammars, learning, and the future", *Language and Linguistics Compass*, 5(4), pp. 153–168.

Heinz, J. and Idsardi, W., 2011, "Sentence and word complexity", *Science*, 333(6040), pp. 295–297.

Ho, C.S.H., Chan, D.W.O., Lee, S.H., Tsang, S.M. and Luan, V.H., 2004, "Cognitive profiling and preliminary subtyping in Chinese developmental dyslexia", *Cognition*, 91(1), pp. 43–75.

Hong, J.C., Wu, C.L., Chen, H.C., Chang, Y.L. and Chang, K.E., 2016, "Effect of radical-position regularity for Chinese orthographic skills of Chinese-as-a-second-language learners", *Computers in Human Behavior*, 59, pp. 402–410.

Hrastinski, I. and Wilbur, R.B., 2016, "Academic achievement of deaf and hard-of-hearing students in an ASL/English bilingual program", *Journal of Deaf Studies and Deaf Education*, 21(2), pp. 156–170.

Hung, K.C. [洪國鈞], Lee, S.H. [李姝慧], Chen, S.Y. [陳修元] and Chou, T.L. [周泰立], 2010, 語意部件與關聯強度對成人與國小五年級孩童漢字語意處理效應的差異 [Effects of semantic radical and semantic association on semantic processing of Chinese characters for adults and fifth graders]. 中華心理學刊 [Chinese Journal of Psychology], 52(3), pp. 327–344.

Jameson, K., 1994, "Empirical methods for evaluating generative semiotic models: An application to the roman majuscules", in W.C. Watt, ed., *Writing systems and cognition: Perspectives from psychology, physiology, linguistics, and semiotics*, pp. 247–291, Springer, Dordrecht.

Jelinek, F., 2005, "Some of my best friends are linguists", *Language Resources and Evaluation*, 39(1), pp. 25–34.

Jiang, X. [江新] and Liu, Y. [柳燕梅], 2004, 拼音文字背景的外国学生汉字书写错误研究 [A study of character writing errors by foreign learner using alphabetic writing]. 世界汉语教学 [Chinese Teaching in the World], 67(1), pp. 60–70.

Jin, H.G., 2003, "Empirical evidence on character recognition in multimedia Chinese tasks", *Concentric: Studies in Linguistics*, 29(2), pp. 36–58.

Jusczyk, P.W., Cutler, A. and Redanz, N.J., 1993, "Infants' preference for the predominant stress patterns of English words", *Child Development*, 64(3), pp. 675–687.

Kahneman, D., 2011, *Thinking, fast and slow*, Farrar, Straus and Giroux, New York.

Karmiloff-Smith, A., 1990, "Constraints on representational change: Evidence from children's drawing", *Cognition*, 34(1), pp. 57–83.

Ke, C., 1996, "An empirical study on the relationship between Chinese character recognition and production", *The Modern Language Journal*, 80(3), pp. 340–349.

Kim, S.Y., Qi, T., Feng, X., Ding, G., Liu, L. and Cao, F., 2016, "How does language distance between L1 and L2 affect the L2 brain network? An fMRI study of Korean-Chinese-English trilinguals", *NeuroImage*, 129, pp. 25–39.

Kirby, S., 2000, "Syntax without natural selection: How compositionality emerges from vocabulary in a population of learners", in C. Knight, M. Studdert-Kennedy and J.R. Hurford, eds., *The evolutionary emergence of language: Social function and the origins of linguistic form*, pp. 303–323, Cambridge University Press, Cambridge.

Kwok, E. [郭婉儀] and Chan, L. [陳莉莉], 2008, 學前兒童對中文字的視覺記憶 [Preschool children's visual perception of Chinese characters]. 基礎教育學報 [Journal of Basic Education], 17(1), pp. 59–71.

Law, N., Ki, W.W., Chung, A.L.S., Ko, P.Y. and Lam, H.C., 1998, "Children's stroke sequence errors in writing Chinese characters", *Reading and Writing: An Interdisciplinary Journal*, 10, pp. 267–292.

Lee, H.H., 2016, *A comparative study of the phonology of Taiwan Sign Language and Signed Chinese*, Ph.D. thesis, National Chung Cheng University.

Leung, K.N.K. and Ho, C.S.H., 2009, "Semantic radical awareness in Chinese dyslexic children and its role in Chinese word reading", *Journal of Psychology in Chinese Societies*, 10(2), pp. 169–189.

Li, A.Y.H., 2015, Facilitating language learning: A generative perspective", in H. Tao, Y.H. Lee, D. Su, K. Tsurumi, W. Wang and Y. Yang, eds., *Proceedings of the 27th North American conference on Chinese linguistics*, vol. 1, pp. 1–21, UCLA, Los Angeles.

224 *Implications and applications*

Li, L., Wang, H.C., Castles, A., Hsieh, M.L. and Marinus, E., 2018, "Phonetic radicals, not phonological coding systems, support orthographic learning via self-teaching in Chinese", *Cognition*, 176, pp. 184–194.

Lin, P.Y. [林佩怡], 2011, 漢字辨識中的部首部件處理歷程：一般與弱讀兒童的比較 [Semantic radical processes of Chinese characters in normal and poor readers]. MA thesis, National Chung Cheng University.

Lindblom, B., 2000, "Emergent phonology", *Annual Meeting of the Berkeley Linguistics Society*, 25(1), pp. 195–209.

Liu, C.L., Kim, I.J. and Kim, J.H., 2001, "Model-based stroke extraction and matching for handwritten Chinese character recognition", *Pattern Recognition*, 34(12), pp. 2339–2352.

Liu, D., Li, H. and Wong, K.S.R., 2017, "The anatomy of the role of morphological awareness in Chinese character learning: The mediation of vocabulary and semantic radical knowledge and the moderation of morpheme family size", *Scientific Studies of Reading*, 21(3), pp. 210–224.

Liu, M. [劉敏], 2013, 中文兒童組字規則覺識發展 [Development of Chinese character orthography awareness of Taiwanese children]. MA thesis, Taipei Municipal University of Education.

Liu, M., Duan, C. and Pi, Y., 2009, "Basic elements knowledge acquisition study in the Chinese character intelligent formation system", *Journal of Software Engineering and Applications*, 2(5), pp. 316–322.

Liu, P.D., Chung, K.K., McBride-Chang, C. and Tong, X., 2010, "Holistic versus analytic processing: Evidence for a different approach to processing of Chinese at the word and character levels in Chinese children", *Journal of Experimental Child Psychology*, 107(4), pp. 466–478.

Luo, L., Tai, Y.-T. and Su, I.-F., 2018, "Meta-linguistic awareness skills in Chinese-speaking children with hyperlexia", *Talk presented at The 17th International Conference on the Processing of East Asian Languages and the 9th Conference on Language, Discourse, and Cognition*, Taipei.

Macri, M.J., 1996, "Maya and other Mesoamerican scripts", in P.T. Daniels and W. Bright, eds., *The world's writing systems*, pp. 172–182, Oxford University Press, Oxford.

McBride-Chang, C., Chow, B.W., Zhong, Y., Burgess, S. and Hayward, W.G., 2005, "Chinese character acquisition and visual skills in two Chinese scripts", *Reading and Writing*, 18(2), pp. 99–128.

McBride-Chang, C., Lam, F., Lam, C., Chan, B., Fong, C.Y.C., Wong, T.T.Y. and Wong, S.W.L., 2011, "Early predictors of dyslexia in Chinese children: Familial history of dyslexia, language delay, and cognitive profiles", *Journal of Child Psychology and Psychiatry*, 52(2), pp. 204–211.

McBride-Chang, C., Shu, H., Zhou, A., Wat, C.P. and Wagner, R.K., 2003, "Morphological awareness uniquely predicts young children's Chinese character recognition", *Journal of Educational Psychology*, 95(4), pp. 743–751.

McBride-Chang, C., Tong, X., Shu, H., Wong, A.M.Y., Leung, K.W. and Tardif, T., 2008, "Syllable, phoneme, and tone: Psycholinguistic units in early Chinese and English word recognition", *Scientific Studies of Reading*, 12(2), pp. 171–194.

Medler, D.A., 1998, "A brief history of connectionism", *Neural Computing Surveys*, 1(2), pp. 18–72.

Mielke, J., Baker, A. and Archangeli, D., 2016, "Individual-level contact limits phonological complexity: Evidence from bunched and retroflex /ɹ/", *Language*, 92(1), pp. 101–140.

Miles, E., 2000, "Dyslexia may show a different face in different languages", *Dyslexia*, 6(3), pp. 193–201.

Mintz, T.H., 2013, "The segmentation of sub-lexical morphemes in English-learning 15-month-olds", *Frontiers in Psychology*, 4, Article 24.

Morford, J.P., Grieve-Smith, A.B., MacFarlane, J., Staley, J. and Waters, G., 2008, "Effects of language experience on the perception of American Sign Language", *Cognition*, 109(1), pp. 41–53.

Morin, O., 2018, "Spontaneous emergence of legibility in writing systems: The case of orientation anisotropy", *Cognitive Science*, 42(2), pp. 664–677.

Muter, V., Hulme, C., Snowling, M.J. and Stevenson, J., 2004, "Phonemes, rimes, vocabulary, and grammatical skills as foundations of early reading development: Evidence from a longitudinal study", *Developmental Psychology*, 40(5), pp. 665–681.

Myers, J., 2012, "Cognitive styles in two cognitive sciences", in N. Miyake, D. Peebles and R.P. Cooper, eds., *Proceedings of the 34th annual conference of the cognitive science society*, pp. 2067–2072, Cognitive Science Society, Austin, TX.

Myers, J., 2016, "Knowing Chinese character grammar", *Cognition*, 147, pp. 127–132.

Neeleman, A. and van de Koot, H., 2010, "Theoretical validity and psychological reality of the grammatical code", in M. Everaert, T. Lentz, H. De Mulder, Ø. Nilsen and A. Zondervan, eds., *The linguistics enterprise: From knowledge of language to knowledge in linguistics*, pp. 183–212, John Benjamins, Amsterdam.

Novembre, G. and Keller, P.E., 2011, "A grammar of action generates predictions in skilled musicians", *Consciousness and Cognition*, 20(4), pp. 1232–1243.

Pereira, F., 2000, "Formal grammar and information theory: Together again?", *Philosophical Transactions of the Royal Society of London A: Mathematical, Physical and Engineering Sciences*, 358(1769), pp. 1239–1253.

Perfetti, C.A., 2007, "Reading ability: Lexical quality to comprehension", *Scientific Studies of Teading*, 11(4), pp. 357–383.

Perfetti, C.A., Liu, Y., Fiez, J., Nelson, J., Bolger, D.J. and Tan, L.H., 2007, "Reading in two writing systems: Accommodation and assimilation of the brain's reading network", *Bilingualism: Language and Cognition*, 10(2), pp. 131–146.

Pinker, S., 1994, *The language instinct*, HarperCollins, New York.

Pinker, S. and Jackendoff, R., 2005, "The faculty of language: What's special about it?", *Cognition*, 95(2), pp. 201–236.

Pinker, S. and Prince, A., 1988, "On language and connectionism: Analysis of a parallel distributed processing model of language acquisition", *Cognition*, 28(1–2), pp. 73–193.

Pothos, E.M., 2007, "Theories of artificial grammar learning", *Psychological Bulletin*, 133(2), pp. 227–244.

Pothos, E.M. and Bailey, T.M., 2000, "The role of similarity in artificial grammar learning", *Journal of Experimental Psychology: Learning, Memory, and Cognition*, 26(4), pp. 847–862.

Ritner, R.K., 1996, "Egyptian writing", in P.T. Daniels and W. Bright, eds., *The world's writing systems*, pp. 73–84, Oxford University Press, Oxford.

Rude, N., 1986, "Graphemic classifiers in Egyptian hieroglyphics and Mesopotamian cuneiform", in C. Craig, ed., *Noun classes and categorization*, pp. 133–138, John Benjamins, Amsterdam.

Saffran, J.R., Pollak, S.D., Seibel, R.L. and Shkolnik, A., 2007, "Dog is a dog is a dog: Infant rule learning is not specific to language", *Cognition*, 105(3), pp. 669–680.

Sahin, N.T., Pinker, S., Cash, S.S., Schomer, D. and Halgren, E., 2009, "Sequential processing of lexical, grammatical, and phonological information within Broca's area", *Science*, 326(5951), pp. 445–449.

Samuels, B., 2009, "The third factor in phonology", *Biolinguistics*, 3(2–3), pp. 355–382.

226   Implications and applications

Sandler, W., Aronoff, M., Meir, I. and Padden, C., 2011, "The gradual emergence of phonological form in a new language", *Natural Language & Linguistic Theory*, 29(2), pp. 503–543.

Scarf, D., Boy, K., Reinert, A.U., Devine, J., Güntürkün, O. and Colombo, M., 2016, "Orthographic processing in pigeons (*Columba livia*)", *Proceedings of the National Academy of Sciences*, 113(40), pp. 11272–11276.

Schmidhuber, J., 2015, "Deep learning in neural networks: An overview", *Neural Networks*, 61, pp. 85–117.

Shen, H.H., 2005, "An investigation of Chinese-character learning strategies among non-native speakers of Chinese", *System*, 33(1), pp. 49–68.

Shu, H. and Anderson, R.C., 1999, "Learning to read Chinese: The development of meta-linguistic awareness", in J. Wang, A.W. Inhoff and H.C. Chen, eds., *Reading Chinese script: A cognitive analysis*, pp. 1–18, Lawrence Erlbaum, Mahwah, NJ.

Shu, H., Chen, X., Anderson, R.C., Wu, N. and Xuan, Y., 2003, "Properties of school Chinese: Implications for learning to read", *Child Development*, 74(1), pp. 27–47.

Silfverberg, M. and Hulden, M., 2018, "Initial experiments in data-driven morphological analysis for Finnish", in T.A. Pirinen, M. Rießler, J. Rueter and T. Trosterud, eds., *Proceedings of the fourth international workshop on computational linguistics of Uralic languages*, pp. 100–107, Association for Computational Linguistics, Stroudsburg, PA.

Simons, F., 2011, "Proto-Sinaitic: Progenitor of the alphabet", *Rosetta*, 9, pp. 16–40.

Snowling, M.J., 2013, "Early identification and interventions for dyslexia: A contemporary view", *Journal of Research in Special Educational Needs*, 13(1), pp. 7–14.

Sproat, R., 2000, *A computational theory of writing systems*, Cambridge University Press, Cambridge.

Stobbe, N., Westphal-Fitch, G., Aust, U. and Fitch, W.T., 2012, "Visual artificial grammar learning: Comparative research on humans, kea (*Nestor notabilis*) and pigeons (*Columba livia*)", *Philosophical Transactions of the Royal Society B*, 367(1598), pp. 1995–2006.

Su, T., 2013, *Chinese handwriting recognition: An algorithmic perspective*, Springer, Heidelberg.

Taft, M. and Chung, K., 1999, "Using radicals in teaching Chinese characters to second language learners", *Psychologia*, 42(4), pp. 243–251.

Tamaoka, K. and Yamada, H., 2000, "The effects of stroke order and radicals on the knowledge of Japanese kanji orthography, phonology and semantics", *Psychologia*, 43(3), pp. 199–210.

Taylor, J.S.H., Plunkett, K. and Nation, K., 2011, "The influence of consistency, frequency, and semantics on learning to read: An artificial orthography paradigm", *Journal of Experimental Psychology: Learning, Memory, and Cognition*, 37(1), pp. 60–76.

Tollini, A., 1994, "The importance of form in the teaching of kanji", 世界の日本語教育 [Japanese Education in the World], 4, pp. 107–116.

Tong, X. and McBride-Chang, C., 2010, "Developmental models of learning to read Chinese words", *Developmental Psychology*, 46(6), pp. 1662–1676.

Treiman, R. and Kessler, B., 2011, "Similarities among the shapes of writing and their effects on learning", *Written Language & Literacy*, 14(1), pp. 39–57.

Tsai, K.C. and Nunes, T., 2003, "The role of character schema in learning novel Chinese characters", in C. McBride-Chang and H.-C. Chen, eds., *Reading development in Chinese children*, pp. 109–125, Praeger, London.

Tzeng, Y.L., Hsu, C.H., Huang, Y.C. and Lee, C.Y., 2017, "The acquisition of orthographic knowledge: Evidence from the lexicality effects on N400", *Frontiers in Psychology*, 8, Article 433.

Tzeng, Y.L., Hsu, C.H., Lin, W.H. and Lee, C.Y., 2018, "Impaired orthographic processing in Chinese dyslexic children: Evidence from the lexicality effect on N400", *Scientific Studies of Reading*, 22(1), pp. 85–100.

van der Hulst, H., 2010, "A note on recursion in phonology", in H. van der Hulst, ed., *Recursion and human language*, pp. 301–342, Mouton de Gruyter, Berlin.

von Ahn, L., Maurer, B., McMillen, C., Abraham, D. and Blum, M., 2008, "reCAPTCHA: Human-based character recognition via web security measures", *Science*, 321(5895), pp. 1465–1468.

Wang, C.C. [王瓊珠], Hung, L.Y. [洪儷瑜], Chang, Y.W. [張郁雯] and Chen, H.F. [陳秀芬], 2008, 一到九年級學生國字識字量發展 [Number of characters school students know from grade 1 to G9]. 教育心理學報 [Bulletin of Education Psychology], 39(4), pp. 555–568.

Wang, T.Q., Yin, F. and Liu, C.L., 2017, "Radical-based Chinese character recognition via multi-labeled learning of deep residual networks", *2017 14th IAPR International Conference on Document Analysis and Recognition (ICDAR)*, IEEE, pp. 579–584.

Watt, W.C., 2015, "What is the proper characterization of the alphabet? VII: Sleight of hand", *Semiotica*, 2015(207), pp. 65–88.

Weekes, B.S., 2012, "Acquired dyslexia and dysgraphia across scripts", *Behavioural Neurology*, 25(3), pp. 159–163.

Wiebusch, T., 1995, "Quantification and qualification: Two competing functions of numeral classifiers in the light of the radical system of the Chinese script", *Journal of Chinese Linguistics*, 23(2), pp. 1–41.

Williams, C., 2013, "Emerging development of semantic and phonological routes to character decoding in Chinese as a foreign language learners", *Reading and Writing*, 26(2), pp. 293–315.

Xiao, X. [肖奚强], 2002, 外国学生汉字偏误分析 [An analysis of character errors of foreign learners of Chinese]. 世界汉语教学 [Chinese Teaching in the World], 2002(2), pp. 79–85.

Yamaguchi, S., Yamagata, S. and Kobayashi, S., 2000, "Cerebral asymmetry of the 'top-down' allocation of attention to global and local features", *Journal of Neuroscience*, 20(9), Article RC72.

Yang, C., 2011, "Computational models of language acquisition", in J. de Villiers and T. Roeper, eds., *Handbook of generative approaches to language acquisition*, pp. 119–154, Springer, Dordrecht.

Yeh, S.L., Li, J.L., Takeuchi, T., Sun, V. and Liu, W.R., 2003, "The role of learning experience on the perceptual organization of Chinese characters", *Visual Cognition*, 10(6), pp. 729–764.

Yin, L. and Treiman, R., 2013, "Name writing in Mandarin-speaking children", *Journal of Experimental Child Psychology*, 116(2), pp. 199–215.

Yin, W., He, S. and Weekes, B.S., 2005, "Acquired dyslexia and dysgraphia in Chinese", *Behavioural Neurology*, 16(2–3), pp. 159–167.

Zhang, H.Y., 2006, "The evolution of genomes and language", *EMBO Reports*, 7(8), pp. 748–749.

Zhang, H.Y., 2014, "A review of stroke order in *hanzi* handwriting", *Language Learning in Higher Education*, 4(2), pp. 423–440.

Zhang, X.Y., Yin, F., Zhang, Y.M., Liu, C.L. and Bengio, Y., 2018, "Drawing and recognizing Chinese characters with recurrent neural network", *IEEE Transactions on Pattern Analysis and Machine Intelligence*, 40(4), pp. 849–862.

228 *Implications and applications*

Zhang, Y., 2017, "Categorical perception", in R. Sybesma, W. Behr, Y. Gu, Z. Handel, C.T.J. Huang and J. Myers, eds., *Encyclopedia of Chinese language and linguistics*, vol. 1, pp. 340–345, Brill, Leiden.

Zhao, G. [赵果] and Jiang, X. [江新], 2002, 什么样的汉字学习策略最有效?对基础阶段留学生的一次调查研究 [What is the most effective strategy for learning Chinese characters: A survey among CSL beginners]. 语言文字应用 [Applied Linguistics], 2002(2), pp. 79–85.

Index

abstractness 17, 21–22, 24–25, 161, 208–210; *see also* iconicity; recursion; semantic bleaching

acceptability judgments 18, 27, 177–178

affixation: in signed languages 21; in spoken languages 47–48, 50–51; *see also* semantic radicals

allomorphy in spoken languages 32; *see also* idiosyncratic allomorphy in characters

alphabetic writing systems 24, 26–27, 203; history of 3; psycholinguistics of 150, 163, 213, 214–215

analogy in characters: across typefaces 144, 147; in corpus linguistics 122; in hooking 100, 102, 195; in prominence 93; in psycholinguistics 184, 188, 195–196; in reduplication 64, 184; in simplified characters 142–143; in small seal script 135–136

artistic and playful characters 151–154; *see also* typefaces

assimilation: in simplified character strokes 141, 147; in small seal script strokes 134–135; in spoken and signed languages 19–20, 87; in traditional character strokes 89, 103, 106, 147

calligraphy 4, 128, 137, 151; *see also* artistic and playful characters; typefaces

character axis 58–59, 77–80; experiments on 178–186; *see also* strokes

character constituents 11–13; positions of 50–54, 76–79, 169–170, 172; *see also* phonetic components; semantic radicals

character history 3–6; *see also* oracle bone script; simplified characters; small seal script

character phonetics: in character processing 175–177, 195; contrasted with character phonology 31, 87, 93–94, 103–104, 108; influence on character phonology 88–89, 104–106, 151–152; variation in 148; *see also* handwriting; phonology; reading; stroke order

character types 7–10, 43; *see also* semantic compounds; semantic-phonetic characters

chữ nôm 字喃 *see* Vietnamese script

circumfixation 58–61

combinability of character constituents 121–122, 169–172

compounding 47–48, 61; *see also* semantic compounds

computational linguistics 6–7, 211, 218–219; *see also* productivity; quantitative modeling; Unicode

consistency *see* phonetic components

corpus analysis 17–18, 43, 120, 148–151; *see also* computational linguistics

counterdiagonal strokes (*tí* 提 and *piě* 撇) 84–86, 88–90, 94, 109–110, 113; *see also* diagonalization

cuneiform 204–206, 215

curved strokes (*wān* 彎) 14, 80, 87, 94–99, 106; *see also* curving

curving 94–99, 104, 115–116, 146–147; productivity of 154, 188, 190–191, 195; in simplified characters 142–143; in small seal script 135–137; *see also* curved strokes

decomposition of characters 28–30, 43–47, 68, 204; across character styles 145–146; corpus-based evidence for 120–122; psycholinguistic evidence for

230   *Index*

165–168; in small seal script 128; *see also* affixation; character constituents; compounding; morphemes
determinatives 204–205
diagonalization 55–56, 66, 79, 81, 83, 87, 100, 102–103; productivity of 146, 180; in simplified characters 141; in small seal script 130; and stroke order 107–108, 144; *see also* counterdiagonal strokes
diagonal strokes *see* counterdiagonal strokes; main diagonal strokes
dictionaries 5–6, 10, 24, 48–49, 131, 151
diétǐzì 叠體字 *see* reduplication
dots (*diǎn* 點) 14, 84, 88–90, 92; in simplified characters 139, 142; and stroke order 113; variation 146–147; *see also* dotting
dotting 55–56, 66, 79, 81, 83, 89, 102–103; productivity of 180; in simplified characters 141; in small seal script 130; and stroke order 107; *see also* dots
duality of patterning: in characters 30, 73–74, 121, 134, 141, 204; in spoken and signed languages 17, 20
dysgraphia 150, 168, 217–218
dyslexia 216–217

Egyptian hieroglyphs 3, 82, 204–206
ERP *see* event-related potentials
event-related potentials 164–165, 166–167, 173, 177, 213–215

fMRI *see* functional magnetic resonance imaging
fonts *see* typefaces
frequency *see* lexical frequency
functional magnetic resonance imaging 164, 176, 214

glyphs 2–3; *see also* Egyptian hieroglyphs; Mayan glyphs
grammar 14–15, 31–32; generative 30–32, 81, 106, 211; lexical 16, 18, 46, 68, 102–103, 177; psychological reality of 15–16, 18; types of evidence for 17–18; *see also* morphology; orthographic grammar; phonology; syntax
grammaticalization 48, 55, 58–59, 131, 139–140
graphemes 25–26

handwriting 25–26, 74, 87, 205; character learning and 162–163, 168, 211–212,

215; computer models of 6, 219; experiments on 3, 168–169, 176–177; physiological constraints on 104–106, 206; variation 111, 148–151; *see also* dysgraphia
Hangul *see* Korean script
hieroglyphs *see* Egyptian hieroglyphs
hiragana *see* Japanese script
hooked strokes (*gōu* 鉤) 14, 83, 85–86; hooking 99–102; productivity of 87, 100–102, 127, 192–195; in simplified characters 142–144; in small seal script 136–137; and stroke order 107, 112
huìyì 會意 *see* semantic compounds

iconicity 17, 205; in characters 8–9, 46–47, 64; experiments on 21–22, 161–162
idiosyncratic allomorphy in characters 55–60; across styles 145, 153; and character phonology 79–81, 99, 103; in compounding 62–63; in psycholinguistics 169; in reduplication 66, 84; in simplified characters 139, 141, 143; in small seal script 130–131; and stroke order 108, 113, 114–115

Japanese script 2, 4, 62; character constituents 12–13, 28, 121; hiragana and katakana 26; learning 163, 216; stroke order 108, 111; variation 150–151
jiǎgǔwén 甲骨文 *see* oracle bone script
jiǎjiè 假借 *see* character types

kǎishū 楷書 *see* regular script
kanji 漢字 *see* Japanese script
katakana *see* Japanese script
Korean script 2, 62, 204; Hangul 81, 94, 214–215

learning characters: by native-speaking children 162–163, 211–214; by non-native-speaking adults 214–216
lexical frequency 16, 18, 20, 27; character constituent frequency 28, 122, 167, 169, 181, 184–186; character token frequency 57–59, 121; character type frequency 4–5, 82, 121–127
lexical grammar *see* grammar
liù shū 六書 *see* character types
logographemes *see* character constituents
logographic writing systems 3, 203–206

Index 231

magnetoencephalography 171
main diagonal strokes (*nà* 捺) 80, 84–85,
88–89
Mayan glyphs 3, 204–205
MEG *see* magnetoencephalography
morphemes 17, 23, 43–44, 204;
character constituents as morphemes
31, 43–47, 103, 128, 134, 170–171;
monomorphemic characters 47, 138,
145–146, 151; morphemic awareness
213, 217; in signed languages 21; in
spoken Chinese 2–3, 6, 8, 15, 129,
131; *see also* affixation; compounding;
decomposition of characters; semantic
compounds
morphemic awareness *see* morphemes
morphological decomposition *see*
decomposition of characters
morphology 18, 25, 45, 82; in character
grammar 31, 43, 47, 56, 62; interactions
with (character) phonology 75–76, 79, 92,
102–103, 114–115; in simplified characters
138–141; in small seal script 128–133;
in spoken and signed languages 15, 19,
75; *see also* affixation; compounding;
decomposition of characters; morphemes;
semantic compounds
music 22–23, 210

oracle bone script 3, 5, 9–10, 28, 128,
131–133
orthographic grammar 23–27; in Chinese
characters 28–32; *see also* grammar

phonemes 23, 26, 74, 86, 208; phonemic
awareness 213
phonetic components 10–12, 43–45;
compared with semantic radicals
49–50, 53–56; consistency of 172–173;
regularity of 173; in simplified characters
138; in small seal script 129; *see also*
character constituents; semantic radicals
phonetics *see* character phonetics
phonograms *see* semantic-phonetic
characters
phonological constraints: in character
grammar 84, 86, 88–89, 186, 188; in
signed and spoken languages 16, 19–20,
27, 86
phonological features: in character
grammar 84–87, 89, 190–192; in spoken
and signed languages 19, 23
phonology 17, 103–104; in character
grammar 31, 73–74, 90, 93–94;

interactions with (character)
morphology 75–76, 79, 92, 102–103,
114–115; in simplified characters
141–144; in small seal script 132–137;
in spoken and signed languages 15,
18–22, 25–27, 32, 75–77, 86–87; *see
also* character phonetics; duality of
patterning; phonological constraints;
phonological features; prosody in
character grammar; reduction of
constituents; syllables
phono-semantic characters *see* semantic-
phonetic characters
productivity 16, 18; of character grammar
67, 102, 120; evidence from coinage
6–7, 122–127, 131–132; evidence
from experiments 177–178, 188, 196;
evidence from variation 147–148; *see
also* artistic and playful characters;
pseudocharacters; slips of the pen
prosody in character grammar 74–76;
effect on stroke shape 95–99; effect
on stroke size 91–94; interactions
with reduplication 81–84; interactions
with semantic radicals 76–81;
phonetic and cognitive motivations
for 104–105, 207; in small seal script
135–137; templates 76–78, 80, 82–84,
91–93, 95, 98–99; weight 77–79,
82–83; *see also* phonology; prosody
in spoken and signed languages;
syllables
prosody in spoken and signed languages
19, 22, 27, 54, 75, 208
pseudocharacters 153, 161; in studies on
adults 164, 166–167, 169, 172–174,
179; in studies on children 162–163,
213, 217

quantitative modeling 6–7, 25, 28, 120;
using Menzerath's law 121, 177; using
Zipf's law 121–123, 126, 210; *see also*
lexical frequency; productivity

radicals 10–11; lexicographic 10, 49–50,
62, 68, 77, 185; other usages of the
term 10, 160–161; *see also* character
constituents; semantic radicals
reading: computer models of 6, 218–219;
effect of handwriting on 162–163,
215; perceptual constraints on 105–
106, 175–177, 206–207; *see also*
decomposition of characters; dyslexia;
learning characters

232 *Index*

recursion 16, 208; in characters 11, 29, 76, 139, 141
reduction of constituents 54–59, 66–67, 79–81, 146; experimentation on 180, 183–184; in small seal script 130–131
reduplication 8–9, 63–64; analysis of 29, 81–84; contrasted with mirroring 63–64, 131; corpus-based evidence for productivity of 125, 146, 149–150, 152–153; experimental evidence for productivity of 175, 184–189; reduction in 66–67; in simplified characters 139–141; in small seal script 131–132; splitting in 64–66; in spoken and signed languages 75
regular grammar 25, 29, 82–83, 208–209
regularities *see* grammar
regularity *see* phonetic components
regular script 4–6, 9–10, 13, 128, 131–132

seal script *see* small seal script
semantic bleaching 48–50, 58, 61, 206
semantic compounds 8–9, 61–63; compared with reduplication 67–68; compared with semantic-phonetic characters 10, 50–51, 56–58, 60, 67; history of 8–9, 28; productivity of 152–154, 173; in small seal script 128–129
semantic-phonetic characters 8–11, 44–45; compared with reduplication 66–68; compared with semantic compounds 10, 50–51, 56–58, 60, 67; productivity of 122–127, 153–154, 168–174; in simplified characters 138–140; in small seal script 128–131; *see also* affixation; phonetic components; semantic radicals
semantic radicals 10–11, 44; as affix-like 47–48, 67–69, 121–125, 205; bound and closed-class nature of 49; positions of 50–54; reduction of 54–58; in simplified characters 138–140; in small seal script 128–131; *see also* character constituents; grammaticalization; phonetic components; semantic bleaching
semantic transparency 11, 46, 63, 128–129
shrinking of strokes 55, 79, 83, 100, 103; in small seal script 130
sign languages 19–23, 208–209; and learning Chinese orthography 215; morphology of 21, 51; phonology of 19–20, 86–87, 206; production of 168
simplified characters 4–5, 137–138; reduplication 140–141; semantic radicals 138–140; strokes 141–144;

see also analogy in characters; curving; diagonalization; dots; dotting; hooked strokes; idiosyncratic allomorphy in characters; morphology; phonetic components; phonology; reduplication; semantic-phonetic characters; semantic radicals
slips of the pen 149–151; *see also* handwriting
small seal script 4–5, 128; reduplication 131–132; semantic radicals 128–131; strokes 132, 134–137; *see also* analogy in characters; assimilation; curving; decomposition of characters; diagonalization; dotting; hooked strokes; idiosyncratic allomorphy in characters; morphology; phonetic components; phonology; prosody in character grammar; reduction of constituents; reduplication; semantic compounds; semantic-phonetic characters; semantic radicals; shrinking of strokes; stretching of strokes
stretching of strokes 55, 80–81, 92, 114–115, 174–175; in small seal script 130
stroke groups 11–12, 87–89; morphemic status of 46, 59–60, 63–64, 128–129, 134; as units of character phonology 73, 90–91, 95–98; variation in 114, 145–146, 151
stroke order 14, 108–109; in character learning 211–212, 215; experiments on 163, 175–177; relevance to character grammar 30, 100, 105, 106–108, 114–115; variation in 111–114
strokes 13–14, 84–87; axis of 84–85, 89, 89–90, 94, 141–142, 147; processing of 121, 175–177; *see also* counterdiagonal strokes; curved strokes; diagonalization; dots; dotting; hooked strokes; main diagonal strokes; shrinking of strokes; stretching of strokes; stroke groups
syllables: analogs in character grammar 77, 88; in signed languages 19; in spoken languages 2, 204, 208, 213–214
symmetry 27, 90, 101–102, 113, 135–136, 143–144, 206; *see also* reduplication
syntax 15–17, 19, 25, 122, 208; relevance beyond spoken and signed language 22–23; *see also* grammar

teaching characters *see* learning characters
traditional characters 4; *see also* simplified characters
typefaces 4–5, 74, 144–148

Unicode 3, 6, 28–29, 79–80, 85–86
universals and innateness: across writing
 systems 78–79, 105–106, 110, 151–152,
 206; as reflected in character grammar
 86, 135, 174, 184; in spoken and signed
 languages 20, 24, 86

Vietnamese script 2, 62–63, 204
Visual Word Form Area 25, 163–165,
 176–177, 209–210
VWFA *see* Visual Word Form Area

writing *see* handwriting
writing systems *see* alphabetic writing
 systems; logographic writing systems

xiàngxíng 象形 *see* iconicity
xiǎozhuànshū 小篆書 *see* small seal script
xíngshēng 形聲 *see* semantic-phonetic
 characters

zhǐshì 指事 *see* iconicity
zhuǎnzhù 轉注 *see* character types